Text and Interpretation

— The Indian Tradition —

Text and Interpretation

– The Indian Tradition –

Kapil Kapoor

DK PRINTWORLD
Publishers of Indian Traditions

Cataloging in Publication Data — DK
[Courtesy: D.K. Agencies (P) Ltd. <docinfo@dkagencies.com>]

Kapoor, Kapil, author.
Text and interpretation : the Indian tradition/by Kapil Kapoor. — Third impression.
pages cm
Includes words in various Indic languages (roman).
"First published in India in 2005" – Title page verso.
Includes bibliographical references and index.
ISBN 9788124603376 (Hb)

1. Indic literature – Explication. 2. India – Languages – I. Title.

LCC PK2903.K276 2024 | DDC 891.4 23

ISBN 978-81-246-0337-6 (Hb)
ISBN 978-81-246-1274-3 (Pb)
First published in India in 2005
Second impression in 2019
Third impression in 2024

Description of the cover photo: Ancient sculpture from Chidambaram Naṭarāja temple, Tamil Nadu, representing from left to right three celebrated exegetes, the sages Jaimini (composer of Mimāṁsāsūtra, 2nd -3rd century BC), Vyāghrapāda ("having tiger paws," a siddha, a grammarian and composer of Daśaka, 2nd century BC) and Patañjali (composer of Mahābhāṣya, later part of 2nd century BC).

Printed and published by:
D.K. Printworld (P) Ltd.
Regd. office : Vedaśrī, F-395, Sudarshan Park
(Metro Station: ESI Hospital) New Delhi - 110015
Phones: (011) 4172 2626, 98713 94815
e-mail: indology@dkprintworld.com
Web: www.dkprintworld.com

"This book is humbly offered to
my father, Papa ji,
who was
the happiest, the kindest, the most forgiving man
I have known in my life."

Preface

LINGUISTIC communities are also interpretative communities — they have shared frameworks and strategies to fix the meaning of what is experienced through senses or communicated through language. This is how a whole people think alike. India presents one such interpretative community in which the three major contending schools of thought — the Brāhmaṇa, the Buddhist and the Jain — contributed, flourished and "fought." The presence of a strong interpretative tradition suggests not only the existence of "a community" but also the existence of texts and issues that are perennially important and certain freedom of mind that the community has enjoyed in handling those texts. India's interpretative tradition, with a history of more than 2500 years, has addressed itself to the problem of fixing the meaning of Śrutis (the Vedas), Smṛtis (philosophical and technical treatises, i.e., Śāstras) and Kāvyas (literary compositions).

The present study is a comprehensive, though not an exhaustive analysis of this tradition, which involves the status and nature of texts, the tasks and types of interpretation, and the mode or strategies of interpretation (*śāstra-Paddhati*) such as theories of language and of meaning, conventions or meta-rules of interpretation, the structure of argument and disputation and the science of exposition or etymology (*nirvacana*).

Its principal concern is the problem of determining the meaning of verbal texts. Though the same principles are involved in the interpretation of sculpture, painting and architecture. It examines the nature of the texts and the typology of textual situations in the context of which a system of interpretation developed and was refined from Yāska to Kumārila Bhaṭṭa and which became a shared mode of interpretation in the tradition — the *śāstra-Paddhati*. The book sets up several typologies — of meaning, of textual situations that invoke the process of interpretation and of the interpretative strategies. The book then proceeds to briefly describe the devices or instruments of interpretaton — verbal testimony, *śārvabhauma śiddhānta, saṅgati Paribhāṣā, laukika nyāya, vyākaraṇa, śabda-śakti* and theory of verbal symbolism and illustrates the use that is made of them (i) in different kinds of texts, Śruti, Smṛti and Kāvya, and (ii) by different exegetes such as Śaṅkara. The text situations — contradictions, transparency and opacity, etc., and the interpretative methodologies are sought to be illustrated through an example analysis, in the last chapter of, Ādi Śaṅkara's commentary on chapter 2 of The *Bhagavad-Gītā*. On account of the centrality of meaning, *artha,* and language in our civilization, and the great value attached to knowledge, a science of interpretation involving theories of meaning, principles of judgement and modes of disputation developed in India, which is unequalled elsewhere in its rich methodological framework and in its wide, continuous application.

The present study originated as a series of lectures to the research students at the Jawaharlal Nehru University, and then appeared, in its first birth, as a long article in *The Journal of the School of Languages*, J.N.U. This book is a comprehensively revised and extended version that has resulted from a series of question and answer sessions with my students. I am grateful to them for their searching, and always significant, questions and for the great interest they took in this subject. It is still an ongoing study, as far as I am concerned, for its essential content — the problem of meaning — is an endless inquiry. And in the Indian context, it involves so many intellectual giants — Yāska, Kātyāyana, Patañjali, Śabara, Bhartṛhari, Kumārila Bhaṭṭa, Ādi Śaṅkara — that a student like *me* has to approach this subject with humility and piety. The purpose has been to disseminate among the young Indians, some ideas and the method of inquiry of these important Indian thinkers.

Finally, a word about the word "tradition." The word "tradition" has these days been used in opposition to "modernity." But, this is a motivated use, to which we need not and must not subscribe. "Tradition" is the mechanism of transferring ideas from one generation to the other. As such, it represents the cultural and intellectual continuity of an ancient civilization and only a few cultures have such heritage of a rich tradition. The Indian tradition is continuous and pervasive and lives in the minds and lifestyles of the average Indian. It has been marginalized for the educated by our educational system, particularly since 1947, producing in the process a whole generation of rootless, de-culturized, subordinated minds. For the mind to be free and innovative, it is necessary to relocate ourselves in this scholarly tradition.

I am very thankful to my former student and now a distinguished colleague, Dr. Rajnish Kumar Mishra, who read the manuscript over and over again and has contributed in so many ways that are difficult to acknowledge. I also thank Tulsi, my Ph.D. student, for preparing a scholarly index.

Finally, how can I thank Susheel ji of D.K. Printworld sufficiently for all the care and 'affectionate' interest he took in this book? It has been a very good experience, this working with Susheel ji.

Contents

1

Language and Interpretation

Language and Reality

EVERY act of making sense of the reality of an object is an act of interpretation — the object may be our external environment, the inner landscape of our mind or a linguistic statement made about either of them. Thus one may distinguish two kinds of "interpretation" — (i) the first order interpretation, which is a direct statement or description of existing objects, external or internal and (ii) the second order interpretation, which is a statement ("paraphrase" or "explanation") about an already existing linguistic statement. It is the second kind of interpretation that has been traditionally called 'exegesis,' while the first kind of interpretation takes the form of "disciplines" that are severally named as Psychology, History, Philosophy, Literature, Linguistics, Literary Theory, etc.

Language is involved in both kinds of interpretations, though in crucially different ways. In the first order interpretation, language is assumed to be either a fixed, invariant element which can be correlated one to one with the objects it describes or a system of elements that relate in a very loose way to the objects they refer to. It is assumed to constitute in an absolute way the knowledge of the object, for all cognitive acts are assumed to be determinate (Bishnupada Bhattacharya, 1962: 20). Disputes, if any, relate to its particular conceptual categories, its technical terminology, have to be settled before the statements are made. In the second order interpretation, the certainty of knowledge as constituted in the language is questioned and the language itself is treated as a fluid object. The status and denotation of technical terms and their fitness for the objects described become the subject-matter of interpretation besides of course the propositional content of the statements. True understanding, valid knowledge, then always rests in the exact knowledge of what the linguistic expressions mean. "Interpretation" thus is a method by which true knowledge is to be gained, and it is essentially a linguistic exercise in *artha-nirdhāraṇa* (the determination of meaning) by examining a given discourse at all its levels of language organization — the lexical, the grammatical, the propositional, the pragmatic and the discoursal. "Interpretation" therefore is essentially a linguistic act, an act of proposition-making in which language functions as the medium as well as the instrument, and in "second order" interpretation language is also the object of interpretation.

In this chain of relationship that binds knowledge, interpretation and language, language has been the primary concern that has shaped the Indian intellectual tradition. We know that interpretation or exegesis has always been a major intellectual activity right from the *Ṛgveda* itself and the exegetes, realizing that all branches of knowledge share the same basic concerns about the nature of interpretation, evolved in the course of time what may be called a common mode of interpretation, what the tradition calls *śāstra-Paddhati*. Evolution of this shared mode of interpretation depended, quite understandably on, and in fact presupposed, a knowledge of the structure and nature of language, and its relationship to thought and knowledge of reality.

The Indian thinkers appear to have had a clear grasp of the two-fold relation of language to knowledge — it is through language that we know what we know, and it is in language that we express what we know. This accounts for the conceptual, cognitive and communicative centrality of language in the Indian consciousness as attested by the innumerable reflections on language in the ancient Śruti-literature and almost continuously, ever since, down the centuries in a variety of linguistic and non-linguistic texts. The Upaniṣads, to give one example, make some of the most insightful statements about this centrality of language. The *Aitareyopaniṣad* says that knowledge and intra-subjective relationship is made possible only by speech (*vāk*) —

> The teacher Pāñcālacanda considered speech itself as the Saṁhitā. . . . 'By speech the Vedas are strung, by speech the metres are made, by speech friends are united, by speech all beings (establish their intra-subjective knowledge and relation) and hence all this is speech.'
>
> — *Aitareyopaniṣad*, III.1.6

The *Chāndogya Upaniṣad* puts language at the foundation of ethics —

> Without speech who could explain right and wrong, good, evil; pleasant, unpleasant ? Speech explains all.
>
> — VII.2

Chāndogya at another place, arranges individual self, intellect or cognition, perception and speech in a hierarchy of relationship (VII.3). The same idea finds expression in the *Kaṭhopaniṣad* as well, with a significant extension to include a new category "the real self of man," the *śānta-ātman* which is the ultimate awareness, made possible by language.

> The wise should merge the speech (Language) in the mind, and that (mind) in the intellect, and that (intellect) in the Great-Self and that (Great-Self again) in the Self of Peace (*Śānta-Ātman*, the real self of man). — III.13

The *Ṛgveda*, replete with reflections on language, in one of its hymns identifies language with all cognition — language is naming, it gives "names to object" (*Ṛgveda*, 10.71.1), and thus is the instrument of giving shape and form to reality. This conception is expressed clearly in *ṚV* (1.164.41), particularly on the *pada, takśati* "forming the water floods," V.S. Agarwala says.

> The real significance is that the principle of Vāk creates or fashions out the manifold forms out of the waters of the infinite Ocean of the Ultimate Reality.
>
> — V.S. Agarwal, 1963

Language "fashions forms" out of the "Ocean of . . . Reality." Why "Ocean"? Because it is not possible to draw lines in water or to divide water; we cannot segment it — everything is merged with everything else, every particle is like every other and indistinguishable. But — and this is important — man makes sense of this flux by positing discrete entities, by segmenting one from the next, or else he would be "drowned" and wouldn't know what is what. The discrete forms and shapes are cognized through language which gives them "names," for language is "naming" and naming is knowledge. Discreteness and sequentiality that are the properties of language get imposed on and appear as the attributes of the reality.

Linguistic Thought and Grammar

Since it is seen to be so crucially involved in the structure of thought and reality, language has come in for sustained study and analysis in the Indian history of ideas. In this sustained thinking, Pāṇini's model of language structure, Jaimini's method of analysis (*mīmāṁsā*) and Bhartṛhari's conception of the linguistic sign (*sphoṭa*) provide the framework for interpretation of texts, for *śābda-bodha*, comprehension of the meaning of words.

The history of linguistic thought in India shows movement from the empirical to the transcendental, the concrete to the abstract, from the investigation in the Prātiśakhyas of the production of the concrete, variant sounds to the conception of *Śabda-Brahman* in Bhartṛhari. The grammarians, it has been said, went to the sea-shore and examined the sands (examined the speech behaviour of ordinary people) for cowrie-shells (sounds) and ended up by finding a pearl, *śabda-brahman*. Fairly early, around seventh century BC, the pre-Buddha time of Pāṇini, language became the object of close analysis and description — language as ontology and as epistemology, its physics as well as its metaphysics. And the tradition has continued down to Nāgeśa Bhaṭṭa (eighteenth century AD) and even modern times. The whole tradition may be divided into four phases:

PHASE I

From the Beginning to Pāṇini : roughly up to seventh century BC.

Includes language-speculations in the Śruti literature (see, Shivnarayan Sastri, 1971: 1-53), the grammarians cited by Pāṇini, at least the *Ṛk-Prātiśakhya* and possibly others (see, Mahulkar, 1981) and the work of Yāska.

PHASE II

From Pāṇini to Ānandavardhana: from seventh century BC to ninth century AD.

Include the work of three major grammarians, Pāṇini Kātyāyana and Patañjali, the philosophers and exegetes, and also of Jaimini (*Mīmāṁsā-Sūtra*), Śabara (*Śābara-Bhāṣya* on *Mīmaṁsā-Sūtra*), of the grammarians and exegetes, Candragomin and Vāmana-Jayāditya, of Bhartṛhari, a philosopher of language and of grammar, and of several poeticians from Bharata and Bhāmaha to Ānandavardhana, the theorist of verbal symbolism.

PHASE III

From Rāmacandra to Nāgeśa Bhaṭṭa: eleventh century AD to the eighteenth century.

Includes the grammarians who rearranged and recorded Pāṇini's rules to suit their understanding of the pedagogical needs — Rāmachandra and Varadarāja, those who investigated the principles of grammar, Bhaṭṭoji Dīkṣita, Kauṇḍa Bhaṭṭa, and Nāgeśa Bhaṭṭa and those who adapted the Pāṇinian system to describe languages other than Sanskrit, viz., Hemacandra and Jainendra, and of exegetists who also analysed the assumptions of grammar, viz., Haradatta.

PHASE IV

Nineteenth century to now; from F. Keilhorn onwards.

The phase of modern, textual and interpretive scholarship includes the work of a large number of well-known German, European, American and British scholars, whose major contribution is the reconstruction, editing and publishing of primary texts of classical Sanskrit literature, including grammar and philosophy, and also a well-argued exposition of the heritage. Here the work of Keilhorn, Bhandarkar, Abhyankar, Charudeva Shastri, Katre and Dandekar is worthy of mention.

This isolation into phases is a matter of convenience to foreground and focus. Otherwise, there is a continuity and each line of investigation extends into subsequent phases.

Thus all the dimensions of linguistic study are to be found to have been explored or touched upon in the very first phase itself — (i) the structure of language, its phonetics and phonology, (ii) its morphology and syntax, (iii) the nature of sound change and change in the meaning of words, (iv) the synchronic variation in linguistic usage, and (v) the philosophy of language, its relationship to thought and reality. In the work of Yāska, almost all of these aspects are found to have been discussed, though he is chiefly concerned with systematically fixing the meaning of certain words used in the Vedic texts — words that have become multivalent or opaque with the passage of time — by deriving them from the verb-roots. Development of this concept of establishing the meaning of words in terms of the verb-roots and a demonstration of the processes of derivation that these words undergo with corresponding changes in meaning and must be ranked as one of the major contributions of this first phase in the history of linguistics.

Yāska also initiated the discussion of change in the meaning of words. In *Nirukta* (2.1), he draws attention to the historical and geographic factors in the diversity of meaning. He also discusses the question of why certain words become opaque or difficult to interpret, and mentions sound-change, and processes of derivation as factors in this, and in fact says that the science of "Exposition" (etymology) is needed to determine the meaning of such words. Thirdly, Yāska while commenting on *R̥V* 1.1.1 and 1.10.1 takes note of ambiguity and polysemy. Finally, Yāska treats certain changes in meaning as figurative extensions, and in the process presents the first formal analysis of figurative language.

In Indian linguistic tradition language change including change in meaning is seen as an instance of language variation which has been the subject-matter of long debate. The study of language as a social phenomenon also begins with Yāska who records extensive social and geographic diversity in the language of his times.

Early in ninth century BC Yāska, while enunciating his etymological/exegetical principles drew attention to the processes of change leading to diversity in usage that comes to mark historical, geographical and registeral "dialects." On account of the existence of an ancient body of texts — the world's oldest — held all through in high esteem and preserved intact, one of the important divergences in the Indian context is that between the language of the texts and the language of current use. Yāska cites (*Nirukta* 2.2) two kinds of example:

(i) the verb-root √*dam* is in current use both as verb and as a nominal, while in the literary texts only its primary derived nominal formation (*damūnas*) is found employed, and conversely.

(ii) only the derived nominal form is in current use, while in the text the verb-root is widely employed, viz., *uṣṇa* and *uṣ*.

Yāska also cites instances of geographic variations:

(i) In the north-west (Afghanistan) √*śav* is used only as a verb in the sense of "go;" while in the middle-land (northern Indian plains), *śav* is used as a noun in the sense of a "dead-body" (an extended meaning based on death as "a great journey").

(ii) √*dā* is used in eastern India in the general sense of "to cut," while in the north, derived nominal *dātra* is used in the restricted sense of "cutting crops."

This fact of variation is involved in the grasp of right meaning of words.

Pāṇini's *Aṣṭādhyāyī* records extensive diversity. Pāṇini lived and worked in times of great intellectual and social ferment and in the rising tide of the Nanda empire and notes six different kinds of variation in a widespread area of usage spread from Assam to Afghanistan:

(i) First, there is the usage restricted to the texts (Vaidikī) — cf. 1.1.18. This includes a good deal of specific ritual enunciation, cf. 1.2.34.37, and ritual performances as well (8.2.88).

(ii) Second, there is the difference in usage between the Vaidika language and *bhāṣā,* the contemporary language — cf. 3.2.107, 3.2.108, 4.1.62, 6.1.180, 6.1.181, 8.2.98.

(iii) Thirdly, there are specific instances of geographically distributed variation — cf. 2.4.20, 4.1.160, 6.3.10, 6.3.32.

(iv) Fourth, there is the stylistic variation, i.e., specific usages "in uninterrupted flow of speech" — cf. 6.3.115, 6.3.122.

(v) Fifth, there is the "free variation," differences in usage not ordained by any rules of grammar but that occur in the usage of *śiṣṭa,* the cultivated speakers.

(vi) Finally, and most importantly, the optionality in living usage, *loka-vyavahāra,* captured and described by rules that explicitly or by *anuvṛtti* include the term *vibhāṣā,* which even as a non-technical term conveys the meaning of "option."

Though Pāṇini's grammar as a set of codification, a laying down of a single, albeit internally complex standard, yet it is not intended to be a prescriptive norm. It is Patañjali who argues for a norm. His arguments for the norm are rich and interesting, though controversial. He addresses himself (*MB* 1.1.) directly to the question — "What is the purpose of the science of grammar?" And in answering the question, he sets up the opposition of (i) *sādhu-asādhu,* and (ii) *śabda-apaśabda,* and the guiding criterion of *dharma-niyama* in the context of the vast area and the immense variety of usage.

He begins by mentioning six central purposes of grammar — three of them exegetical and two epistemological and one related to language use. The science of grammar, says Patañjali, ought to be acquired for its own sake because a man of learning or whose profession is learning, must seek knowledge as an end in itself. Also, grammar is the best means of gaining knowledge of language. Among exegetical goals, he includes: (i) understanding of the sacredotal texts: (ii) correct reading or enunciation of these texts, and (iii) disambiguation or determination of the nature of specific use.

And, lastly and most importantly, we must study this science so that the language we speak successfully communicates only the meaning we intend to communicate, use of inaccurate words would fail in communicating the intending meaning, and language after all is just communication of meanings. Later Bhartr̥hari's theory of meaning would claim that only *sādhu* words have *sphoṭa* (*Vākyapadīya* 10). It is this from that Patañjali sets up his heavily loaded construct of *apaśabda* — words that fail in their necessary purpose of communicating meaning. He employs the word *mleccha* as an alternative to *apaśabda*, thereby suggesting that the speech of non-native communities (*anārya*) is to be classed as *apaśabda* because words that are mispronounced in their sound-substance, pitch or vocalicity (*duṣṭa śabda*), due also some time to carelessness or incapacity, will necessarily fail to communicate the desired meaning. This is the hearer's point of view, and suggests a situation of contact or interaction between different communities of speakers. Hence Patañjali's injunction that the 'brāhmaṇa', the man of learning, the speaker belonging to the main cultural community, must not do *apabhāṣaṇa*, must not allow his own speech to be influenced by the *anārya* modes. Just as there is benefit, fulfilment of purpose (*dharma*) in right knowledge, the knowledge of right words, there is disadvantage (*adharma*) in the knowledge of the *apaśabda* or variant forms. In fact, says Patañjali, there is greater possibility of failing in communicative goals because *apaśabda*s are far more numerous than *śabda*s, i.e., there are innumerable dialectal variants. So what the Grammar does is to lay down, generate, *śabda*s such as *gau*, cow, the right forms, and says Patañjali, by implication excludes the dialectal variants such as *gavi*, very much as by specifying what is edible we exclude by implication everything else as inedible. The grammar could follow the other path and specify all the excluded variants but that would be uneconomical because the universe of variants is much larger than that of the norm — each word such as *gau*: cow, has several *apabhraṁśa* — *gāvi, goṇi, gopa, gopotalikā*, etc. So, the Grammar generates the right word which, the Grammar assumes, have given associated meanings (it being not the function of grammar to assign meanings to words). The "associated meanings" are known from *loka*, the use of language, wherein available words are used in given meanings. But then, even *apśabda*s, the variant forms are similarly, and widely, employed effectively, to successfully denote associated meanings. And if both *śabda*s and *apaśabdas*, in actual use, equally effectively perform the function of communicating meaning, then in terms of which overriding principle does the grammar restrict itself to generating *sādhu śabda*s alone? Patañjali's answer is: *dharma niyama*, discipline, injunction of the desirable. He explains this by analogy — one can satisfy one's hunger by dog's flesh as well as by jungle fowl. So a *niyama* is laid down — the injunction of the desirable, eat this, not this. In the same way when it is possible to communicate meaning by both *śabda*s and *apaśabda* then the grammar enjoins — communicate meaning through *śabda*, not *apaśabda* (*Mahābhāṣya* 1.1). To be able to do this — to use *śabda*s, the right forms, one needs the knowledge of what is *apaśabda*, so as to be able, knowingly, to excise them from one's speech.

The other major contribution in the first phase is in phonetics and phonology. In fact, speech sounds are studied and analysed in this phase, and the study finds its maximum systematization in the Prātiśakhyas which not only fix the sound-patterns of each school of the four Vedas, but also propound finished theories about the articulation and properties of speech sounds in isolation and in the dynamic context of actual utterance. To this perfection of phonetic and phonological studies, we owe the fact of the oral texts having come down intact.

The second phase is the richest in the linguistic history of India. It is marked by theory building in at least four major areas — (i) grammar, (ii) language in philosophy, (iii) literary language, and (iv) the interpretation of verbal texts. In the field of grammar, Pāṇini gives an explicit and exhaustive rule-bound description of the Sanskrit language and sets in motion a long tradition of grammatical analysis and exegesis. In philosophy, each of the six major theistic schools of Indian philosophy employ *śabda* as means of knowledge, while the atheistic schools — the Cārvākas, the Buddhists — while rejecting language as evidence, necessarily talk of the non-existent or illusory relationship between language and reality. Besides, Bharata and Bhāmaha, Vāmana, Daṇḍin and numerous other poeticians investigate the nature of literary language, a question that is central to Indian poetics because of the very definition of literature as *vāṅmaya*, "that which has existence in language." While Bhāmaha and Vāmana examine at length the lexical and syntactic properties of literary meaning, both direct and indirect, and Kuntaka examines the devices of defamiliarization of literary language. Finally, Jaimini in his *Mīmāṁsā-Sūtras*, handles the all important questions of meaning of a proposition and the relationship that holds between linguistic meaning and existence — the reality of objects that language talks about. The questions that Jaimini raises and answers, make great sense to the modern mind —

(i) isn't every linguistic proposition necessarily ambiguous if not multivalent?

(ii) does the text not have intrinsic potential to generate all the meanings that potential readers may read into the text?

(iii) when a reader confronts more than one meaning of a given text, how does he select, provided he wants to select, one meaning from them ? What are the processes and devices involved in the exercise ? And this leads to the next question, one with which, in fact, Jaimini's analysis of the problem of interpretation necessarily begins?

(iv) what are the structures of meaning and what conditions or factors are involved in denoting and connoting meaning?

Jaimini's *Mīmāṁsā* is a philosophy of performance and therefore it sets up a system for interpreting the injunctive sentences, *vidhi vākya*. It is particularly directed towards interpretation of the Vedic texts which are composed in a figurative language, its mode being *rūpaka*, as Sāṁkhya enjoins. The method is needed to make sense of a discourse that transfers the abstract conceptions of intuition into concrete images. Its system of interpretation allows for assumptions of the interpreting school, contexts of the age and thought, the principles of disputation (*vāda*), the logical structure of argument (subject, doubt, the opposed point of view, the counter argument and the principle). Its locus of interpretation is the sentence and therefore it organises linguistic exegesis in terms of word-meaning, sequence of statement, meta-rules and *eka-vākyatā*, the interdependence of all sentences in a discourse.

Jaimini expounded his interactive system of interpreting or determining meaning — in which the reader and the text interact — sometime in the third century BC and his work must be ranked among major contributions of the Indian mind.

In this long history, language has been studied, as we have mentioned above, both as an object as well as means of knowledge. The ontological study has examined language in its three aspects —

(i) as an abstract system,

(ii) as an organism that has its own laws of change,

(iii) as a social phenomena involving communication and variation.

The epistemological study is an intrinsic dimension of the study of language in relation to thought, the cognitive process, and reality and proceeds on the foundations of the knowledge of language as an abstract system. Two major theories of the grammarians, the *kāraka* theory and the *sphoṭa* theory, enunciated to analyse language structure, necessarily concern themselves with these questions — how the relational reality (of the *kāraka*-theory) and essentially a linguistic construct (the *sphoṭa* theory). Later, Bhartṛhari (fifth century AD) was to argue at length) that reality is cognized as a linguistically evoked conceptualization.

The ***Kāraka*** theory, as a theory of grammar, specifies the possible semantic relations that hold between nouns and the verb in grammatical sentences, how these relations are to be identified for particular verbs, and the system of inflectional expression of these relations. The theory originates with Pāṇini who lays it down at three places in the *Aṣṭādhyāyī* — (i) the *kāraka* relations in 1.4.23 to 1.4.55; (ii) the *vibhaktis*, inflections for *kārakas*, and the choice of *vibhaktis* in 2.3.1. to 2.3.73 and 4.1.2; (iii) the surface forms in which the different *vibhaktis* are realized in 7.1.45 to 7.1.103. It is extended in the *Mahābhāṣya*, *Āhnika* III, in Patañjali's discussion of Kātayāna's *Vārttikas* on twenty of the Pāṇinian *kāraka* rules (1.4.23 to 1.4.32, 1.4.37; 1.4.42; 1.4.48 to 1.4.55). It is fully expounded in Bhartṛhari's *Vākyapadīya*, III.7.

The word *kāraka* is formed the root *kṛ* "to do" with agent (*taddhita*) suffix *ṇvul* and like the word *kāraka*, has the same literal meaning, "doer" or "agent." The word is used in Pāṇini's *adhikāra*-rule, 1.4.23, *karake*, a heading rule which says that "The phrase *kāraka* (meaning in the special relation to a word expressing an action)" is to be understood in the following aphorisms" (S.C. Vasu, tr., *The Aṣṭādhyāyī of Pāṇini* I, p. 177) in the technical sense of given noun-verb relations. Six such relations or *kāraka*s, are recognized in all treatises of grammar — *apādāna* (ablative), *karman* (accusative) and *kartṛ* (nominative). Discussing the meaning of *kāraka* under 1.4.23, Kātyāyana in *vārttikas* 7 to 11, says that the *kāraka*s other than the *kartṛ*, nominative, may also be used as the agents or doers. Thus in "*Devadattaḥ* cooks," Devadatta is the agent, but in "The pot cooks," "The pot," which is normally locative, is the agent, and so on. Hence, the definition *karotīti kārakam*, "that which does, the doer of the activity of the verb, or that which is the means or instrument of the activity denoted by the verb," applies to all the *kāraka*s. *Kāraka*, therefore, as the *Kāśikā* (p. 1.4.23) says, is a synonym for *nimitta*, the circum-stance or means, the *hetu* (cause) of the activity, or "being," denoted by the verb, although *kāraka*, as Bhartṛhari shows (III.7.24-25) is to be distinguished from both *nimitta* and *hetu* as also from *karaṇa*, instrument (III.7.26). The relationship between *kāraka* and *kriyā* (verb) is complex. On the other hand, a noun necessarily enters into a *Kāraka* relationship with reference to some activity or the other. So, a relationship of expectancy (*ākāṅkṣā*) holds between *kāraka* and *kriyā*. But which one is the determinant and which is the determinate? The tradition accommodates both points of view — the *kāraka* as the determinant in definitions of *kāraka* such as *kriyājanakam kārakam* (instrumental in bringing about action), and the *kriyā* or verb as the determinant in definitions of *kāraka* such as *kriyām anvetīti kriyāmnveyī kārakam* (that which comes after or whose coming into being depends on that of the verb). Thus the relationship between *kāraka* and *kriyā* is one of mutual expectancy, both determining each other.

The capacity by which things become instrumental in bringing about an action is seen to be of six kinds — the six *kārakas*:

> *kartā karma ca karaṇañca sampradānam tathaiva ca* ।
> *apādānadhi yāhu kārakāṇi ṣaṭa* ॥

> The nominative, the accusative, the instrumental, the dative, etc., the ablative, the locative — these are the six *kārakas*.

Whatever the speaker presents as the independent entity in the accomplishment of or as involved in the action is *kartā* or agent (*Aṣṭādhyāyī* 1.4.54) and that which is the inspirer (*prayojaka*) of the object of *karma* (*Aṣṭādhyāyī* 1.4.55). That which is specially desired by the agent to be accomplished or most affected by the action is called the object of *karma* (*Aṣṭādhyāyī* 1.4.49). That which is the instrument of production of any action is called instrument or *karaṇa* (*Aṣṭādhyāyī* 1.4.42). The person or entity whom one wishes to connect with the object of giving or towards whom the object of giving is directed is called recipient or *sampradāna* (*Aṣṭādhyāyī* 1.4.32). A noun whose relation to an action is that of a fixed object being in that place is called location or *adhikaraṇa* (*Aṣṭādhyāyī* 1.4.45). The relation between a noun and another noun, the genitive of Western grammar, is not included as a *kāraka* because *kāraka* is the relationship of the substantive with the verb. The genitive is subsumed under the sixth case affix by the *Aṣṭādhyāyī* rule 2.3.50 which says —

> The sixth case-affix is employed in the remaining cases, that is to say, where there is a sense, such as the relation between property and its owner, etc., different from that of a word related to a verb and from that of a nominal-stem.
>
> — S.C. Vasu, *The Aṣṭādhyāyī of Pāṇini* I, p. 296

For the same reason, Sanskrit grammarians do not include

vocative as a *kāraka*. It is categorically laid down that there are only six *kāraka*-relations and no more —

> According to others, there reside, powers like the universals in all objects. Those powers seem to be unlimited according to the shape, etc., of objects. The truth about them is that it does not go beyond the number six.
>
> — *Vākyapadīya* III.7.35, 36

Pāṇini introduces these *kāraka*s in a significant order: In the *kāraka* sections of Pāṇini, of *Kātantra*, and in the other grammars that distinguish between *kāraka* and *vibhakti*, the order of the cases is as follows: Ablative, Dative, Instrumental, Locative, Accusative and Nominative. This order is fixed according to Pāṇini's *Paribhāṣā*: *vipratiṣedhe param kāryam* (1.4.2), i.e., in case of conflict between two rules the latter is to prevail over the earlier — "Thus the order of the cases in Pāṇini shows the relative importance of the cases according to the viewpoint of Indian grammarians" (Kshitish Chandra Chatterji 1964, p. 375). The progression is from the *apādāna*, which is least controlled by the *kartā* to *karman*, the *kāraka* most affected by the action of the *kartā*, with *kartā* heading the list, an arrangement in which every succeeding *kāraka* is stronger (by virtue of its nexus with the *kartā*) than, and therefore, prevailing (by *Aṣṭādhyāyī*, 1.4.2) over the preceding one.

The *kāraka* relations are formally expressed by *vibhakti*s, *su-*, *au-*, *jas-*, etc. For each *kāraka*, there is a corresponding *vibhakti* — *prathamā*, the first one, for *kartā*, *dvitīyā* (second) for *karman*, *tṛtīyā* (third) for *karaṇa*, *caturthī* (fourth) for *sampradāna*, *pañcamī* (fifth) for *apādāna*, *ṣaṣthī* (sixth) for *sambandha* (genitive), and *saptamī* (seventh) for *adhikaraṇa*. Each *vibhakti* has three forms according to the three numbers of Sanskrit — singular, dual and plural. The twenty-one *vibhakti*s are listed in *Aṣṭādhyāyī* (4.1.2). It is important to distinguish between *kāraka* and *vibhakti*. *Kāraka* is a semantic category and *vibhakti* is a syntactic category that corresponds to *kāraka*. But the domain of *vibhakti* is larger than that of *kāraka*: thus, while the *prathamā vibhakti*, the first case-ending, is employed to mark the *kartā*, agent or doer, it is also employed where the sense is that of the nominal stem, i.e., mere existence (*Aṣṭādhyāyī* 1.2.45) (as in "*The table* is in the corner") or of gender only or measure only or number only (*Aṣṭādhyāyī* 2.3.46), in which case no *kāraka*-relation is expressed. Also, *vibhakti*s are employed under purely syntactic conditions (cf. *Aṣṭādhyāyī* 1.4.38). However, the *kāraka* assigned by grammar in such cases, the grammatical *kāraka*, is not always the semantic *kāraka* — in a sentence such as *paraśu: vṛkṣam chinatti, paraśu:* axe, is assigned *kartā* as the grammatical *kāraka* though, semantically, it has a *karaṇa* relationship to the action. The *prathamā-vibhakti* is, however, employed because it is the grammatical-*kāraka* which functions as the condition for the introduction of the case-affixes. The grammatical *kāraka* is assigned by Pāṇini's ordered *kāraka*-rules, which first assign *karaṇa-kāraka* to *paraśu* (by *Aṣṭādhyāyī* 1.4.42), then *kartā* (by *Aṣṭādhyāyī* 1.4.54) but by *Aṣṭādhyāyī* 1.4.2, a meta-rule, *paraśu* is uniquely classed as agent, *kartā*, thus requiring the *prathamā-vibhakti* to be employed. *Kāraka* thus is a semantic category that controls syntactic behaviour, while *vibhakti* is a purely syntactic category. In Pāṇini *tantra*, system, each *vibhakti* subsequently, is realized as a different surface, form, depending on the phonologic shape or morphological structure or the external context. The *prathamā vibhakti, su*, for example, may be realized in different context as — zero, *-am, a*, etc. The *kāraka* theory therefore involves three systems in Pāṇini's grammar — the semantic relations, the syntactic or functional affixation system and the system of phonological representation.

In the derivational system of Pāṇini's grammar, *kāraka*s determine the "voice" of the verb, concord with adjectives and the concord with the participial verb form. By *Aṣṭādhyāyī* 3.4.69, the L-suffixes, the tense-affixes, are chosen to denote the *kartā* or the *karman* in the case of transitive verb-roots, to denote the *kartā* or *Bhāva* (impersonal "voice") in the case of intransitive verb roots and by *Aṣṭādhyāyī* (3.1.87), to denote the *karma-vadabhāva*, a passive like construction.

The *kāraka vibhakti*s of nouns are also employed for the co-occurring adjectives under the wider law of *samānādhikaraṇa* which states (*Aṣṭādhyāyī* 1.2.42) that words which have got the same individual object (*dravya*) referred to by means of their sense and which are in apposition are put in the same case. In the terminology of Sanskrit grammar — the *viśesaṇa* (qualifier) accords with the *viśeṣya* (qualificand), viz.

dr̥ṣṭAM pustak AM

The *kāraka*-theory in this way is at the heart of Sanskrit syntax — it gives the requisite surface form to nouns, and then controls the forms of co-occurring verbs and adjectives. The topic, particularly its *vibhakti*-aspect, is so complex that to explain it, a large number of compendiums and treatises were composed in the tradition. Some of the major ones are: *Kārakakārikā* (Puruṣottamadeva), *Kārakapariccheda*, *Kārkakavāda* (Kr̥ṣṇaśāstrī Arada), *Kārakaviveka* (Jayarāmabhaṭṭācārya).

Outside grammar, the *kāraka* theory is rooted in significant metaphysics. This has been established by Bhartr̥hari in his important discussion of *sādhana*, the means, in *Vākyapadīya* (III.7). In the metaphysics of the grammarians, the ultimate Reality is endowed with infinite power (*śakti*) a construct which is the source of the infinite variety of cosmic phenomena. An infinite number of concrete objects exist in the cosmos. These objects are dynamic — they interact and bring about innumerable actions and processes which in their turn produce new objects which also act in the same way and become instruments — thus the chain of being proceeds. The objects are able to bring about actions and processes by virtue of their *śakti*, the power to do so. In fact, a concrete object is nothing but a bundle of powers. (*Vākyapadīya* III.7.2). The concrete objects are called *sādhana*, means, by Patañjali and Bhartṛhari. Actually it is one of the powers or capacities of the object that is the *sādhana* or means, for, the object is fixed and determinate and yet it seems to function in a variety of ways in the accomplishment of action — thus the same object can become an instrument (*karaṇa*) or an agent (*kartā*) as in.

> *usane* ***dimāga se*** (*karaṇa*) *ye socā*
> 'He thought of this with his brain'
>
> *usake* ***dimāga ne*** (*kartā*) *ye socā*
> 'His brain thought of this'

This is because of the powers or capacities latent in objects. An object is a bundle of powers and it is up to the speaker how he perceives its role in the accomplishment of the action, to emphasize its one power or the other in different contexts. It is a matter of the speaker's cognition and his intention, *vivakṣā* (*Vākyapadīya* III.7.3.). These *sādhana*s are called *kāraka*s "doers," in grammar because they all play some part in the main action. As noted above six such "doers" are recognized in grammar on account of the particular function performed by them such as that of the instrument. Therefore, with regard to the main action, the same object is *kāraka* in a general sense, and *karma, karaṇa,* etc., in a special sense (*Vākyapadīya* III.7.18). The grammarians' metaphysics then, makes a distinction between a *sādhana, karaṇa, hetu,* cause, *lakṣaṇa,* sign and *tadārtheya,* "What is meant for something else." A *sādhana* performs an operation and brings about an effect; a *hetu* is looked upon as a cause irrespective of whether it performs an operation or not, as *bīja,* the seed, in — *bījāṅkuraḥ,* the seed, the sprout (*Vākyapadīya* III.7.25,27). *Lakṣaṇa,* sign, on the other hand is that which makes something known, although a cause with a predictable effect is also a *lakṣaṇa* of the effect (*Vākyapadīya* III.7.24). The other word for *sādhana* is *nimitta,* the finished object that is looked upon as cause for the sake of rendering help. *Kāraka* literally describes it as "do-er." *Hetu* is cause — it does not perform an operation. *Lakṣaṇa* is neither cause nor a performer of an operation, but a *dyotaka*, one that makes known. Thus in *vṛkṣaṁ anu vidyotate vidyut*, "the lightning flashes off the tree," 'The tree,' is the *lakṣaṇa*. Distinction is also made between *tadārtheya*, purpose, and *hetu*, cause which seems to include purpose. *Tadārtheya* is a manifest relation of causality between "that" and "this," as for example between "earrings" and "gold" in the compound *kuṇḍala-hiraṇyam* which means that gold is the material cause of earrings which are formed by transforming the "cause" itself.

The *kāraka*-theory of the grammarians is thus a part of their larger metaphysical framework which explains the cosmos as an interaction of objects and events, defines objects in terms of their powers or capacities to bring about events, and classifies objects into types according to the nature of their causal relationship to the events. Some of the other schools of Indian philosophy, however, do differ from the grammarians' in this conception of reality, particularly in the conception of the nature of objects (*sādhana*). The Vaiśeṣikas, for example, who are understandably concerned with the ontological reality rather than with the grammarians' linguistic reality do not postulate a power (*śakti*) apart from the object. The Mīmāṁsakas, on the other hand hold that power is different from what has power and that this power is an abstraction and beyond the range of senses. The grammarians, indifferent to this controversy, go by what the words convey, and the words to present objects and powers as distinct entities — the stem presents the objects, and the affix the power (*Vākyapadīya* III.7.38,43), although "in reality. . . . It is unity (*tattva*) which shines as distinction and identity" (*Vākyapadīya* III.7.39).

Thus on one hand the *kārakas* as *sādhanas* are cognitive categories that make an ontological statement about being and thereby constitute the boundaries of human thought. On the other hand, as perceptual/linguistic categories that are entirely dependent on the speaker's *vivakṣā,* intention, they constitute the mechanism for man's creative prediction about the universe around him, about the way he may see the instrument as agent, or purpose as instrument, etc. The *kāraka* theory, therefore, has an explanatory value for man's conception and perception of reality.

Sphoṭa-theory is the second major theory of the grammarians, a theory that defines the essential nature of language in order to explain the relationship that holds between *śabda*, the signifier, and *artha*, meaning, and the signified position between the two, a *sphoṭa*, the entity that signifies meaning. Its meta assumption is that communication of meaning is the function of language and its consequence is the highly complex theory of reality (also all knowledge) being a linguistic construct.

The word *sphoṭa* is derived from the *bhavādi* root *sephuṭ* and means literally "that which becomes manifest" or "that which blossom or develops." *Sphoṭa* is used by the grammarians to name "the essential word or language" (*śabda-tattva*), the radical *śabda* which is distinguished from, and opposed to, *dhvani*, the articulated word realized as a structure of sound. According to the Indian grammarians, the manifest language, which is discrete and sequential, is only a realization in sound of the essential linguistic reality, the essential language, which is non-discrete (*akhaṇḍa*) and universally unchanging (*nityā*) in a speech-community. It is this *śabda-tattva, sphoṭa*, non-partitive and invariant, which makes successful linguistic communication possible in spite of infinite phonetic variation, transitoriness of sound (spoken words) and the mismatch between the spoken language's segmented and sequential organization of meaning and the integral holistic meaning in reality. As Prof. K.A. Subramania Iyer explains —

> . . . the *sphoṭa* doctrine arose as a solution to the problem of the understanding of meaning. The problem was how to explain the understanding of meaning from the sounds which are uttered in a temporal sequence. As they are not simultaneous and cannot co-exist, they cannot co-operate in order to convey the meaning. The doctrine of *sphoṭa* is the grammarian's solution of the problem.
>
> — K.A. Subramania Iyer, *Bhartṛhari*,
> University of Poona, 1969, p. 160

Behind infinite variety of forms, the grammarians posit an indivisible, invariant unit (which underlines all the variant forms). This abstract unit is the signifier of meaning. It is *sphoṭa.*

Sphoṭa is the meaning-bearing element — the unit that correlates with meaning:

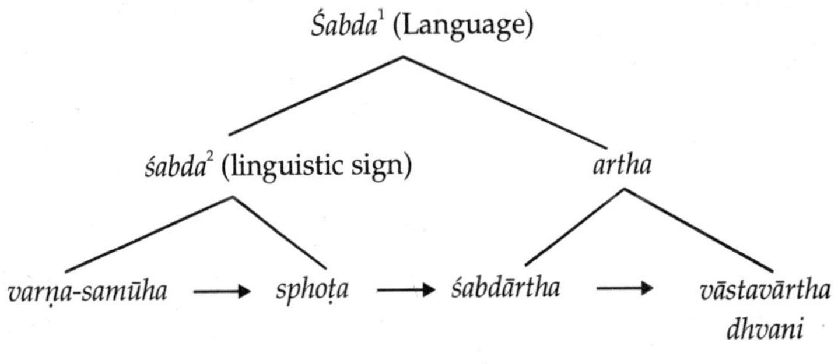

In a speech act, the speaker begins with *sphoṭa* and expresses it through *dhvani,* which the hearer grasps and then reinterprets in terms of the *sphoṭa*:

Speaker ***Hearer***

Sphoṭa ⟶ *Dhvani* ⟶ *Sphoṭa*

Patañjali is credited to be the first to set-up the construct of *Sphoṭa*. In his famous definition of *śabda*, he says: "that which when made manifest in articulated sounds brings to reader's mind the cognition of an object, is called *śabda*" (*Mahābhāṣya* 1.1).

But it is the grammarians headed by Bhartṛhari who have discussed in depth and introduced by way of deduction from Pāṇini's grammar the theory.

> that *śabda* which communicates the meaning is different from the sound which is produced and heard and which is merely instrumental in the manifestation of an internal voice which is called *sphoṭa*.
>
> — K.V. Abhyankar, 1977, p. 436

Bhartṛhari's exposition of the *sphoṭa*-theory begins with *kārikā* 44 of the first *kāṇḍa* (Chapter) of *Vākyapadīya* and proceeds through to *kārika* 120. Defining the scope of grammar, Bhartṛhari says it is concerned with that *śabda* which in one form (*rūpa*) is the *nimitta* (formal cause) of the manifest word produced by the organs of speech and hearing, and in the other form (*rūpa*) is the abstract meaning-signifying unit. Between *sphoṭa* and the manifest word a cause and effect relationship is said to hold (*Vākyapadīya* I.45), according to the point of view accepted by Bhartṛhari. Just as fire which is inherent in the wood becoming manifest after rubbing becomes a source of light and burning, in the same way the *sphoṭa* that inheres in the intellect of the speaker becomes manifest in a sequence in the form of produced and heard words (*VP* I.46). There is oneness, a correspondence, between the meaning-*sphoṭa* and word-*sphoṭa* — the speaker having made up his mind about the meaning-*sphoṭa*, makes effort then to make manifest, articulate the corresponding word-*sphoṭa* (*VP* I.47).

While there is *varṇa-sphoṭa*, *pada-sphoṭa* and *vākya-sphoṭa* (*VP* I.72), *vākya-sphoṭa* is the only reality — the idea exists as an undifferentiated whole, and the divisions like word and sound are facts of segmentation and sequence peculiar to *dhvani*, the manifest speech, and exist only in terms of the *vākya*, the whole utterance (*VP* I.73). The ultimate, indivisible, sequenceless *sphoṭa* is unaffected by these partitive units, just as it is unaffected by the phonetic variations such as length in *dhvani* (*VP* I.76-77).

Bhartṛhari is of the view that the knowledge of the sound-structure of the word and of the *sphoṭa* is inter-dependent and simultaneous and both are cognized in association with each other, and are integral — the *dhvani* leaves a super — or trans-sensory impression of both. Also a series of sounds constitute the structure of a word, and all of them have a role to play in the cognition of *sphoṭa* — each sound separately is not a revealer of *sphoṭa*, but all succeeding sounds that build up a cognition of a word which is fully established when the last sound is uttered and heard are as a whole the revealers, and then the *sphoṭa* is clearly cognized (*VP* I.83). The cognition of *sphoṭa*, therefore, is made possible by the structure of the word — the given number of sounds in a fixed sequence closed by a particular sound. Though it is the last sound that finally reveals the *sphoṭa*, the preceding sounds are equally necessary in that in the order they appear, they enable the hearer to conceptually grasp or imagine a possible word, with the possibilities getting narrowed down with every successive sound, till the last sound restricts the certainty of realization to be particular word (*VP* I.84). The cognitive process, therefore, is one of proceeding from ignorance through progressive elimination of error (the awareness of parts such a sounds, *pada*, etc.) to certain knowledge (*VP* I.85). So although *sphoṭa* is *abheda*, non-partitive, it cannot be cognized except through parts (*VP* I.86). If the sound and *pada* are seen and understood separately, we cannot get any meaning — it is only when they are seen as one, that the *sphoṭa*, the holistic conception can emerge (*VP* I.88). Through the two analogies of milk turning into curd and the seed becoming a full grown tree, involve successive transformations (*vikāra*) in a fixed order, Bhartṛhari demonstrates how *sphoṭa* is cognized by passing through several cognitive stages in a fixed sequence (*VP* I.90-91). But these stages are simply means to the final true knowledge, no more (*VP* I.92).

This brings Bhartṛhari to the important philosophical consequence of his *sphoṭa*-theory — what is the essential substance of the word (*śabda*)? Bhartṛhari reports three positions: (i) it is air that takes the form of words, (ii) it is atoms that take the form of air, and (iii) it is knowledge that takes the forms of words (*VP* I.108). The phoneticists took the first position, the Jaina thinkers the second (*VP* I.109-111). But the grammarians led by Patañjali hold that the intellect (*antaḥkaraṇa*) is knowledge, and there is in the human mind the power to communicate this knowledge in the form of meaning: therefore, word, *śabda*, is but the result (*pariṇāma*) of knowledge, the intellect (*antaḥkaraṇa*), with the birth of desire to communicate meaning, becomes the mind (*mana*) and associating itself with energy (*jaṭharāgni*) pushes the life-breath (*prāṇa-vāyu*), i.e., the same air which is also the breath, upward, and dividing itself into speech sound such as *ka*, *kha*, manifests itself as a *śabda* (word) and then subsequently dissolves itself into the speech itself (*VP* I.113, 115). Thus both the life-breath and the mind have an inherent power (*śakti*) to express meanings and it is this power that manifests itself as segments of sequential speech which enable us to cognize the reality as made up of so many different objects or forms (*VP* I.118). Therefore all meaning and all difference (*bheda*) is the product of language (*VP* I.119). Hence the sages have said: "all this world (*jagat*) is the result (*pariṇama*) of language" (*VP* I.120).

Thus the *sphoṭa* theory, like other theories in the Indian tradition, begins by accounting for and explaining a given physical, perceptible phenomenon — that of the speech act — and ends up by building an explanatory theory of reality. However, the *sphoṭa*-theory is not accepted by all the philosophical system. The Jainas, the Mīmāṁsakas, the Naiyāyikas and even Vedāntists disagreed with its formulations. The construct of *sphoṭa* is rejected outright as illogical by Mīmāṁsā, Nyāya and Cārvāka systems and as unnecessary by Vedānta as represented by Ādi Śaṅkara. The Mīmāṁsakas reject the constancy (*nityatā*) of *sphoṭa*, reject in fact along with Cārvākas the principle of oneness (*ekatva*) behind multiplicity and argue that it is the sounds themselves that communicate meaning. The Naiyāyikas reject *sphoṭa* and assert that the word (*śabda*) is merely a structure of sounds. The Sāṁkhyas do not accept the existence of any subjective knowledge independent of external reality and argue that the grammarian's intellect (*antaḥkaraṇa*) merely reflects images of external reality and that there is nothing like abstract meaning *baudhārtha*. The Jaina thinkers similarly reject the grammarians' nexus between knowledge and language and argue that words are products of atoms (*paudgalika*).

But the grammarians upheld the doctrine of *sphoṭa* by offering a variety of arguments against each of their contenders. Apart from Bhartṛhari, a number of grammarians either wrote specific treatises on *sphoṭa* or also argued *sphoṭa-vāda* in their commentaries on the *Aṣṭādhyāyī* of Pāṇini and the *Mahābhāṣya* of Patañjali. Some of the major works are — *Sphoṭaśataka* (Kṛṣṇaśāstrī Arade); *Sphoṭacandrikā* (Kṛṣṇabhaṭṭa); *Sphoṭatvanirūpaṇa* (*Kṛṣṇaśeṣa*); *Sphoṭanirūpaṇa* (Āpadeva); *Sphoṭavāda* (Kaunḍabhaṭṭa); *Sphoṭavāda* (Nāgeśa); *Sphoṭasiddhi* (Bharata Miśra); *Sphoṭasiddhi* (Maṇḍana Miśra). Haradatta's *Padamañjarī*, a commentary on *Kāśikāvṛtti*, and Kaiyaṭa's *Pradīpa*, a commentary on the *Mahābhāṣya* also need to be mentioned.

The study of **language as an abstract system** produced a number of schools of grammar in India (see Belvalkar, 1915, 1976: 47-95). But the Pāṇini-Tantra, the Pāṇinian School represents the culmination of Indian grammatical science. Pāṇini's *Aṣṭādhyāyī* evokes wonder in the minds of even modern students of linguistics, for its completeness and for its aphoristic brevity. It is the first — and so far the only one — complete structural analysis of a language whose categories and operations have an abstractness and a generality that invests them with the power to represent and explain even modern Indian languages and whose transdisciplinary cognitive categories and operations are used as constructs in the schools of philosophy as well as the sciences. It is in this sense that Pāṇini's grammar acquired the status of a general modelling device for the acquisition and structuration of all knowledge. The tradition, therefore, calls Vyākaraṇa the Veda (knowledge) of Vedas (all knowledge). In its overt form and organization the *Aṣṭādhyāyī* is a finished system that looks deceptively simple (see *fig.* on p. 29).

This is Pāṇini's analysis of the structure of Sanskrit. The entire store of words is divided into two large grammatical classes, the Bases and the Affixes, and all utterances are seen as built up by successive affixation, which is the central grammatical operation in the *Aṣṭādhyāyī* at all levels. The Bases are divided into two classes, the Nominal and the Verb-roots, and the corresponding two classes of Affixes are also distinguished — the inflectional affixes, *sup* and *tiṅ*: *sup* the nominal (*kāraka*) affixes, and *tiṅ*, the verb-affixes. Besides, there are the derivational affixes too, from (i) the derived nominal bases, (ii) the feminine bases, and (iii) the derived verbs. For a given utterance whose grammaticality is to be established (to show how it is *siddha*), the process of formation/generation (*niṣpatti*) begins with the formation of the nominal bases which are then assigned a *kāraka*-relation which becomes a condition

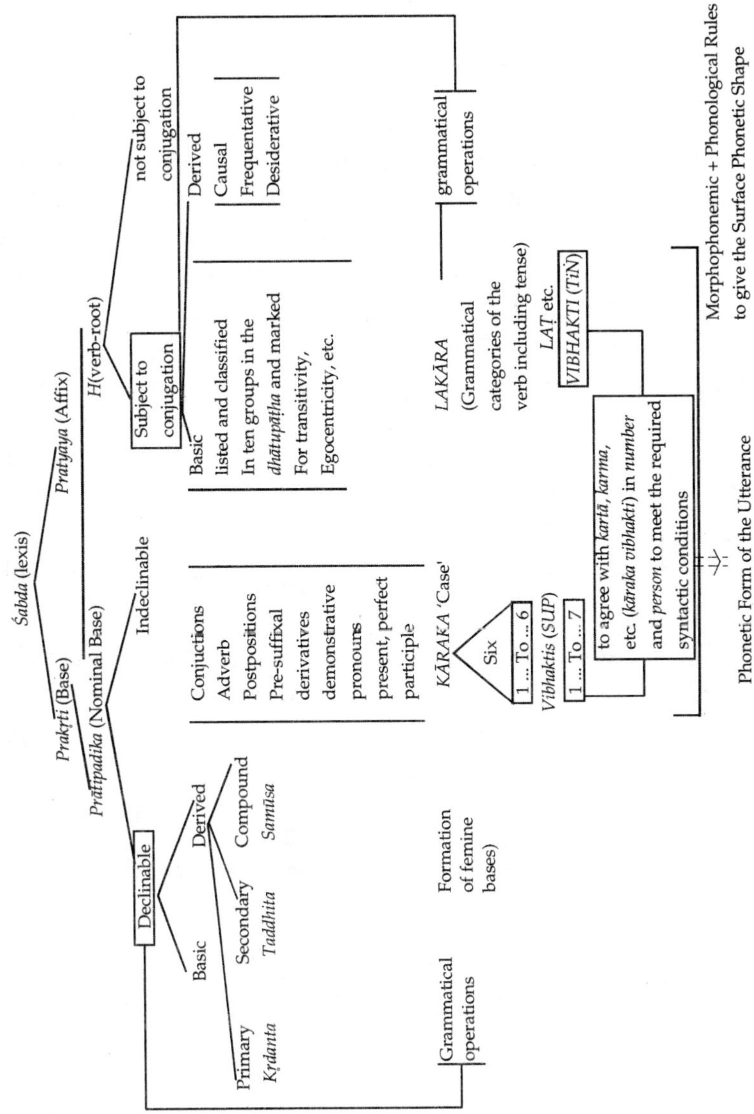
Śabda (lexis)
Prakṛti (Base)
Pratyaya (Affix)
Prātipadika (Nominal Base)
H(verb-root)
Declinable
Indeclinable
Subject to conjugation
not subject to conjugation
Basic
Derived
Primary *Kṛdanta*
Secondary *Taddhita*
Compound *Samāsa*
Conjuctions
Adverb
Postpositions
Pre-suffixal derivatives
demonstrative pronouns
present, perfect participle
Basic
listed and classified
In ten groups in the *dhātupāṭha* and marked
For transitivity,
Egocentricity, etc.
Derived
Causal
Frequentative
Desiderative
Grammatical operations
Formation of femine bases)
KĀRAKA 'Case'
Six
1 ... To ... 6
Vibhaktis (*SUP*)
1 ... To ... 7
LAKĀRA
(Grammatical categories of the verb including tense)
LAṬ etc.
VIBHAKTI (*TIṄ*)
grammatical operations
to agree with *kartā*, *karma*, etc. (*kāraka vibhakti*) in *number* and *person* to meet the required syntactic conditions
Phonetic Form of the Utterance
Morphophonemic + Phonological Rules to give the Surface Phonetic Shape

for the choice of a particular *vibhakti* (case-affix) which would reflect the number of the base as well. The *gaṇa* (class) of the verb-root (√*bhū-ādi*) interacts with the tense of the utterance subsumed by one of the *lakāra* (*laṭ*, etc.) to act as a complex condition for the choice of nine-term set of *tiṅ*-affixes structured 3 × 3 in terms of person and number. Choice of one particular affix from this set of nine is made — and this is the syntactic heart of this grammar — depending on the noun in the utterance with which the verb "agrees" to reflect the syntactic-semantic relations that hold between the verb and the nouns in the utterance. The *tiṅ*-affix so selected reflects the syntactic-semantic relations that hold between the verb and the nouns in the utterance. The *tiṅ*-affix so selected reflects in its form the nominal categories of the "governing" noun, its number and person. At different stages of this operation the (base+affix) composition is given successively changing phonological shape through sets of morphophonemic rules, till the rules of *sandhi* (putting together of sounds in context) operate finally to yield the phonetic form.

Pāṇini distributes this information over his eight chapters. The *Aṣṭādhyāyī* has three main divisions :

I. *Chapters. 1 and 2*: Pāṇini enumerates "words," *pada*, and introduces his terminology, i.e., the categories of his grammar.

II. *Chapters. 3 to 5*: The *pada* or words are separated into roots and affixes and their classes and sub-classes are identified.

III. *Chapters. 6-7*: Through operational rules he puts together roots and affixes by establishing the Āgama (what appears or is put in place) and *ādeśa* (saying what happens to which element as a consequence of the Āgama).

The first quarter — each chapter has 4 quarters — of chapter VIII, deals with the pronunciation of words. Quarters 2 to 4 called *Tripadi* or *Asiddha Kāṇḍa* also deal with the phonetic form and handle phenomena not handled in chapters 6 and 7 for the sake of brevity. The total system of Pāṇini Tantra consist of : (i) The *Dhātupāṭha* (verb-lexicon); (ii) the *Gaṇapāṭha* (nominal-lexicon); (iii) the *Śiva-Sūtras* (morphophonemic classification of Sanskrit speech-sounds); (iv) the *Sūtrapāṭha* (rules proper), and (v) the *Liṅgānuśāsana*, gender-lexicon.

Evidently, the simplicity of the overall structure conceals the complex structural analyses of classes of elements (such as "types of bases") and of the categories of grammar (such as "types of primary derivational affixes," etc.). Besides the complexity of operations — rules, conditions and contexts of application, and number, and order of the application of rules — is also not revealed. It is the rigorous discrimination of classes, categories and operations on the basis of their nature and function that enables Pāṇini to organize an extremely complex, though seemingly simple, and a completely explicit grammar of Sanskrit.

This structure of language and its categories are part of the interpretative frame work, the *śabda-bodha*, and as we have noted earlier Patañjali has argued the role of grammar both in effective communication and in the establishment of meaning. But it must be noted that the Buddhists challenged, among others, the role of grammar in the inerpretation of texts. This challenge is represented as the *pūrva-pakṣa* in *Adhikaraṇa* 9, of *Tantra-Vārttika* of Kumārila Bhaṭṭa (seventh century AD).

Attention is drawn by them to usages that are at variance with what the science of Grammar lays down but which cannot be classed as *apaśabda* or *mleccha*, viz., anomalies in the Vedas, usage of excellent writers such as Nārada and Jaimini, the language of Pāṇini's own rules, the forms employed by Kātyāyana and Patañjali himself are cited in support (*TV* pp. 271-76).

The exegetical role of grammar is also rejected. Vedas are rather preserved, understood and analysed by the students and teachers with the help rather of the Prātiśākhyas which deal with "accent, conjunction of letters, hiatus, explanations, precedence and sequence, etc., all of which are directly connected with the study of the text of the Veda itself. And as such this fact distinctly points to the fact of the Prātiśākhyas, and not the grammar of Pāṇini, etc., being the real "subsidiary" of the Veda (Vedāṅga)" (*TV* p. 282).

And, the last major use of grammar mentioned in *Mahābhāṣya, asandeha, artha-nirdhāraṇa*, determination of the meanings of the texts, is also rejected. First of all, many doubts regarding meanings "are set aside by the observation of the usage of experienced and learned people; and the few that are still left are cleared by the help of commentaries, etymological explanations . . . because all these latter deal with the meanings (of words and sentences). On the other hand, Grammar takes no notice of the meanings of words, dealing with merely verbal forms. . . ." (*TV* p. 283) In fact, when we have doubts about the meaning of the grammatical rules themselves, we have to take the help of the commentaries, which address themselves to specific problems and bring about specific ideas.

However, grammar is the third major aspect of language-study in its epistemological dimension. Statements and theories about the epistemological status of language, we have noted above, flowed from the investigation of language as an abstract system. The categories, assumptions and operations of Pāṇini's grammar and its theoretical foundation, when examined in principle, were found to be powerful explanatory mechanisms that would account for language and much more. The first such pertinent theory of the grammarians is the *kāraka* theory. Finally, the abstract structure of Pāṇini's grammar, its inter and intra-categorical relations, came to serve as a model for organizing knowledge in other disciplines as well. So also did the assumptions of his grammar — such as the goal of exhaustively and explicitly describing the empirical data — contribute to the development of sciences.

Further, his numerous constructs and conceptions — the zero, *anuvṛtti*, "recurrence," elision, deletion, modification, affixation, condition for an operation to take place, context bound versus context free operations, functional typology of operations, typology of the "result" of operations, contra-diction-resolution, exception and restriction, etc. — and his formal devices of statement, such as a meta language, a nominalist style, several devices of abbreviation, and the intrinsic ordering of the statement (rules) could be and were seen to be related fundamentally to the way the human mind processes, organizes and describes experiences and therefore had the potential validity and explanatory power to transcend the domain of language and become general explanatory modes. In relation to reality, language is seen to have two axes — the ontological and the epistemological. The store of words, the lexis, names the objects and events and therefore belongs to the ontological axis. The "discipline of words" — *śabdānuśāsana* — is grammar, and its categories, operations and its assumptions constitute the epistemological axis of language in that they are the means of knowledge of the language. In a more fundamental sense also they are epistemic — when marked by sufficient generality they constitute explanatory constructs for a wide range of phenomena outside the linguistic domain as well. For example, the case category *karaṇa*, instrument, is a term in logical and philosophical systems as well. Grammar therefore has the dual function of being an instrument of knowledge of both language and reality:

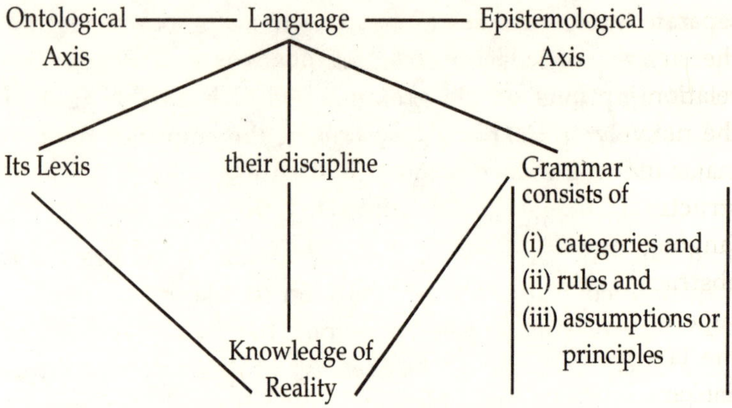

In the Indian thought grammar is the first among the six auxiliary exegetical disciplines (Vedāṅga), because it is the discipline of other disciplines, the foundation of all disciplines of learning (*vidyā*). "All knowledge," says Bhartṛhari, "takes the form of words, exists in words . . . *vāṇī* (language) makes possible the cognition of all disciplines, arts and crafts and is responsible for cognition of separate existence and identity of all objects such as "pot" and "cot" (*Vākyapadīya* 125). In fact, ". . . language constitutes the consciousness in all animate beings; there can in fact be no conscious animate beings that have no language" (*Vākyapadīya* 126). Language, therefore, is the system in terms of which knowledge exists and through which knowledge is gained and as grammar is the system of language it is the key system, a general semiotic framework for the cognition (*bodha*) of meaning (*artha*), universe/existence (*jagat*) and organized bodies of information about particular aspects of existence (*vidyā*). Grammar may in fact have not just this passive, instrumental relationship to reality by which it helps us to understand and make sense of things. It may also be an active principle which imposes itself as the creative, shaping system of the reality so that we perceive the structure of reality in terms of the grammatical structure. It is difficult to really separate these two roles — the passive instrumental role and the active explanatory role of grammar. This complex relationship between thought and reality is quite evident in the nexus between the Pāṇinian grammar and some of the major Indian philosophical positions. Pāṇini's grammar in its structural analysis of the roots and affixes of the Sanskrit language into a hierarchy of levels of increasingly general, abstract classes or arrangements terminating in the single superordinate entity, *śabda*, is the first formal illustration of the later Advaita philosophy associated chiefly with Ādi Śaṅkara, whereby this visible, multiple and multifarious world of reality is seen to be a transformed manifestation (*vivarta*) of the one superordinate principle — *Brahman*:

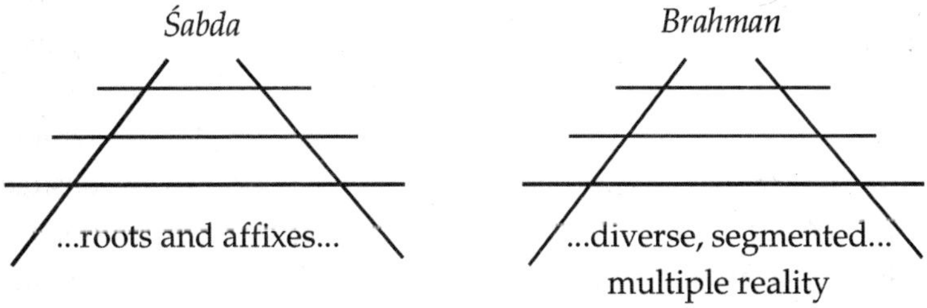

The ultimate explanation of empirical facts or phenomena would be some philosophical construct, philosophical in the sense of being abstract and general. *Vivarta*, visible world is the transformed manifest appearance of a transcendental construct. The innumerable linguistic forms of the empirical reality of language getting successively classified into a hierarchy of increasingly general and abstract constructs are finally absorbed in the single construct *śabda*, "language." Thus, for example, consider the domain of *kāraka*-affixes. The third person nominative singular affix takes several empirical forms: zero, — *-am*, *a*, or simply *visarga* (:), a kind of breathy *h*. Each of these has as many phonetic tokens as the instances of their articulation by innumerable speakers. These four are classified at the next higher level of categorization as *prathamā vibhakti*, or "the first case affix," along with the dual and plural nominative affixes. The twenty-one *prathamā*, etc., *vibhakti*s, case affixes, are categorized at the next higher level as *sup* in opposition to all the verbal affixes, *tiṅ*. *Sup* and *tiṅ* are categorized as *pratyaya*, "affix," in opposition to *Prakṛti*, "stem." *Prakṛti* and *pratyaya* together are then subsumed under *Śabda* "language."

In the domain of case-affixes (*kāraka*-affixes), the *nirākāra*, abstract, *sup* is the essential reality — this changeless formless concept manifests itself as different *vibhakti*s or forms (*Vākyapadīya* III.3.87). In this way, there are several underlying layers or levels of constructs behind the manifest grammatical categories, constructs that have no physical existence, but exist as real entities in our mind, in our linguistic competence not only as categories of linguistic organization but also of thought. For this reason, several categories of grammar are, as we pointed out, transdisciplinary. Prof. K.C. Chatterji (1964) and Prof. B.K. Matilal (1985) have discussed this explanatory potential of several grammatical categories — *kartā* (agent), *karaṇa* (instrument), *dravya* (substance), *jāti* (class), *guṇa* (attribute) — by analysing their status in philosophy and grammar. Some of these categories, such as *karaṇa*, instrument, in fact, originated in grammar and were then borrowed into other disciplines such a Nyāya School of Philosophy (Matilal 1985: 372). The Vaiśeṣika categories of *dravya* (substance) and *guṇa* (attribute) are evidently related to the same grammatical categories. Again a category may appear in other disciplines in an allied sense — thus, *upasarga*, the dynamic derivational verb-prefix that modifies the meaning of the verb-base to which it is attached, is employed in *Āyurveda*, the science of medicine, to have the allied meaning of an ailment that is superimposed on another, and in Yoga philosophy to mean "a hurdle" or "obstacle." These *upsarga*s, prefixes, such as *vi* —

appear as inital components of a wide range of terminology in the nine major philosophical systems (Vedānta, Mīmāṁsā, Sāṁkhya, Yoga, Vaiśeṣika, Buddhist, Jain and Cārvāka) and in Indian poetics (Heimann, 1951: 1-2).

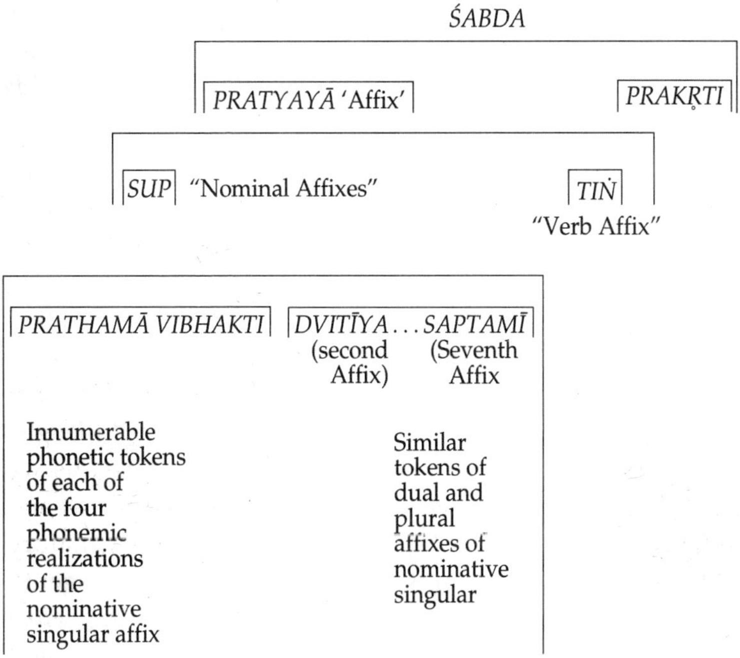

Finally, the principles of grammar, the foundation of categories and rules, are the general and universal principles of thought, the primary models of intellection (thought processes). All systems or models of knowledge of particular segments of reality make use of these general principles along with local principles restricted to particular domains. To give some example —

(1) The *prakṛti-pratyaya* opposition is the radical-catalyst opposition involved in the principles of particularization and of derivation. By the principle *sandhi* rules,

the *pragṛhya*-vowels for example, exemplify the powerful principle of assimilation. Corresponding to the *pragṛhya* vowels, we have the "inert" gases in chemistry that don't "mix" with other gases.

(5) The meta-rules of grammar, the *Paribhāṣā-Sūtra*s, all too evidently represent principles of judgement that help one interpret or select unequivocally from several, or contradictory choices and they are widely employed in philosophy as well as in ordinary life.

(6) Finally, we must refer to Pāṇini's use of Sanskrit and its grammatical categories to describe the grammar of Sanskrit itself — the meta-use. The conception of "meta," particularly, "meta-language" is again an important general principle.

This multi-dimensional analysis and understanding of the structure of language, its relationship to cognitive processes and reality and the semantic status of its categories, operations and principles, put language at the centre of India's intellectual tradition.

Since all interpretation is making sense of things, it is language that is the chief instrument and object of India's interpretative tradition. Exegetic exercise in this tradition is, therefore, essentially a linguistic exercise.

2

Texts and Commentary Tradition

The Interpretative Tradition

THE presence or absence of a powerful interpretative tradition is an index of the degree and extent of the liberty of thought and discussion available in a given civilization more so if the tradition has or hasn't produced and has or hasn't accorded respect to competing and even conflicting interpretations. India, on this count has a long and continuous interpretative tradition that has facilitated liberty of thought and expression.

Pāṇini's *Aṣṭādhyāyī* (seventh century BC[1]) indicates the presence of a literature of commentaries, *vyākhyāna*, in his *sūtra*, rule, IV.3.66: *tasya vyākhyāna iti ca vyākhyātavya namana*: "an affix comes in the sense of its commentary, as well as, in the sense of what occurs there." Patañjali in his *Mahābhāṣya*, lays down the broad rudiments of the process of *vyākhyāna* or explanatory interpretation (I.I.). Commentaries were written

---

1. Indians have not worried much about or attached much significance to "dates," nor to "who" or "by whom"; but, "what;" and "why" and "how" matter. However, the dates satisfy certain curiosity. They are subject to much debate and a person or an event can be located anywhere in a wide temporal span. On the basis of internal and external evidence, it is possible to estimate the time, roughly. Pāṇini does not mention the Buddha. In Indian scholarship, not to mention Buddha is not to have known him; and not to have known Buddha is to have been born before Buddha. Hence Pāṇini is at least seventh century BC. Most Western scholars put him in the sixth or fifth century BC while Indian scholars place him further back.

on almost all the major texts belonging to different types of literature, *vāṅmaya* (literally, "that which is permeated by speech"). Classical typology divides all literature into three classes:

(1) ***Śruti***: literature dealing with knowledge that is not contingent on any given person, or time (the Vedas and the Upaniṣads belong here).

(2) ***Smṛti***: literature dealing with knowledge that has already been known or cognized through any or all of the different means of knowledge, belong here.

(3) ***Kāvya***: compositions dealing with imaginary themes and localized in the understanding of one individual or a set of individuals.

The Śruti-Smṛti opposition is also described as the Nigama-Āgama opposition. Śruti-literature is Nigama, a word in which the meaning of certainty (of the truth of statement) is inherent, as is the meaning of received (knowledge). Āgama on the other hand, is "what has come," i.e., has had a known origin.

Pāṇini has mentioned five classes of Sanskrit literature that existed in his time. The five types are based on the relationship of the author and the text and also on the nature of knowledge embodied in the text. The five classes are —

1. *Dṛṣṭa*: that which is "seen" or visualized. In this class Pāṇini includes compositions which are neither known to have been "created" (by an individual) nor are adaptations of already existing works. All *mantra*-literature is considered *dṛṣṭa*, directly realized or intuited and not created. It contains a body of knowledge of the kind that is constant and absolute (like the fact that "anything that is thrown up must fall down"). Pāṇini refers to an instance of this body of literature in 4.2.7.

2. *Prokta*: means "expressed" or "taught." One expounds or teaches both one's own compositions and the compositions of others (Pāṇini, 4.3.101), and in Sanskrit the names of the two kinds of expositions will be inflectionally distinguished (see Pāṇini, 4.3.116). Five kinds of instrumental affixes are used in Sanskrit to name authors of such texts (Pāṇini IV.3.102-111). A vast body of *prokta*-literature was extant in Pāṇini's time, if we go by his evidence — explanatory Saṁhitā, *Brāhmaṇas*, Kalpa-Sūtras, Śikṣā texts, *Vyākaraṇa*, Prātiśakhyas, *Nirukta*, Chanda texts, Joytiṣa texts, texts of dramaturgy, *Itihāsa*, Purāṇa texts, Astronomy texts, Mathematics, texts of architecture and sculpture, and those dealing with animals and birds (see Yudhisthira Mimamsaka, pp. 7-24).

   Prokta literature deals with a body of knowledge that has been formulated earlier by a teacher and enounced again by someone.

3. *Upajñāta*: is that body of knowledge which has been conceptualized or laid down by an individual, that is, knowledge acquired by oneself without being taught as such. (Pāṇini, 4.3.115) Pāṇini's own grammar is an example of this in those portions where he has made an advance over previously available knowledge, for example in the organization of tenses of Sanskrit (Yudhisṭhira Mimamsaka, 1963:25)

4. *Kṛta*: Pāṇini has mentioned compositions, *ākhyāyikas* and poetical compositions, in two separate *sūtras* IV.3.87 and IV.3.116. The *Kāśikā* mentions the compositions dealing with the life and times of Yayāti, Subhadrā, Vāsavadattā etc., as examples for the rule 4.3.87.

> For the rule 4.3.118, various compositions such as *Vararūci Kāvya* are mentioned. Pāṇini himself is supposed to have composed a long poem — *Jāmbavantavijaya.* The epic *Mahābhārata* also belongs here. Apart from imaginative compositions, concordances of the Vedas also belong here.

To this, he adds the fifth class of literature, Vyākhyāṇa, the commentary, thus attesting to the existence of this tradition prior to him. He refers to a particular affix which comes "in the sense of 'a commentary,' after the name of a work to be explained. . ." (Vasu, 1980: 1.772, 4.3.66). The *Kāśikā* illustrates the formations in a series of rules (4.3.66 to 4.3.73) and names several disciplines whose commentaries are subsumed under these rules — and also cites the *ṛgayana-gaṇa* from the *Gaṇapāṭha* which includes metrics, Nyāya, grammar, Purāṇas, architecture, astronomy, Dharma-Śāstras, Upaniṣads, phonetics, etc. So as early as Pāṇini's time, a vast body of commentary literature must have been in existence.

Even when a culture is not *bibliolatorous*, it would often accord a special status to a text. A distinction may be proposed between a text that is repeatedly made to accord with, "produce," one given 'conformist' reading and a text that has provenly generated competing philosophies, viz., the *Ṛgveda* as the source of different philosophic systems and a text like Bādarāyaṇa's *Brahma-Sūtras* which, among many more, has produced, through commentaries, at least five major schools — monism, qualified monism, theory of difference and non-difference, dualism and "Pure." Where the interpretative traditions originate and are built around such "sacred" texts — sacred in the sense of being the source-books for ideas, customs and practices — understandably, a rigorous system of interpretation tends to develop, a science of exegesis, for, great store is laid by the knowledge of the exact meaning of these texts. From the very beginning, three paths have been laid down to guide an individual's conduct in life — *karma* (action), *upāsanā* (belief), *jñāna* (knowledge) — a distinction of great universality that rules the conduct of people. People may believe in performance and practice, in doing, and aim at success without being tied down to their conduct; or they may believe in something and let that belief rule ideas, without being tied to one belief and without feeling obliged to gain salvation, meaningfulness or fulfilment. Of these, "knowledge" is held to be superior though it is recognized that it is a highly complex entity and that *dharma* is the superordinate principle of life; it is *dharma* which determines the validity and value of knowledge and conduct.[2]

The importance of properly acquired valid knowledge was no doubt responsible for creating the scholarly pursuit of interpretation. Hence, we note the growth and development of a *darśana* known as Mīmāṁsā. Thinkers tried to impart to the process a particular rigour and precision and created a work of great merit in the systematization and generality it achieved.

Most of the object texts — except for Śrutis — are themselves reasoned expositions. The Śāstras which have come in for extensive interpretation, deal not with the supernatural, but with the rules of conduct, or modes of daily life or with the theses of different disciplines. The task of interpretation, as such, is three-fold : (i) to determine and explain the meaning of the text; and (ii) to establish the relevance and significance of, and sometimes to amend, the rules of conduct or the thesis of a Śāstra — whichever applicable — in case where they grow out of tune with either the usage or the knowledge of the time; and (iii) to articulate the rationale and the rationality of

2. Patañjali talks of *jñāna-dharma* and says that *adharma* results from the absence of correct knowledge, cf. *Mahābhāṣya*, I.1.

the assertion and defend them against counter philosophies or objection.

What sets the interpretative process in motion, therefore, is not only the symbolic and the seemingly irrational text alone, but also the ambiguous, the contradictory, the apparently meaningless texts and the clear and direct statements as well. The Śrutis are a special case. An important predication about them is that they are *apauruṣeya*, that is, not linked to a person, a place or a time. Their meaning is not contingent on local or shifting variable. They are expressed in a language that is almost a code — a symbolics, a language that is obscure in places (*parokṣa*) because it has undergone change or, because it has been originally so expressed. R̥gvedic or Śruti exegesis stems in part from this obscurity of language and seeks establishment of the indirectly expressed meaning, reconciliation of the irrational with the visible and the logical, i.e., the identification of obscure meanings. A long line of interpreters addressed themselves to this task.

Characteristics of the Tradition

The tradition of interpretation in India is (i) continuous, and (ii) cumulative, originating as it does in the R̥gvedic exegesis.

It is hoary because in any case while dealing with this tradition we are dealing with the world's earliest poetry and the earliest prose. The attested tradition begins with Yāska,[3] the eighth century BC *Nairukta*, the "expositionist," who

3. We say Yāska is the first attested exegete because (i) Yāska himself refers (in *Nirukta*, I.1.3) to earlier exegetes who debated the major premise of his discipline — the assumption that all Sanskrit nouns are derived from verb-roots; (ii) Patañjali says in the *Mahābhāṣya* (I.1) that the grammars were in the form of lists, whose each word was analysed and explained separately. The earlier work has been lost; its parts and portions are now available only as incorporated in subsequent texts.

composed his *Nirukta* to explain and determine the meanings of 2041 *parokṣa*, "obscure," uses in the Ṛgveda.

It is known[4] that the tradition of interpretation, in the sense of determination of meaning in the particular use and context, begins in the *Ṛgveda* itself. There are, in the Sākala recension of the Saṁhitā, 1240 instances of nirvacana,[5] "a full exposition of meaning through analysis of the word." Thus in the same expression we find used together a noun and a verb both derived from the same verb-root, with the verb- root establishing the meaning of the noun as well, viz.

Uṣā uccheda (I.48.8) — "the dawn that destroyed" — that destroyed (darkness). Thus *uṣā*, "dawn" — destroyer of darkness.

Both the noun and the verb are from the root $\sqrt{uṣ}$ — which means "to burn."

Out of the 1240 *nirvacanas*, "etymologies," 675 help establish the meaning and also suggest the derivation from a given exposition (we are avoiding the familiar word etymology on account of its inapplicability) of words that are not obscure and whose meaning is directly expressed — the *pratyakṣa vṛtti* words.

If we trace this particular line of exegesis — interpretation of the *mantras* — the line is traceable next to the prose *Brāhmaṇas*[6] which give an interpretation through minimal

4. Cf. Shivnarayana Shastri, *Nirukta*, p. 30, see also by the same author — *Ṛgveda saṁhitā mē vyutpatti cintan* in B.N. Tewary (ed.), 1972, pp. 24-118.

5. *nirvacana, nir* +($\sqrt{vac}$)+*lyut* affix — "a full exposition."

6. *Brāhmaṇas*, prose commentaries, vehicles of sacerdotal and esoteric disputations corresponding to the Saṁhitās. More important among them are the *Aitareya, Taittirīya* (*Kṛṣṇa Yajurveda*), the *Śatapatha* (*Śukla Yajurveda*), *Pañcaviṁśa* (*Sāmaveda*) and *Gopatha* (*Atharvaveda*).

paraphrase. Next come the Vedāṅgas.[7] Among them, the school of etymology (*Nirukta*) with its task of verbal interpretation, as we have already noted. Among them we have also to mention Pāṇini and his *Śabdānuśāsana*, grammar: his eight-chaptered grammar generates the Vedic language too, *Vaidiki*, besides generating *bhāṣā*, the current speech, which of course is his primary concern. Pāṇini's rules have been intimately involved in the Ṛgvedic exegesis (Devasthali, 1967).

Above all, we have the great school of Mīmāṁsā, analysis, one of the six Vedic schools of philosophy, which originating around fourth century BC, spans almost a thousand years through a long line of thinker-exegetists ending in the authoritative work of Kumārila Bhaṭṭa (seventh century AD) and Prabhākara Miśra seventh-eighth century AD). A number of medieval commentators followed, without much originality, the traditional line finally culminating in Sāyaṇa — a fourteenth-century exegetist, whose school gave "the last extant complete interpretation of the Vedas and *Brāhmaṇa*s in a systematic way" (Anirvan, 1937: 320).

This tradition of Ṛegvedic interpretation, one of exegesis in the ritual and the philosophic context, is essentially eclectic: (i) it allows for a deeper (spiritual) interpretation as well,[8] (ii) it allows and accepts the possibility of other meanings, interpretations; and, above all, (iii) it bases itself, to a large extent, on an objective linguistic methodology. It is definitely not dogmatic.

---

7. Vedāṅgas, literally "limbs of the Vedas," i.e., disciplines auxiliary to the study of Vedas. They are six in number : phonetics, etymology, ritual and conduct, metrics, astronomy and grammar.
8. Cf. Yāska, in *Nirukta* (VII.4; I.20), he discuses the significance of gods, for example, and relates them to the process of naming the attributes of Nature and the attributes held desirable, and relates them then to the Self.

Further, this tradition is cumulative — every succeeding commentator builds on the work of his predecessor. What we get is a kind of collective interpretation.

But first we must consider the broad typology of interpretation.

Types of Interpretation

We are here concerned chiefly with the learned tradition.

There is a parallel popular tradition. Its elements are the folk modulations of literature and the widespread *kathā*, narrative, practices. The folk literature performances "interpret" the themes of scholastic literary texts through modifications/extensions and generally the "divine" element is transmuted into "human" in such replays. The *Śrīmadbhāgavata* themes for example are retold in *ākhyāyikas*, the oral narratives. There is also in the rural countryside the customary *saptāh*, a weekly get together of a group of villages for commercial and cultural exchange, at which *Bhāgavata-kathā*, narration of the *Bhāgavata Purāṇa* dealing with the life and times of Lord Kṛṣṇa, is an integral element. *Kathā* tradition is very pervasive and *itihāsas*, epics and mythological histories, supply the content of this tradition, which in turn has provided a narrative model for imaginative compositions in almost all modern Indian languages. The narrators, the *vācakas*, generally men and women learned in different degrees, are familiar with and are quite often trained in the learned commentary tradition. They are chiefly instrumental in the dispersal of learning, and have played a seminal role in making the core substance of Indian thought a common property of the masses, in transforming the vocabulary of learning into the ordinary vocabulary of the ordinary people. This popular tradition no doubt enters into a two-way interaction with the learned tradition — arguments, examples and interpretations travel both ways, though one can safely postulate, that the learned tradition remains the source for the popular tradition.

The learned tradition has, as we pointed out above, a threefold task of:

(i) determining the meaning

(ii) establishing the relevance, and

(iii) articulating the rationality (of belief, etc.)

One typology is yielded by the types of texts commented upon:

(i) interpretations of Śruti-texts: the Vedas and the Upaniṣads[9]

(ii) interpretations of the Smṛti-literature

(iii) interpretations of the Śāstra-literature, i.e., of ancillary *Vedāṅgas* such as grammar and etymology and astronomy.

To this we may add

(iv) the interpretations of *kāvyas* (including *Itihāsa-Purāṇa*).

These differ broadly — the interpretative exercises on Śrutis have handled questions of metaphysics and have been instrumental in generating diverse schools of philosophy; the Smṛti interpretations have been concerned chiefly with modulating and adapting the rules of conduct and elements of thought for the changed times and different places. Of these, the *śāstra*-interpretations have been concerned with rigorous

---

9. Upaniṣad, literally means "teaching imparted by the teacher to the pupil who sits (*ṣad*) near him (*upa*) in a closed, select (*ni*) group . . . also called Vedānta . . . first . . . systematic philosophizing . . . over 200 Upaniṣad . . . usually, thirteen . . . are regarded as the principal. *Īśa, Kena, Kaṭha, Praśna, Muṇḍaka, Māṇḍukya, Tattirīya, Aitareya, Chāndogya, Bṛhadāraṇyaka, Śvetāśvatara, Maitrī* and *Kauṣītakī.*" (Dandekar, 1937:27-29).

determination of meaning of words and sentences specifically their refrential domains; the *kāvya* interpretation has chiefly addressed itself to the problem of indirect language.

According to the nature of statement, the interpretations take these forms:

(i) *annotations*: brief comments, viz., Kātyāyana's *vārttika*s on *Aṣṭādhyāyī*

(ii) *paraphrase*: as in the *Brāhmaṇa*s and in *Kāśikā*, a commentary on *Aṣṭādhyāyī*

(iii) *elaboration* (paraphrase and/or explanation with example and counter example)

(iv) *exposition*: detailed, critical discussion, *vyākhyāna* and,

(v) a new text out of a section in the original, viz., the Upaniṣads

(vi) finally, a creative variant on a given theme, literary as well as folk.

All these, barring the fifth and the sixth one, take the format of a commentary called *ṭīkā* in the tradition. Commentary is the major form that interpretation takes in the tradition. The commentator, the exegete, is the *ṭīkākāra* who holds a place of much honour. According to the controlling metaphysics, the commentators are classified into "Schools" viz. *advaitavādī ṭīkākāra*, the Non-Dualist Interpreter, etc.

The Commentary Tradition

The commentary tradition is a cumulative tradition, i.e., a long line of commentaries on a given text generally follow each other, each succeeding commentary taking into account and building on the preceding one. We may illustrate this with reference to two disparate texts — the *Mīmāṁsā-Sūtra* of Jaimini and Pāṇini's *Aṣṭādhyāyī*. These two offer examples of (i) interlaced commentaries which interpret and build up the meaning of the object — text from within a single school of thought. On the other hand, we have (ii) chronologically sequential commentaries that take into account the preceding commentaries but which differ in their basic assertions from each other in some ontological category or categories and epistemologically also in the relative ordering of the means of knowledge. Major commentaries and interpretations of The *Bhagavad-Gītā*, are thus not commentaries on each other but independent commentaries on the same text, contending with each other.

It is not possible to understand a text without an equally close study of the commentaries. Thus for a proper understanding of the *Mīmāṁsā-Sūtra*, we have to fall back on its major commentaries, and the commentaries on·commentaries. Sir Ganganath Jha has recorded and reviewed the major ones in his introduction to his own English rendering of Kumārila Bhaṭṭa's *Śloka-Vārttika* (Ganganath Jha, 1983: rpt. ii-iii). Mīmāṁsā is a science of judicial interpretation of the sacrificial portion (*karma-kāṇḍa*) of the Veda just as Vedānta is that of the *jñāna-kāṇḍa*, the portions dealing with knowledge. The oldest commentary now available is the *Bhāṣya* by Śabara Svāmī, popularly known as *Śābara-Bhāṣya*.[10] This *bhāṣya* mentions older, now available, commentaries chief among which is the *Vṛtti* of Upavarṣa. Śabara's commentary is divided into *adhikaraṇa*s (topic-division) and each *adhikaraṇa* has been given head-notes. Further, Śabara has given lucid and copious notes on each *sūtra*.[11] Each topic — *adhikaraṇa* — is defined and briefly explained and he has discussed the for and against of the

10. See References under Sir Ganganatha Jha, 1933 (1973 rpt.)

11. *Sūtra* is a highly precise, abbreviated, generally verbless statement. The Vedāṅgas are all written in these aphorisms and this nominal style became the style of scholastic disputation. see, R.G. Bhandarkar, 1883.

author's views. Above all, he develops in a systematic manner the system of word-meaning relationships, and is a major contributor to the recognition of links that bind, and that had long been developing between interpretation and language.[12] Next we come to Kumārila Bhaṭṭa[13] who wrote his great commentary on *Śābara-Bhāṣya*. His work is divided into three parts, known under three different names: (1) *Śloka-Vārttika*, which discusses the first section of the first discourse (*adhyāya*) dealing with *tarka*, principles of argumentation; (2) *Tantra-Vārttika*, dealing with the last three sections of *Adhyāya* I and whole of *Adhyāya*s II and III; and (3) *Tupṭīkā*, a short commentary dealing with *Adhyāya*s IX-XII. Kumārila has often dissented from Śabara's readings and his major focus is on valid epistemology — valuation of the means of knowledge. He has discussed at great length the nature and status of *śabda* as a means of knowledge, the nature of cognition involved therein, the sentence meaning and the shift in the meaning of words (*Śloka-Vārttika*, V.6; VI-XIII; XXIV-XXVI) and the role of grammar, *Vyākaraṇa*, in interpretation and its limitations (*Tantra-Vārttika*: *Adhikaraṇa* 9). In his work, Kumārila Bhaṭṭa displays an astounding range and command of linguistic knowledge.[14] On *Śloka-Vārttika*, there were two well-known subsequent commentaries, and on *Tantra-Vārttika*, there were

---

12. See, for example, Śabara's exegesis on the first and second *sūtra* 1.2.4 and part of his comment on *sūtra* 5.

13. For Kumārila Bhaṭṭa's work, see references under Sir Ganganatha Jha for *Śloka-Vārttika* and *Tantra-Vārttika*. *Tupṭīkā* is not available in English translation. The original has been published in the Benaras Sanskrit Series.

14. For a detailed statement on Kumārila Bhaṭṭa's linguistic knowledge, see Pt. Gopinath Kaviraj, "*Tantra-Vārttika* and its Author" in Sir Ganganatha Jha, 1903-24; 1983 (rpt.) pp. v-xx. (also see, *Tantra-Vārttika*, 295, 298-9, 260).

six well-known commentaries.[15] This closes the list of major interlinked commentaries on Mīmāṁsā.

Besides these interlaced commentaries, we also have chronologically sequential, direct commentaries on the *Mīmāṁsā-Sūtra*. Prabhākara Miśra's commentary on *Śābara-Bhāṣya* called *Bṛhati* (available only as an incomplete *MS*) and is being mentioned here separately, for he interpreted *Mīmāṁsā* and *Śābara-Bhāṣya* differently according to his own school.[16] Śālikanātha's *Ṛjuvimalā* is a ninth-century commentary on this. Śālikanātha's work gives an insight into the Prabhākara system. Among indHependent works on the Mīmāṁsā may be mentioned the *Śāstradīpikā* of Pārthāsārthi Miśra (fourteenth century). Mādhavācārya (fourteenth century) also wrote a commentary on the *Jaimini Sūtra* known as *Nayāyamālā*. He has not, however, commented upon each *sūtra* as was done by Śabara and Kumārila. This work is very valuable and ranks first amongst the works of those writers who commented upon

---

15. These are not all available in print; nor are all available intact. The two major *Śloka-Vārttika* commentaries — *Kāśikā* by Suchārita Miśrā, and *Nyāyaratnākara* by Pārthāsārthi Miśrā have been published by Chaukhamba Sanskrit Series. Of the *Tantra-Vārttika* commentaries, only *Nyāyasudhā* by Someśvara Bhaṭṭa is published (Chaukhamba Sanskrit Series). The rest — *Tautātitamatatilaka* by Bhāvadeva Bhaṭṭa and commentary on this by Pārthāsārthi Miśrā; *Nyāyaparāyaṇa* (fragment) by Gangādhara Miśrā and a commentary on this by Kamalākara Bhaṭṭa; *Subodhinī* by Annām Bhaṭṭa; *Mitākṣarā* by Gopāla Bhaṭṭa; *Ajita* by Paritoṣa Miśra — are available, in Government Sanskrit Library Benaras or the Government Oriental MSS Library, Madras. (For details, see Ganganatha Jha, 1983 rpt. Introduction.)

16. Gaurinath Sastri says : "Both the *Mīmāṁsā-Sūtra* and the *Bhāṣya* were interpreted differently by three different schools of thought associated with the names of Prabhākara, Kumārila and Murāri. The school of Murāri is known by name alone." (Gaurinath Sastri 1987 rpt., p. 183).

the *adhikaraṇa*s as a whole but not on each *sūtra* separately. The seventeenth century saw a renewed interest in the Mīmāṁsā system: Appaya Dīkṣita wrote *Upakramaparākrama*, Āpadeva, *Mīmāṁsanyāyaprakāśa*; Khaṇḍadeva, *Mīmāṁsā Kaustubha*; Gāgābhaṭṭa, *Bhaṭṭacintāmaṇi* and Nārāyaṇa Bhaṭṭa, *Mānameyodaya*. In the eighteenth century, Kṛṣṇayajvan wrote *Mīmāṁsā-Paribhāṣā*.

Turning now to *Aṣṭādhyāyī*, Pāṇini's grammar, we have the same picture — two kinds of commentaries: interlaced and independent. However, there is one difference. While in philosophy, for each competing school there is a distinct *sūtrapāṭha*, a primary text, in grammar though there were more than one school there is only one primary text. The *Aṣṭādhyāyī* holds a unique central position in the grammatical literature and, therefore, all subsequent grammatical texts — whatever be their concern — in one way or another interpret and reinterpret Pāṇini. Grammar as a branch of literature has always held an important place in the Indian mind and its study has been continued through centuries with deepest reverence and consummate application. It is worthy of notice that in India, the study of grammar ultimately led to a system of philosophy, the Pāṇini-*darśana*, which is the thirteenth system in the sixteen discussed by Mādhavācārya (fourteenth-century) in his *Śarvadarśanasaṁgraha*. Pāṇini's *Aṣṭādhyāyī* describes both Vaidikī and Bhāṣā and it has eight chapters each of which contains four sections.

Kātyāyana, also known as the *vārttikakāra*, assigned to third century BC, is the first commentator of Pāṇini. His *vārttika*s are "supplementary rules" framed to account for new forms which had developed in the language after Pāṇini had written his *sūtra*s (of his *vārttika* 4.3.105). In some cases, Kātyāyana has evaluated Pāṇini's rules with reference to their domain and found it necessary to modify or reject them (*P*. 8.4.4; 7.3.69). In other cases, he has improved upon the text of *Aṣṭādhyāyī* to meet the demands of a living language (6.1.142). In all he has commented on 1245 *sūtra*s (K. Madhavakrishna Sharma, 1968: 7) Kātyāyana's exegetical purpose and substance can be understood only in conjunction with a subsequent work — Patañjali's *Mahābhāṣya*, the great commentary. As R.G. Bhandarkar has pointed out (1877), Kātyāyana explains and supports the *sūtra*s of Pāṇini both by raising questions and answering them and also without resorting to this procedure. He also amends certain rules, finding them inadequate or inaccurate, and at other places, he simply extends the rules by adding another or by introducing a modification. Patañjali's starting point is very often, but not always, Kātyāyana. In fact, Kātyāyana's *vārttika*s are available only as cited by Patañjali (second century BC). Patañjali approaches Kātyāyana's own definition of *vyākhyāna*[17] (*Mahābhāṣya,* 1.1). Sometimes he agrees with Kātyāyana (cf. *P*. 3.2.111; 8.4.44), sometimes he refutes him (*P*. 6.1.142). Sometimes he recasts Pāṇini's rule (6.4.121 and 122) and sometimes says that the rule or a word or words in the rule are not wanted, even in cases when Kātyāyana justifies them or defends Pāṇini. Elsewhere, he discusses and explains *sūtra*s even where there is no *vārttika* on them. Finally, Patañjali gives supplementary rules called *iṣṭi*s which, however, occur very rarely. On the basis of this, Prof. Bhandarkar concludes:

> The only tenable theory is that Kātyāyana's work is an edition of Pāṇini with notes; explanatory, critical and supplementary, and that Patañjali's is a commentary on this edition, explaining in detail the notes of Kātyāyana, but discussing at length all points connected with the system

---

17. In the first *āhnika,* Patañjali says that we know/learn language not only with "rules of grammar" but also through *vyākhyāna,* which consists in "analysis of the rule, example counter-example, and contextualised use (in a sentence or sentences) requiring reconstruction of what is absent". (*MB* I.1)

> of Pāṇini and with grammar generally, whether Kātyāyana notices them or not, in a manner favourable or otherwise to his author. The object of both was the same, viz., to teach grammar by following and explaining the system of Pāṇini, endeavouring to perfect it . . . and to complete it by supplying the omissions and bringing up the knowledge of Sanskrit grammar . . . to their own times. —Bhandarkar, 1873

Patañjali's *Mahābhāṣya* is a work unequalled in its range of scholarship, its methodology and its inimitable prose of much grace, brevity and perspicuity. Kaiyaṭa (eleventh century) wrote his commentary on *Mahābhāṣya* — known as *Pradīpa*. At the end of the eighteenth and the turn of the nineteenth century, Nāgeśabhaṭṭa, who has also written major treatises on grammar, poetics and philosophy, wrote *Uddyota*, a commentary on *Pradīpa*.

Another independent commentary on *Aṣṭādhyāyī* was written by the Buddhist scholars Vāmana and Jayāditya (seventh century). It is known as *Kāśikā-Vṛtti*.[18] As we will explain below, being a *vṛlli* its scope is self-defined as different from Patañjali's work, which is a *bhāṣya*. Coming so many centuries after *Mahābhāṣya*, *Kāśikā* has the avowed purpose of integrating *Cāndra-Vyākaraṇa*, the Buddhist recension of Pāṇini, with *Aṣṭādhyāyī*. In the process of interpretation, it differs with the *Mahābhāṣya* in the reading of several *ṣātras*, viz., 1.1.29; 3.1.96; 3.1.143; 3.2.56; 3.2.78; 3.2.87; 3.2.138; 3.2.141; 3.2.172; 4.1.150; 6.1.136; 6.3.84; 7.2.101; 7.2.102. Although this commentary is much briefer, yet it follows the tradition of explanation showing the applicability of rules on actual language objects, giving examples and counterexamples, and spelling out the meaning of the rules.

---

18. There are many other commentaries — some of them quite important for the scholar — in both the *Mahābhāṣya* and the *Kāśikā* streams. We have mentioned only the major works — works that give a definition to the tradition.

In the eighth century, another Buddhist scholar, Jinendrabuddhi, wrote his commentary Nyāya (also known as *Kāśikā-vivaraṇa-pañjikā*) on *Kāśikā*. And in the twelfth century, Haradatta wrote his commentary *Padamañjarī* on the *Kāśikā*.

The third body of literature about *Aṣṭādhyāyī* comprises the reordered grammars — the *Prākṛta Kaumudī*s. Fifteen century onwards, some scholars changed the order and arrangement of Pāṇini's rules — they rearranged them according to the topics selected for discussion. This in effect is a pedagogical re-interpretation of Pāṇini governed by a new understanding of what is called in the tradition *prakaraṇa-saṅgati*: the mutual consistency of ideas and topics. Rāmacandra's *Prakriyā-Kaumudī* (fifteenth-century). Bhaṭṭojī Dīkṣita's *Siddhānta Kaumudī* (early seventeenth-century), and Varadarāja's *Madhya* and *Laghu-Siddhānta Kaumudī* (nineteenth-century) are major works in this line and are widely read by all learners of Sanskrit, and are often looked upon as somehow inadequate pedagogical alternatives to Pāṇini's *Aṣṭādhyāyī*.

The fourth, the last but very significant body of work on *Aṣṭādhyāyī* concerns the philosophy and the theory of grammar. Bhartṛhari's *Vākyapadīya* (sixth-century.) belongs here, though this line also actually begins in Patañjali's *Mahābhāṣya* which first discussed many general questions pertaining to the theory of grammar and the philosophy of language. There are four major commentaries on *Vākyapadīya* — (i) Bhartṛhari's own *Vṛtti*; (ii) Helarāja's *Prakāśa*; (iii) Puṇyarāja's commentary (nameless, as the first portion is missing), and (iv) Vṛṣabhadeva's *Paddhati*, and these belong here. Bhaṭṭojī Dīkṣita's *Prauḍha-Manoramā* (basically a commentary on his own *Siddhānta Kaumudī*) and *Śabda-Kaustubha* (basically, a commentary on *Aṣṭādhyāyī*) — the two seventeenth-century works come next. Finally, Nāgeśabhaṭṭa at the turn of the nineteenth century wrote *Vyākaraṇasiddhānta Mañjūṣā* (*Bṛhatī* and *Laghu*), an outstanding work on various topics of Sanskrit grammar, and *Paribhāṣenduśekhara*, a work devoted to the *Paribhāṣā*s or meta-rules of Pāṇini's grammar.[19]

To sum up : The commentary tradition in India has been alive, continuous and cumulative. This is the way sense has been made of important books — by explicitly building one reading on the other.

Types of Commentaries

In our above statement, three generic words for commentaries have appeared as parties of titles of different commentaries — *vṛtti* (e.g., *Kāśikāvṛtti*), *vārttika* (e.g., *Śloka-Vārttika* and Kātyāyana's *vārttika*s) and *bhāṣya* (e.g., *Śābara-Bhāṣya* and *Mahābhāṣya*).

Basically, there are two types of commentaries: first, the one that analyses the rules and explains their operations and their domain. This is called *vṛtti*. The other is the comment on the rule — that brings out the unexpressed or the implicit content of the rule. These are, therefore, in effect, two kinds of explanation — one descriptive, and the other analytic. The two together constitute vyākhyā, "explanation." *Bhāṣya* in Pāṇinian school is an expanded *vyākhyā*, akin to *vārttika*, based on Kātyāyana's *vārttika*s. In general, *bhāṣya* is simply a critical commentary — such as *Śābara-Bhāṣya*.

Rajaśekhara in *Kāvya-Mīmāṁsā* gives a complete list of different kinds of commentaries. He distinguishes eight —

> Commentary that explains the ideational content of a *sūtra* is called *vṛtti*; analysis of a *vṛtti* is *paddhati*. *Bhāṣya* is a detailed analysis that takes into account the possible objections and counter-arguments. *Samīkṣā* gives an explanation of the intended and deeper meanings and issues implicit in a *bhāṣya*-analysis. A mere indication of meaning

19. The tradition comes down uninterruptedly from Nāgeśa Bhaṭṭa to our own times.

> in the simplest and briefest language is *ṭīkā*. Explanation of only the difficult words is *pañjikā*. A brief statement of the meaning of a *sūtra* is *kārikā*. In the same manner, an analysis of the unexpressed or suggested meanings and implications of a *sūtra* is called *vārttika*. These are *sūtra* divisions.
>
> — Rājaśekhara, p. 12

Purpose and Value of Commentaries

Sri K.A. Subramania Iyer has very concisely and cogently explained the value of commentaries (K.A. Subramania Iyer, 1969). Commentaries are needed to understand serious works — the Śāstras — because of the style in which they were composed[20] and because they "serve the purpose of bringing about specific ideas . . . true meaning is ascertained through explanatory commentaries." (Kumārila Bhaṭṭa, *Tantra-Vārttika*, p. 285). Most of them are composed either in *sūtra*s or in *kārikā*s. *Kārikā*s are different from *sūtra*s in that the author does not deliberately achieve brevity by economising even on syllables and *varṇa*s (sounds). Moreover *kārikā*s are complete sentences and clear even without a commentary. Yet, even the *kārikā*s like the *sūtra*s are meant to be understood with the help of explanation.

> These further explanations supplied the context and brought out the full implications of the main idea. . . . In understanding the meaning of a stanza, a knowledge of the context is absolutely essential and it is not always easy to understand it from the stanza itself, it is no wonder that many authors wrote commentaries on their own *kārikā*s.
>
> — K.A. Subramania Iyer, 1969, p. 51

---

20. One motivation for composing abbreviated primary texts was to enable the serious student to keep the whole text in his mind simultaneously.

The context would include basically the philosophical assumptions of the writer and/or the school to which the writer belongs. Thus, for example, Bhartṛhari, the philosopher of grammar and the author of *Vākyapadīya*, was a *vivartavādī*, a fact we come to know from his own *vṛtti* — and not from his *kārikās* — and this knowledge is crucial for a full comprehension of the nature of grammatical categories he postulates. Context helps resolve other problems also. In certain texts, such as *Vākyapadīya*, it is only the context provided by the commentaries which enables us to know when a new topic begins to be treated. It is the context which enables us to understand that in *Vākyapadīya*, the author proceeds from one topic to another in a somewhat logical sequence. It is when the context is known that there is a chance of the significance of the words . . . becoming clear. The commentaries (except the *vṛtti*) give the context for each *kārikā* and sometimes for the *kāṇḍa* or *samuddeśa* as a whole. Sometimes in the middle they recapitulate the points already made and indicate what is coming[21] (K.A. Subramania Iyer, 1969, p. 50).

Again, later commentaries often interpret a text in the light of later developments of thought. This on the one hand requires careful reading to separate the old from the new and on the other it develops the discipline. At the same time, the commentators as also the writers of primary texts, are extremely careful about handling down the old tradition faithfully, and this, in fact, "was also one of the original motives of those writers" (K.A. Subramania Iyer, 1969, p. 50). The commentaries thus perform the dual function of handing down the tradition of knowledge and, at the same time, in a clearly identifiable way, updating it.

---

21. See, for example, for Helarāja on *Vāk* (111.1.42), which examines the concept of universals.

This is particularly true of Smṛti texts — such as the Dharma-Sūtras which unlike the Śrutis were always expected to be reinterpreted and adapted according to the changed context of time and place and the availability of different perspectives.

The commentaries also place the given text in the context of philosophies and compare the discipline — specific categories with the categories of other disciplines. Thus, for example, in the discussion of the denotation of words — "universal or particular" — Helarāja highlights the fact that the grammarians' universal is what Patañjali had long ago posited — that which comes to the mind when a *śabda* (word) is articulated (*Mahābhāṣya*, I.1). This Helarāja says is close to the Vijñānavādin's position who believed only in the reality of the different momentary states of consciousness and for whom "some things figure as common properties while other things figure as distinguishing features" (K.A.S. Iyer, 1969, p. 51). The grammarians' word denotes this thing which figures in the momentary consciousness, the *śabdārtha* and not the object of external reality, the *vāstvārtha*. This interpretation of a Bhartṛhari category would be missed in the absence of Helarāja's commentary.

A telling example of how necessary it is to have access to learned commentaries in order to reach a proper interpretation of the text has been cited by Sri K.A.S. Iyer again from Helarāja on *Vākyapadīya* (III.1.3). Bhartṛhari, discussing substance (*dravya*), the particular denotation of words, says that *ātmā, vastu, svabhāva, śarīra* and *tattva* are synonyms of the word *dravya* (substance). Helarāja points out that all these words including *dravya* are synonyms for the ultimate ontological category, substance, in the different systems of philosophy (*yathādarśanam*). Advaita calls it *ātmā;* Sāṁkhyas call it *vastu* Satadvaitavādins call it *svabhāva* and the Cārvākas call it *tattva*. Thus Helarāja explains that the words are synonyms — but not in Bhartṛhari's system. If this insight is missed, there is bound to be crucial misinterpretation.

In this way, the commentaries, achieving their ostensible purpose of determining the meaning precisely, also accomplish the much greater task of unifying scattered knowledge. Vāmana-Jayāditya say in their first *kārikā* of *Kāśikā* : "The purpose is to bring together and unify the grammatical knowledge that lies scattered in *vṛttis*, *bhāṣyas* and all *śāstras*, analysing verb-roots and nominal-stems." (*Kāśikā, Atha Pratyāhāra*, 1) In fact, in the work of the great exegetes — Jaimini, Śabara, Patañjali, Śaṅkara, Kumārila, Helarāja, Bhaṭṭojī Dīkṣita and Nāgeśa, the discipline-boundaries are transcended and all knowledge is tied up into an interrelated whole.

Status of the Text

The presence of this well-motivated interpretative tradition may be accounted for in terms of the community's collective need and will to understand and to sustain certain texts. For, as our discussion has suggested in Section 1, certain important texts have been the focus of the tradition. But why these text? Why or how does a text acquire a certain status?

The *Ṛgveda*, the Upaniṣads, and the Smṛti texts — Dharma-Śāstras the Darśana-Śāstras,[22] the *Bhagavad-Gītā*, and Pāṇini's *Śūtrapāṭha* — have been repeatedly commented upon, analysed and explained right down to our time.

Obviously, it is the Śāstric literature of knowledge that is the object of perennial study. The two dominant metaphors for these primary texts, and such others, are — (i) of *Kāmadhenu*, and (ii) of *Kalpavṛkṣa*. The first metaphor suggests that they are sources of endless knowledge and the second suggests

22. For the primary texts of six philosophies in one place, see Swami Dvarikadas Shastri, 1984.

that they yield the desired fruit — whatever is most conducive to the community's contentment and welfare.

The tradition evidently attaches great value to knowledge — *jñāna-dharma* — and this lends to the texts of knowledge (Śāstras) a pre-eminent status. The Vedic literature is the first record of the Indian civilization. The word *veda* means "knowledge" and is derived (vide Pāṇini *Dhātupāṭha*) from the Sanskrit *adādigaṇa, parasmaipada* transitive root $\sqrt{vid}$, "to know," which also underlies the English words *visual* and *visualize* that have a meaning which has affinity with the assertion that Vedas represent a kind of knowledge that was the result of direct apperception and that consequently the *ṛṣis* were *draṣṭās*, "seers" in the literal sense. The same root underlies *vedanā* which means "experience" — Pāṇini says *anukūla vedanā* is happiness (*sukha*), and *pratikūla vedanā* is sorrow (*duḥkha*) — the experience that is in harmony with ourself is "joy," and the experience that is not, is "sorrow." Interestingly, the other meaning of *vedanā* is "knowledge." Later, Yāska explicitly praised knowledge and condemned ignorance (I.17) : *arthāpi jñāna praśaṁsā bhavati ajñāna ninda ca*, "Moreover, there is praise of knowledge and censure of ignorance." Sri V.S. Agarwala points out that the period from the fifteenth century BC to the fifth century BC was a time of much intellectual ferment in India, a period of *jñāna-manthana* (churning of the mind) for knowledge — several new Śāstras, sciences, which Pāṇini designates (4.3.115) as *upajñāta* (sciences of discovery) originated at this time. Patañjali in his commentary on 6.4.163 refers to *jña-devatā*, the deity of knowledge. Pāṇini accepts *jña* as an independent word (vide 7.3.79). This *jña* in Sāṁkhya stands for *jñātā* (the knower). Patañjali in his commentary on 4.1.1, *vārttika* 3 has referred to a sect of brāhmaṇas known as *jña*-brāhmaṇas who had created a mass-movement in those days for the acceptance and worship of knowledge (see V.S. Agrawala, 1963). It is quite an easy step from this to the worship of learning (the goddess Sarasvatī) in the Purāṇic period (first century AD onwards), to next, the high regard for brāhmaṇas as custodians of knowledge, to the esteem for a teacher, an *ācārya*, "the friend of students," to *guruvāra* and *bṛhaspativāra* as names of week-days, one named generally after "teacher" and the other after the first mythical teacher in the tradition.

The texts embody knowledge — hence their sanctity. They are a disembodied store-house: being oral — not tied to transient materials that constitute a book. Their constant substratum is the collective Indian mind itself.

Further, many of these texts, in the course of time, acquired the status of *pramāṇa*, testimony, and came to be cited as such. *Śabda* (verbal testimony) is an important epistemology for the six major schools of philosophy, and for certain forms of reality, for the *adṛṣṭa*, non-perceptible being, for example, language as such is the only means of knowledge. In the extreme position adopted by the grammarians, all knowledge is contingent on words — the *pariṇāma* or result of words (Bhartṛhari, 1971 : I.22). Words, therefore, are important and their meaning has to be scrupulously determined. In India, thus, texts enjoy great authority because most major philosophic schools accept *śabda-pramāṇa* — verbal authority. Their meaning therefore has to be determined with great care. This no doubt engendered a scholarly exegetical tradition. It is both responsible for, as well as founded on, the twin assumptions that a final meaning is there, and that it is discoverable — provided we have sufficiently sophisticated instruments of interpretation.

But these texts wouldn't have acquired their pre-eminent position as mere repositories of knowledge. It is the nature of knowledge that ensures the relevance and the continued validity of these texts. These texts of knowledge advance *dharma*, righteousness, as the Indian tradition expects them to. In their fundamental concern with human happiness in the face of odds and with the quality of that happiness, these texts necessarily conceptualize and analyse : (i) the nature of ontological reality, (ii) the existential dimensions of man's state and condition, (iii) the nature and organization of social life, and (iv) the goal and routine modes of individual life. These texts, therefore, are not mere abstractions — they have, in their concerns, sprung from the actual life patterns and routine modes of individual life. As the habit of reading these books grows more and more restricted, modern readers have to be reminded that these texts describe and analysis concrete and ever so small details of daily life as much as some of them discuss the abstract questions of man's existence and the nature of the universe and that an average Indian reader even today pleasantly and unexpectedly recognizes the elements of his daily routine in them. Pāṇini's *Aṣṭādhyāyī* is less a grammar of *Vaidikī*, the Sanskrit of the Vedas, and more of *Bhāṣā*, the language of actual current speech. The *darśana*s are statements of various competing belief systems which were current and which separately commanded respective following — as has already been noted, the Smṛti literature is a record of what is already known.

Of Dharma-Sūtras, Śrauta deal with performances while Gṛhya, deal with ceremonies in individual life, and *dharma* involve the questions of right, duty, law, religion, custom, and usage (R. Sastri, 1937 : 301-2). Take, for example, the *Manusaṁhitā*, "pre-eminent among the Dharma-Śāstra texts," which embraces in its sway the whole of India and the neighbouring countries of South-East Asia. *Manusaṁhitā* is a representative example of how texts in the Indian context not only record but also influence and govern the conduct and beliefs of people in a sustained and pervasive manner. There is extensive record in literature of how Manu's teachings were invoked as authority and were governing the life and conduct of people from the earliest times.[23]

It is said that just as Pāṇini determined the nature of Sanskrit for all times, Manu has determined the code of conduct "the technique employed in both the cases was *saṁskāra*." (Raghavan, 1962 : 33) The detailed descriptions one gets in *kāvya* literature of social and individual life confirm the reality of the contexts of the *dharma*-texts. An eminent scholar has said that a serious student of Indian literature and history cannot but assume the practical nature of these works of *dharma* and that the legal rules contained in them are statements of laws that were actually in force (Julius Jolly, 1885 : 28-9, 32). Till this day, the Indian law, codified by the Britishers, is substantially a codification of the common law which has its roots in Manu. It may be noted that a text does not become unreal because of the presence of ideal elements, just as modern Indian Constitution does not become unreal because of the presence of the directive principles or the fundamental rights. Similarly, a text does not become intrinsically illogical simply because some portions of the text are no more acceptable to one's current reason after two thousand years — only the ignorant, or the motivated, would interpret the texts out of their context or read them without reinterpreting them, if possible or editing them as the historical method demands! As Manu stated he was not merely concerned with what is but also with what ought to be. Thus, though standards and practices of conduct have changed with time, the *saṁhitā*-framework was something which obtained in actual life and not a mere theoretical fabrication. The statements . . . are to be understood some as records of facts, some of such as have obtained a wide vogue, and some . . . as

23. Cf. Yāska's *Nirukta* (111.3); *Taittirīya Saṁhitā* (II.2, 10.2); *ṚV* (II.3.3.13); *Mahābhārata* (XII.336.38-46).

what ought to be done as the most proper thing (Raghavan 1962 : 339; 341). The first chapter introduces the subject-matter and describes the origin of the world, the birth of beings, and the origin of the text. The second discusses the sources and proofs of *dharma*, the person for whom it holds good, and the areas in which it prevails. The code and duties of the first of the four states, *āśrama*s, of life are also laid down. The third and the fourth chapter describe the desirable mode of a householder's life and duties — ways of earning one's livelihood righteously, principles of character and conduct. Chapter five discusses food and eating habits and incidentally the duties of women. Chapter VI discusses the last two stages — *vānaprastha* and *saṁnyāsa*, life of retirement and renunciation. Chapters VII and VIII describe the rulers, their duties, law and justice. Chapter IX describes in detail the duties of and towards women and their importance in the family system and their rights. Chapter X deals with the exceptions to the *dharma* described so far — the codes of people who are outside the system, geographically, culturally or by ethnic heritage, and the code of conduct during abnormal times (the *āpad-dharma*). Chapter XI describes different kinds of wrongful acts, their punishment and their expiation. The last chapter, a brilliant exposition of the goal of a man's life has two parts — in the first part, the theory of *karma*, actions good and bad and their consequences, is discussed; the second part describes and discusses those modes and disciplines of life which help in the realization of the ideal goal — the seeking of *ātma-jñāna*, self-knowledge and attainment of the everlasting good (*niḥśreyas*). Basically and emphatically this text is a life-affirming text, an exhortation of the effort. We can not truly appreciate Manu unless we attend to his *subhāṣita*s, profoundly wise observations — "one does not become an elder by reason of one's grey hair; he who is well read, though young, him the gods deem an elder" (II.156); "Whatever makes one dependent on another is misery; all that helps to rest on oneself is happiness." (IV.161); "Of all kinds of cleanliness, that in monetary affairs is the greatest . . ." (V.106); "Dharma is the only friend that accompanies one even in death; all the rest perishes with the body" (VIII.7); "One's self is one's witness, it is the final resort; do not disregard your own self, the greatest witness of man" (VIII.84). These are some cited by Prof. Raghavan (Raghavan, 1937 : 357). It is this that enthused Nietzsche to say about *Manu-Smṛti* that "it has an affirmation of life, a triumphant, agreeable sensation in life, and that to draw up a law book such as Manu means to permit oneself to get the upper hand, to become perfect, to be ambitious of the highest art of living" (see, Raghavan, 1937).

The text thus discusses the actual and the desirable aspects of man's life. And these are discussed and described as *dharma*. We have had the occasion to mention earlier (cf. I.1) the fact that *dharma* is the superordinate principle of Indian life — the ultimate touchstone of what should be done, of what is right and of what is wrong. *Dharma* is sought called because it holds or sustains everything — is the firm foundation of all: *dhāraṇād dharmamityāhu* (*Mahābhārata*).

> It is an accredited declaration made all through the vast body of our sacred literature that to be born as a human being is rare privilege. The purpose of human life is to emerge from imperfection to perfection. Dharma in its primary sense, . . . is perfection. And the ways and means to which are conducive to this perfection are naturally and necessarily called Dharma. — Sri Seshachalasarma 1985 : 44-49

One of the unfortunate memory lapses of Indian people — particularly the English-educated Indians — is their complete confusion about the concept of *dharma*. In the often repeated ideal of *dharma-nirpekṣa*, *dharma* is equated with religion in the sense of an organized, church-based, priest-ruled belief system.

Nothing could be farther from the meaning of *dharma*. The appropriate expression that captures the intended meaning is *mata-nirpekṣa*. What is this *dharma*, the touchstone of all right meaning? It is necessary to dwell a while on this concept, specially because *dharma* provides the rationale for acquisition of knowledge and thus for the process of interpretation itself. Patañjali, for example, in his *Mahābhāṣya* talks of *jñāna-dharma* and *dharma-niyama* as cardinal principles in the study of the discipline of grammar (I.1). So also in learning — all knowledge and all pursuit of knowledge must promote *dharma*. This *dharma* is from the root *dhṛ* — (*kriyādi, parasmaipada, sēṭ*, vide *Pāṇini Dhātupāṭha*), which means "to support" or "to sustain." In its broadest sense it means "duty," a conception that in its comprehensive meaning supports and sustains a society. Its meaning ranges from the qualities and characteristics of things to the highest virtue possible in man and also what men should or ought to do.

The concept is heterogeneous and, therefore, subject to plurality. Thus the *dharma* described in the *Manu Saṁhitā* pertains not only to civil, religious and spiritual matters, but also includes general rules of prudence, of personal habits, of proper social behaviour and individual conduct. It is important to remember that *dharma* is not laid down as something absolute or universal — it is applicable differently and varies from place to place, and from time to time (*yuga-dharma*). Further, it does not exclude *ācāra*, accepted custom, handed down from generation a generation within a community (*MS* I.107-10). Besides, there are immemorial customs peculiar to places, classes, families, peculiar to guilds, to fringe communities and to republican groups (*MS* I.118; 4.30). While the society is to live as ordained by *dharma* and *ācāra*, in unusual times, the *dharma* may be abandoned for what is called *āpad-dharma*. Finally, the most important feature is the inclusion of the spiritual goal — the final realization of the self as the legitimate culmination of man's worldly efforts which must be harmonized with this spiritual goal.

These *dharmas*, duties, are governed by the abstract concept of *dharma* which, both in its generic (*sādhāraṇa*) and its specific (*viśeṣa*) senses, "contributes to the preservation, progress and welfare of human society, and in a wider sense of the whole world" (Venkateswaran 1962; 1969 rpt. : 287). *Ahiṁsā*, non-violence, *kṣamā*, forgiveness, *dayā*, kindness for all living beings, *śauca*, purity of thought and action, *dāna* or *tyāga*, giving up (renouncing), and *satya* truth, are the principal attributes of generic or *sādhāraṇa dharma* that determine the injunctions with respect to the duty and conduct of the individual and thereby ensure the general good. In this sense, *dharma* is the desired propensity of the social man. Manu says that all activity of man originates in desire for self-gratification but it is not praise worthy to act on that desire (*Manu-Smṛti* II.205); so to enable man to act properly, guided by *samyag-vṛtti*, a total view, *dharma* was promulgated (1.6). The *Bṛhadāraṇyaka Upaniṣad* says (I.4.11-14) that this *dharma* is stronger than even the ruling class and that there is nothing greater than *dharma*.

> Dharma was thus like the rule of law, something above the ruler who was also bound by it. To the extent society respected it, society protected itself; to the extent society made inroads into it, to that extent society was also undermining itself (*Ṛgveda* VIII.15). — Rāghavan, 1963: 342

There is a uniqueness to this conception of *dharma* — it is a principle that needs to be upheld at all times but not through violence; it must not cause suffering to other living beings. (*Manu-Smṛti* II.238). Thus, for example, though one must never compromise truth for being nice, yet truth should be spoken only if it causes no hurt (*Manu-Smṛti* IV.138). As the *Mahābhārata* says categorically:

> Dharma has been postulated only for the welfare and development of living beings; so, that which achieves this is dharma. Such is the definition laid down by the learned.
> — XII.109.10

This principle of *dharma* is superordinate: it is the touchstone of the value of all human pursuits and also their only valid goal. It is because the Śāstras are repositories of such knowledge as is a means to the realization of *dharma*, that they have enjoyed a pre-eminent status in the Indian society.

And, of course, some of these texts would be more important on account of their relation to other texts as they come to be accepted and cited as authority. This is true of such diverse texts as Pāṇini's *Aṣṭādhyāyī*, *Śābara-Bhāṣya* (on *Brahma-Sūtras*). Or, the text may be the source for later texts which extrapolate on the ideas of the source-text. This is the case with *Manu-Smr̥ti* as well, whose legal procedures, for example, came in for a very extensive treatment by Yājñavalkya and which is frequently cited and invoked as an authority even in the epics so much so that even today when the traditional Hindu Sociology is discussed, it is Manu, who is named, praised and blamed. No wonder *Manu-Smr̥ti*, *Śābara-Bhāṣya*, and *Aṣṭādhyāyī*, all the three have had the largest number of commentaries composed on them, and have thus been interpreted and reinterpreted again and again. They have always been important — both in affirmation and in rejection.

Nature of the Texts

Indian texts are situated in India's oral tradition. They range from the brief Śāstra to a *mahākāvya* such *Mahābhārata*. Pāṇini uses the term *kr̥ta* in two ways — one to mean one of the four kinds of literature as opposed to *dr̥ṣṭa upajñāta*, *prokta*, etc. (vide 4.2.7; 4.3.115) and secondly, in a general sense, to mean anything that has an origin, i.e., that has originated (vide 4.3.87 and 116). The derivative *kr̥ti*, therefore is the closest term we can use for the English word text — "Text" is anything that has been brought about or, created. In this sense, a text can be verbal or non-verbal. Our concern here is with verbal texts, but we may as well underline the recognition, explicitly formulated by Bharatmuni in the *Nāṭyaśāstra*, for example, that the body of the dancer, the *mūdrās* (hand-positions or gestures) and words are equally *vācaka*, i.e., expressers of meaning. Not only that, the non-verbal artefacts also function as texts. In the oral tradition, the verbal texts also incorporate or depend on the non-verbal elements in different ways. This is easy to understand in the case of *kāvya*-texts which are mostly *śravya-prekṣā* (aural-visual) texts and come into being in their totality only in a performance or a recitation with the aural and visual elements carrying significant loads of meaning. But even a Śāstric text such as *Aṣṭādhyāyī* is not just the text on the page. In fact, it is essentially an oral text — we are told that Pāṇini read it in *ek śruti svara* and many features of the text structure were marked in the enunciation, the change of subject or topic, for example.[24] Again, the mnemonic compositional devices are also compelled by its orality and are non-verbal. Again "invocation — main text — closing *stuti* or hymn" paradigm of most of the verbal texts is paralleled in dance-performances as well. Then the Indian texts are not at al esoteric nor restricted to a small audience. As texts of the oral tradition, the Indian texts relate very intimately to the life of the people. Through folk exposition and performances, their content, at least the relevant or significant parts become the shared knowledge of the masses. It is therefore quite inappropriate in the Indian context to refer to *Śrī Bhāgavata Purāṇa* or *Rāmāyaṇa* as "elite" literature. In the Indo-Gangetic plains of north India, there is hardly anyone not familiar with the narratives related to Śrī

24. Such as the employment of *svarita* accent (circumflex pitch) in *Aṣṭādhyāyī*, to mark the *adhikāra sūtra*, the rule that introduces a topic and holds till the next topic is signalled.

Rāma or Śrī Kṛṣṇa. Ironically, it is the contemporary urban literature which in spite of its conscious choice of the so-called people's themes — poverty, hunger, etc. — remains "elite," alienated as it is from the oral tradition in its narrative mode, its concern, and its tone and, therefore, from the masses. This is not true only of the *kāvya* texts. Even the Śāstras have always been popularized, and the average Indian's daily language is replete with seminal thoughts of the Śāstras, although the speaker himself is generally unaware of the fact. The Jain *ahiṁsā* and *śūnyatā*, the Buddhist *kṣaṇikavāda*, centrality of suffering (*duḥkha*) and *tyāga*, the Vedāntic *nirākāra*, *ananta Brahman* and *ātma-jñāna*, are not esoteric concepts at all — they have become the basic structures of the Indian mind irrespective of the caste and religious distinctions. The "modern" English-educated Indian is again and again surprised to recognize, provided he can always recognize, in the speech of the ordinary Indian, echoes of the thoughts of *tathāgata*, Ādi Śaṅkara and Veda Vyāsa. The phenomenon is incomprehensible to the Western-oriented India, but makes perfect sense to those who are familiar with the systems of diffusion of ideas in the Indian tradition. The Indian texts, including the Śāstric texts, through community and participative reading, are mass texts.

Thirdly, the syntax of the Indian texts is generally very complex and serves as an index of ideas, as a guide to the study and ritual-rendering of the text, as a guide in the transmission of the text, and as a mnemonic instrument. The structure as a result is sometimes so complex that it needs explication and often alternative principles of arrangement are seen to be exhibited by the text. This is amply illustrated in the case of the *Ṛgveda*, for example. *Ṛgveda*, the oldest book of mankind, is a collection of hymns and is the most important work in the Vedic literature, if not really the entire body of Indian literature, ancient and modern. It has 1028 *sūkta*s (collections of hymns; literally, *sūkta* means "that which is well-expressed") and 10462 *ṛk*s. These have been divided in two ways: (i) according to *aṣṭakas, adhyāyas* and *vargas*, and (ii) according to *maṇḍalas, anuvākas* and *sūktas*. According to the first arrangement the whole of *Ṛgveda* falls into 8 *aṣṭaka*s. Each *aṣṭaka* is a unit of 8 *adhyāya*s and each *adhyāya* is made up of several *varga*s. Each *varga* normally contains 3-5 *ṛk*s. A *varga* is a unit of a lesson for the students to learn by rote. According to the second arrangement *Ṛgveda* is divided into 10 *maṇḍalas*, each *maṇḍala* consisting of several *anuvāka*s, with each *anuvāka* having varying numbers of *sūkta*s. All such arrangements have a basis in the homogeneity of ideas, in the supposed authorship and in the metrical forms (see, for details, S. Ranganatha, 1985, pp. 49-52). A noteworthy feature is the preference for number 8 — books generally have eight chapters, or each chapter in a book has eight parts. And almost uniformly, there is a symmetry of sorts in the arrangement of parts — each section will have a uniform number of sub-sections and so. Thus, the *Ṛgveda* has eight *aṣṭaka*s, and each *aṣṭaka* has eight *adhyāya*s; the *Aṣṭādhyāyī* has eight chapters, and each chapter has four quarters (*pada*). Thus, part of the motivation for interpretation comes from the very nature of the texts. *Sāhityadarpaṇa* of Viswanatha mentions, in Chapter 1, four requisites of a text: *adhikārī* (reader), *prayojana* (purpose/function), *viṣaya* (subject), *sambandha* (relation between the reader and the subject). The texts of the Indian tradition, particularly the Śāstric texts, are very brief and abbreviated. This is no doubt partly due to, as we have already said, the exigencies of the oral tradition which required, for accurate transmission, the texts to be brief and as mnemonically expressed as possible so that they can be stored accurately in the mind. These texts are also called the *sūtra*s, which refers to their linguistic style, the *sūtra*, or an aphoristic statement that is defined as *alpakṣaram asandigdham* (*Vāyu Puraṇa*, 59.142), that is, "unambiguous and expressed in the minimum number of syllables." Through several devices, the writers achieved economy — class-markers, meta-terms, technical terminology, understood repetition, ellipsis, eschewing the verb ". . . and of the cases only a few are to be met. . . . The nominative and ablative singular prevail, and long compounds are constantly employed. All our ideas are thrown into the form of nouns, mostly abstract, and even the participles have become rare. This style is the style of formulas rather than of discourse . . ." (Bhandarkar, 1883, p. 88). This *sūtra*-style was also associated with the movement which began with a less frequent use of verbal forms and the employment of attributive expressions and ended "in making Sanskrit a language of abstract nouns and compound words." Further, the approach of the Indian thinkers also contributed to brevity, and, hence to complexity of the text. "An Indian author does not lead his readers into the processes, his own mind has gone through in arriving at the doctrine he lays down; in other words, he does not tell us how he has come by the opinions he holds, but lays down these doctrines." (Bhandarkar, 1883, pp. 87-88) This, along with the algebraic *sūtra*s with their devices of brevity, made explanatory commentaries necessary. At the same time, it became possible to hold the texts simultaneously in mind and the comprehen-sion process did not have to be linear. *Aṣṭādhyāyī* is a good example of a brief, aphoristic but complete Śāstra — it has 3996 aphorisms (rules) composed in just 32000 syllables.

As the second feature of these texts, we may mention their highly organized structure. Unlike the familiar, rather simple, chapter-and-section arrangement, the Indian texts have a classified, thematic (or topic) organization. Rājaśekhara says that the treatment of specific topics is organized in *prakaraṇa*s; larger subjects, which include these topics, are treated in *adhyāya, sarga, pariccheda* or *maṇḍala*, separately or one woven within another (Rājaśekhara, p. 12). Knowledge of the *prakaraṇa* and *prakaraṇa-saṅgati*, order of treatment of topics, is often necessary for a correct interpretation of particular statements in the text. The textual divisions and subdivisions are usually quite clear, being marked by some device or the other. But when the divisions become obscure, commentaries are needed.

Next we must draw attention to the relationship between texts. There is a known chronology of texts belonging to a given discipline or a *Śāstra,* and the later texts quite consciously, and necessarily, take off from the preceding texts. We have already shown that this is true particularly of the commentary tradition. This is true also of all the primary Smṛti texts — in all the six auxiliary disciplines. This is understandable as this along with the commentaries ensured the development of thought in the disciplines.

In *kāvya* literature, there is a different situation. In the Indian tradition, some major stories or themes have been repeatedly re-worked; each time the new author, through the change and adaptation, instils a new meaning or a new shade of meaning into the original theme. The story of Rāma, for example, is a perennial favourite and has been reinterpreted several times from age to age and from one region to the other, each version adding or deleting an episode and/or shedding a new light on some part or other of the original story,[25] and thus fulfilling either a psychic need of the new age or moulding the text to accord with the changed metaphysics of the age. Thus, Bāṇa's *Rāmacaritamānas* reinterpreted Sītā, and in modern times Karṇa and Draupadī have been the subject of many recreations in modern Indian languages. There is also, of course, the rampant echoic intertextuality in *kāvya* literature — deliberate or unconscious. Rajaśekhara has discussed at length the verbal echoes, the echoing of thought and the replication of emotions in literature (*Kāvya-Mīmāṁsā,* chapter XI and XII). In Indian *kāvya* literature,

25. Cf. A.K. Warder, 1978.

this happens because the major source of imagery with most writers is the same — Indian mythology.

Again, some of the major texts may be available in several redactions as, for example, the *Manu Saṁhitā* (see Raghavan, 1962: 335-36) or in several recensions,[26] as for example, The *Rāmāyaṇa* (see C.P. Ramaswami Aiyar, 1962: 23) and the *Mahābhārata* which, apart from the three literary recensions,[27] is also available in several popular recensions. The *pāṭha* or text in such cases varies considerably, always suggesting the possibility of interpolations. Besides there arise instances of contradiction — both apparent and real. It becomes then a part of the task of interpretation to identify interpolations and borrowings, to resolve contradictions, if they are only apparent, and thus to constitute the critical text. This is a rather recent dimension of the interpretative process, a part of the nineteenth-century European scholars' pioneering work in putting together and reconstructing texts from the manuscripts. We must distinguish from this (i) an intended variation of a text, which amounts almost to a re-interpretation, and (ii) an unstable text which results from interpolations and changes during its oral transmission and performance. Contradictions in a text, therefore, are of different orders, depending on the type of the text, and have to be handled accordingly. One thing is clear — oral texts are no more subject to random contradiction than texts of a written tradition, and, in an oral tradition like India's, the oral texts have proved far more stable and much less subject to corruption than the texts of the written traditions.

---

26. It is quite normal in India to have *trividha-pāṭh* (three variant texts) of any given text — (i) the *uddicya* (north-western), (ii) the *prācya* (eastern), and (iii) the *dākṣiṇātya*, (southern) as is the case, for example, with Pāṇini's *Aṣṭādhyāyī*.

27. The Nīlakaṇṭha, the Kumbhakonam, and the Poona texts.

In this way the nature of Indian texts gives to the tradition of exegesis its several-fold character.

Task and Types of Interpretation

Earlier we had noted that Śruti interpretations concerned themselves with determining the meaning and articulating its rationality. We had also noted that the Śāstric interpretations sought to establish the meaning by making a reference to the original and the changed contexts of the text, and in the perspective of the later thinking and development of thought in that discipline.

Interpretation is the process of matching a code with a text, rather of making a code cohere with the text. The whole exercise of *vyākhyāna*, therefore, resolve itself into *artha-nirdhāraṇa* — the determination of meaning. Two aspects of meaning are clearly distinguished : (i) *yathārtha*, 'meaning as it is or as it means,' and (ii) *tattvārtha*, the significance or purport. To establish both kinds of meaning, the interpreter takes into account the *prasaṅga* or context as an instrument of exegesis, in addition to all the other instruments such as grammar, meta-rules, evidence, etymology, metaphysics and the symbolics of language. The determination of *yathārtha* itself is not always a simple matter, of course. Texts differ in degrees of and nature of complexity — those texts that employ for example figurative language or make recurrent use of symbols would be more complex. Again, when the texts are very old, their language may become archaic. Finally, the nature of ideas itself may be such that the concepts involved are highly abstract and the meaning, therefore, is esoteric.

In all such cases when the *yathārtha* has been stated and we find that it does or does not make sense, it is the "suggestion that lies behind" that is elusive, and when the nature of experience or ideas that have been expressed are metaphysical or mystic — as is the case with the Vedas, or with Yeats, for example — "We need canons of interpretation (other) than mere intellectual ones." (Shrimat Anirvan, 1937:312)

Talking about the problems of interpretation, Yāska identifies (*Nirukta*, 2.1) three tendencies of words — (i) *pratyakṣa vṛtti*, "straight-forward meaning;" (ii) *parokṣa-vṛtti*, obscure meaning or indirectly expressed meaning, and (iii) *atī-parokṣa vṛtti* — opaque words, whose meaning is esoteric. In *pratyakṣa-vṛtti*, the meaning is directly expressed, the text is literal and yet there may be layers of meaning that have to be articulated. Thus "Hari resides in a village on the bank of Gaṅgā" is a straight-forward factual statement about Hari's residence but may also have been offered as an explanation of Hari's piety. Sometimes, again, the establishment of *yathārtha* itself may offer some problem on account of use of some archaic word or grammatical form, or because it is unexpected, its meaning is inappropriate in the given context (immediate and/ or textual) or makes no sense. Then it is the indirectly expressed meaning that has to be culled out. Generally, figurative use and symbolism result in this kind of transparency — the need to look beyond the surface. In *atī-parokṣa vṛtti*, the words are opaque, the meaning is *upaniṣad rahasyam*, esoteric, either because the substance is mystic or metaphysical or because the words used are no longer in use, at least not in the way they are used in the given text or because the context is irretrievably lost. (This often happens in the interpretation of esoteric *mantra*s which have referents that are no longer recognizable or known.)

Once the *yathārtha* has been painstakingly established the interpreter moves to *tattvārtha*, the significance or purport, if there be one — an exercise in which the multiply complex context is necessarily invoked. A classic example is offered by Śaṅkara's lengthy disquisition on the rationale of the use of the world *aśocya* "not to be mourned," for Bhīṣma, Droṇa and such other grand old men of the Kaurava race, an interpretative exercise that invokes the contextual metaphysics of the text.[28]

Artha-nirdhāraṇa, therefore, involves, three things:

(i) explication of a clearly worded statement, focusing perhaps on particular lexical choice, if need be.

(ii) establishment of the meanings of a seemingly clear or of a multi-valent statement.

(iii) determination of the symbolical meaning,[29] of a transparent statement.

Rewording of grammatical rules, the paraphrase, for example, illustrates the first kind of exercise, while the multivalent statements of Indian philosophical texts require the second kind of exercise. The famous *dvā suparṇā sāyuja sakhayā* . . . from *Śvetāśvataropaniṣad* (4.6) is a well-known example in which the expression *dvā suparṇā*, is interpreted as (i) two birds, (ii) *ātmā* "self" and *śarīru* "body," and (iii) *jīva* and *paramātmā*.[30] And where the text is transparent as, for example, several *mantra*s in the Vedas, or portions of *kāvya* texts, the surface has to be transcended and the symbolic meaning, the indirectly expressed meaning has to be deciphered.

There are specific text situations (see *fig.* on p. 81) which

---

28. See *Śāṅkara-Bhāṣya* on *Śrīmad Bhagavad-Gita*, Goendka (ed.) pp. 25-32.

29. Several types of symbolic meaning are recognized in the Indian tradition. Ānandavardhana, a ninth-century poetician has exclusively studied the symbolics of language. We will treat of this below in the section devoted to theories of meaning as instruments of exegesis.

30. *Śvetāśvataropaniṣad*, Swami Tyagishananda (ed., tr.), p. 85.

set these interpretative processes in motion.[31] The content or meaning of a text has an internal validity and an external validity, an inner coherence and an outer coherence. In itself, internally, a text may (i) conform to the visible facts, or (ii) be neutral with respect to them, or (iii) be asymmetrical, (iv) be meaningless, or (v) be ambiguous. A text is meaningless when it does not relate to anything outside: for example, four is 4, or any such tautology or a proposition without reference unlike one as, "The King of India is dead." Ambiguity may be (i) lexical, or (ii) propositional;[32] *asymmetry*, on the other hand may take any of the three forms — (i) *contradiction* within the proposition where one part of the text is asymmetrical with some other part; (ii) *contradiction* between the text, its content, and the world, the known laws of this world (implausibility) and, (iii) between the text and the cultural context, both general and of the whole composition (inappropriateness). With respect to the rest of the text, the statements may be (i) discontinuous, when for example the topic is changed suddenly or when there are a series of apparently unconnected words, (ii) superfluous or repetitive, and (iii) contradictory when it says one thing at one place and something quite the opposite in another place. The Mīmāṁsā theorists use the term *arthavāda*s for the three kinds of statements — those that are in conformity with known facts (*anuvāda*);[33] those that are against the known facts but are consciously made for some purpose (*guṇavāda*),[34] and those

31. Todorov very aptly calls them "Tiggers" in his *Symbolism and Interpretation* (1973, 1982), a book inspired by the Indian tradition, "whose spirit," he says, "informs the pages that follow" (p. 12).

32. Ambiguity results from the manifold signification of words-class, individual, object or quality (see Patañjali *MB*, I.1).

33. viz. "Fire is an antidote of cold."

34. viz., "The Sun is a sacrificial post" said to establish the fact that "The Sacrificial Post has the same qualities or is assumed to have the same qualities as the sun."

Typology of Textual Problems

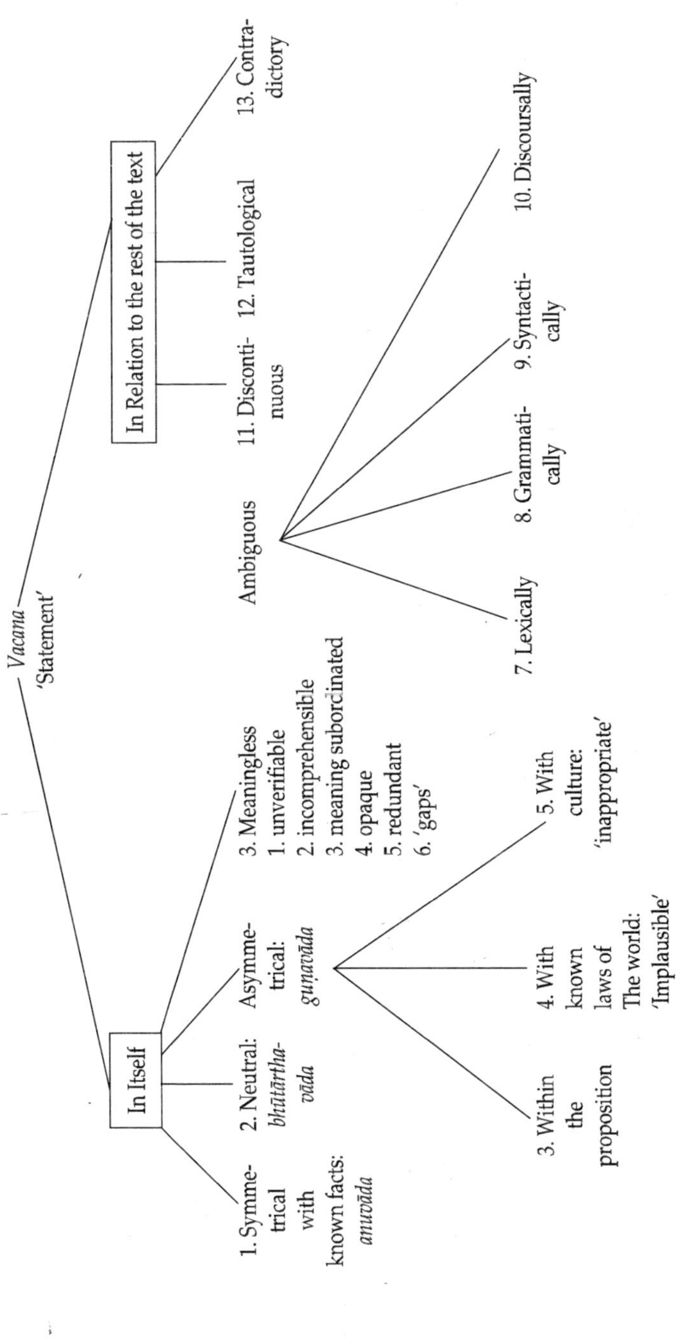

that are neither against the known facts nor are provable by perception (*bhūtārthavāda*), viz., "Indra uplifted his thunderbolt against Vṛtra."

If we evaluate the different sources of difficulty from the point of view of advancement of knowledge, we notice the great importance of *asymmetry* and *contradiction* — it is these two which pose the most frequent and the most definite challenge and thus contribute significantly to the develop-ment of systems of ideas. In response to these, the Indian mind made new efforts to reconcile the unknown with the known and produced new conceptual structures.

A discontinuous text needs "fillers" or explication. For example, Patañjali in 1.1 of *Mahābhāṣya* reads off words of current usage one by one, but cites contextualized words from texts. Why? Because words from texts are in a given form, while words cited from daily use may be found in any of the many forms. Repetition often adds proportion to the idea and is to be justified on that ground. Contradiction may be apparent or real. Apparent contradiction appears in *Mahābhāṣya* (1.1) where it is first said that form (*ākṛti*) is changeless (*nitya*) while *dravya* is *anitya;* later it is said that substance (*dravya*) is *nitya* and *ākṛti anitya* and both these are valid. Real contradictions may be found in the matter of foods, for example, where something is prescribed at one place and barred at another place. Such contradictions are resolved through meta-rules (see below).

The incidence of these elements or "triggers" differs from one kind of texts to another and accordingly we talk of different types of exegesis. We may distinguish between Śruti, Smṛti and *kāvya* exegesis.

The Vedic exegesis overwhelmingly faces the problem of symbolic expression and is marked by a multiplicity of schools, approaches and methods of interpretation. We can thus talk of : two schools — European and Indian; two approaches — tribal/primitive centered and modern empathic; and of two methods — linguistic philological and cultural-mythic. All seek to disambiguate the Vedic meaning. There is an early recognition that this meaning is very complex — "The meaning of speech is called its fruit and flower. . . . So many roots have the same meaning, *dhātu* (root) is derived from the root $\sqrt{d\bar{a}m}$ (to put). So many are the synonyms of this substantive. This is the homonym of so many meanings. This name of a diety is incidental, the other is primary (Yāska, 1.20). The *R̥gveda* repeatedly draws attention to the esoteric meaning of the Vedas — cf. 1.164.39; 4.3.16; 8.100.10; 10.71.3-5; 10.114.8; 10.125.7. Yāska's *Nirukta* insists upon a thorough knowledge of the meaning of the Vedas (1.18). The *Gopatha Brāhmaṇa*, while fully defining the scope of the Vedas, speaks expressly of their *rahasyam* (1.2.10). Modern European interpreters are divided into two schools — one regarding "the (*R̥gveda*) as predominantly an Indo-European document, so that its interpretation demanded the basis of comparative philology and comparative mythology" and consequently keeping the traditional commentators in the background as of little or no help. The other school, however, preferred the orthodox Indian tradition, represented by Yāska and Sāyaṇa, to the modern philological methods. At present, due importance is attached to traditions of ritual and internal evidence serves as a powerful tool in Vedic interpretation in several ways, e.g., in ascertaining the meaning of words, supplying lacunae, etc. (Suniti Kumar Chatterji 1937, 1958 (rpt.)).

In modern India also, several attempts at Vedic exegesis have been made. Some of them, such as the one by the Ārya Samāj thinkers represented "reaction to the uncritical and unjust attacks on the Vedas by ill-informed foreigners of the early 19th century." (Chatterji 1937, 1958 rpt.: iii) In any case in the process, the symbolic nature of the Vedic texts was commented upon and explained as requiring different approaches separately or simultaneously. "According to Sri Aurobindo the Veda is mystic and symbolic poetry, ... Coomaraswamy finds the Veda as containing an original metaphysical tradition." (Chatterji 1937, 1958 rpt.: liii) These two schools, the Ārya Samāj and of Pondicherry, seek to build both on reason and on mystic faith. No doubt, the Western Indologists inducted the rational spirit into the task of Vedic exegesis and often wrote in despair when the text would not yield to modern logic — but it is important to remember that reasoned interpretation had in fact, originated with Yāska himself:

> concerning the *mantras*; none can claim to have perceived their truths if one is not a seer . . . when seers passed beyond, man asked the gods, "who are going to be seers for us?" To them the gods gave reason as the seer. And hence, whatever one speaks with reason, following the track of the word, becomes as good as the utterances of a seer. . . .
>
> — *Nirukta*, XIII.12, 13

Shrimat Anirvan in his essay "Vedic Exegesis" (1962) talks of the mist that veiled the Śruti texts and hopes that this mist will be cleared if we approach the problem of interpretation with a penetrative insight . . . and a sound historical sense that can discover the motive of a great thought movement covering immense stretches in space and time and arrays its events in accordance with the rhythm inherent in it. (Anirvan, 1962: 311) What is needed, he says, is a proper interpretive technique, a technique founded on correct assumptions about the nature of experience embodied in these texts. Anirvan has strongly argued that the evolutionary hypothesis "which can arrange forms in time but cannot explain the timeless spirit that inspires the forces" (p. 312) is "a stumbling block to a correct appreciation" (p. 328) of the content of these texts. The *mantras* portions of these texts are an exposition of an inner reality, of reality experienced as consciousness and seen as "an ocean of reality" (*Ṛgveda*, 1-164-41), a non-segmented and a non-segmentable, a non-discrete and a non-sequential whole. Its external manifestation in the objective world is of course, segmented, discrete and sequential. What is essentially *abheda* becomes characterized by *bheda*. India's intellectual effort has been directed towards characterizing the two levels of reality and explaining the relationship between the two. Consciousness (or awareness or comprehension) of the essential reality constitutes the religious experience. This religious experience has a psychological reality and the forms that appear and are cognized in this reality are projected as gods. The Vedic theory of gods as names of the same one indivisible reality[35] is not therefore an expression of the primitive mind, as the Western evolutionists have assumed, but an explanation of "a supernormal fact," of a reality that can be experienced only in a heightened state of consciousness[36] in which the mind becomes an acutely sensitive interpreting instrument. This content is not amenable to the evolutionary or the historical method and needs to be studied on the basis of "other postulates," as Anirvan explains (Anirvan, 1962: 328).

> It is the epistemological assumption of the Vedānta, laying stress on the concretely realizable identity of the subject, the object, and the transcendant subsuming both, which supplies the motive of the Vedic religion. Its real nature like that of Vāc will be revealed only when, with a clear grasp of

35. See *Ṛgveda*, 1-164-46 and 3-53-8.

36. *Māṇḍūkyopaniṣad* has as its subject-matter, the exposition of different levels of consciousness. *Māṇḍūkya-Kārikā* of Gauḍapāda needs to be read along with the Upaniṣad. Both are available together in the Sri Ramakrishna Math, 1956 edition of *Māṇḍūkyopaniṣad*.

> this identity, one moves up . . . to its source in simple intuition . . . of an integral whole, symbolically described by the seers as the flash of lightning. — *Kenopaniṣad*, IV.4

The Vedic understanding is thus a subjective experience of the objective unified non-discrete and non-sequential reality. It is an intuitive awareness of an order of reality that in its essence and dimensions differs radically from the reality perceived through the spatio-temporal coordinates of our wakeful consciousness. As such it is not possible to

> capture it, or to express it in the ordinary language which is intrinsically discrete, sequential and 'concrete.' The Vedic poets, therefore, like all poets, took recourse to symbolism to embody this reality. Symbolism is the inverse of rationalism — symbol is the sensuous expression of a mystical experience . . . suggestive of something allusively transcendent. . . . It requires an atmosphere quite different from rationalism. While rationalism seeks to translate the concrete into abstract, symbolism as an art tries to transform the abstract of the intuition into concrete images.
>
> — Anirvan, 1962: 312

Everything in the Vedic literature, particularly the *Mantra Saṁhitā*, is couched in images and the reader has to "paraphrase" or decode them, but interpretation of the ancient symbols that embody mystical and often occult experience is an extremely difficult if not an impossible task. But the *Mantra Saṁhitā*, the Vedas, are on the surface virtually opaque, making little or no sense.[37]

---

37. Language, *vāc* for example, in one of the numerous descriptions is portrayed thus — "She the White Deer, shines in the highest Void in an array of thousand syllables which appear as flame-songs in the immutable empyrean in whose depth are seated the universal powers of illumination?" — *R̥gveda*, (1.164.39).

And this was in fact the objection of the early rationalist thinkers of ancient India. Kautsa, mentioned by Yāska, is a known pre-eminent representative of this early anti-Vedic scepticism founded essentially in the apparent meaninglessness and irrationality of the Vedas.

For a brief review of the history of this movement, we may turn to Laksman Sarup's introduction to his translation of Yāska's the *Nighaṇṭu and the Nirukta* (1926; 1967 rpt., pp. 71-80), Kautsa was the leader of a movement

> which may be described as materialistic rationalism, and which was the result of a remarkable literary activity, a characteristic of the epoch of Yāska . . . (and) the beginning of which can be traced to an earlier period
>
> — L. Sarup, 1927: 72

Its origin is to be traced to the sectarian efforts of the followers of the *Atharvaveda* who demonstrated the superiority of the *AV*, by allegorically describing the ineffectual character of the three Vedas. The method of Atharvanas "gave rise to *a movement of inquiry and scepticism*[38] — a movement the traces of which can be discovered even in the Āraṇyakas and the Upaniṣads" (L. Sarup 1926: 74) a fact that leads one to adduce that this rationalist movement was so strong and widespread that even the orthodox thinkers here and there expressed heterodox beliefs. Sarup cites the following passages in this, and in later literature, which question the Vedic belief system: *Bṛhadāraṇyakopaniṣad* (1.5.23); *Kauṣītakī Upaniṣad* (II.5); *Chāndogyopaniṣad* (V.II-24); *Taittīriyopaniṣad* (II.5); *Vivekacūḍāmaṇi* (Śaṅkara) (2); The Jaina *Uttarādhyayana Sūtra* (IV.2, XIV.12); *Gītā* (II.42, 45, IX.21, XI.48, 53). Both in *Kenopaniṣad* (I.2.23) and *Muṇḍakopaniṣad* (III.2.3), the knowledge in Vedas is regarded as *avidyā* (*apara*), i.e., lower knowledge.

38. Emphasis mine.

The Buddhists, the Cārvākas and the Jaina *arhats* continue this line of materialistic scepticism. The Buddha carried out (cf. *Tevijja-Sutta* in *Dīgha Nikāya*) . . . vehement denunciation of Vedic rites and practices. . . . He held them (Vedas) up to ridicule, and discarded them as an obstacle to final emancipation (L. Sarup 1927: 75). The *arhats* and the Cārvākas were obviously influenced by and carried forward the Buddhist arguments against the existence of an omniscient being and the need and validity of the consequent ritual. This line of thought "created in course of time a considerable amount of opposition to the teachings of the Vedas. It was therefore necessary for the followers of the Vedas to answer the objections of their opponents and to re-establish their position." (L. Sarup 1967: 78).

The first thinker at the head of this line of materialist sceptics is Kautsa, and the first Vedic thinker to counter his arguments is Yāska, the *Nairukta.* However it is Jaimini who develops a whole system of thought — Pūrva-Mīmāṁsā — to examine and refute the position held by the diverse non-Vedic philosophies.

The basic objection of the non-Vedic schools, and most of their arguments, emanate from the symbolic mode of expression in the Vedas, a mode that generates transparent statements making no sense on the surface. That this intrinsically provoked reasoned objections is evident from the explicit statements of the Cārvākas on this point — "the Veda is tainted by the three vices of untruth, self-contradiction, and tautology . . . the three Vedas themselves are only the incoherent rhapsodies of knaves . . ." (quoted by Mādhavācārya, 5). It is however Kautsa who formulated the critique that remained the bed-rock of all later non-Vedic thinkers. His criticism is reported and countered by Yāska (Yāska, I.15, 16) and the Kautsa-Yāska controversy is criticially reported by Jaimini in the first chapter of his *Mīmāṁsā-Sūtra.*

Kautsa's objections are reported briefly but essentially and contradicted by Yāska (I.15).

Kautsa says that the Vedic statements are open to any or all of the following objections —

(1) they are "meaningless"

(2) they are implausible

(3) they are self-contradictory

All the objections pertain to the nature of relations that obtain between the expression (*lakṣaṇa*) and the expressed (*lakṣya*). Hence they all fall under the left branch of "statement" (see, *fig.* on p. 81) which includes among other, the relationship of symmetry with the known facts. Statements, accordingly, are classified by Mīmāṁsakas into *aṇuvādas, bhūtārthavādas* and *guṇavādas* (see *fig.* on p. 81), for which we are employing the more familiar English terms above (which, however, are neither translations of, nor correspond to, the Sanskrit terms). The first illogicity (of *guṇavādas*) is identified as "meaninglessness." Now there are no "meaningless" statements as such — this is the credo of Indian linguistic philosophy, for the moment we verbally predicate, we create what we predicate. The only question is the relationship of that predication to the available knowledge of facts. "Meaningless" statements are those that relate to known facts in such ways that they fail to make sense, or we fail to see the reason why such statements should at all have been made in the first instance. There are five kinds of "meaninglessness" (see, *fig.* p. 81).

Thus a statement like "The mind is a thief" (*stenam manaḥ*) makes a proposition the truth or falsehood of which "cannot be verified by the scripture and the sensuous perception." (Mohan Lal Sandal, 1980) Again, Kautsa says the Vedic statements are incomprehensible and one has to employ highly esoteric and technical system of orthoepy, grammar and meta-rules to understand their meaning. So in themselves, they do not mean anything. Thirdly, in any case, in the traditionally handed down system of using the Vedas, meaning is subordinated — thus it is laid down that the sequence of words in a Vedic statement is sacrosanct. Now in ordinary language, one has only to bother about grammaticality and meaninglfulness, but here it is the sequence (*krama*) which is superordinate. Meaning thus is of no consequence. Again, the meaning is shut-off in opaque words. There are word-uses in Vedas, such as *amyak, yādṛśamin, jāryāyi, kaṇuka*[39] whose meanings are completely lost on the readers. Finally, many Vedic utterances are tautological — they repeat known facts — and are therefore redundant or irrelevant. These four arguments are forwarded by Kautsa to show that Vedic *mantras* are *anarthak* (devoid of meaning).

The second textual illogicity is that of implausibility, which may also be realized in one of several ways. Thus Vedic passages often refer to non-existing things — a celebrated, often-cited example is the *Ṛk* about the four-horned bull (*catvāri śṛṅga* . . . *ṚV* 4.5.8.3.). Prohibition of the impossible also belongs here. Shri Sandal cites the example from *Taittirīya Saṁhitā* — ". . . the fire should not be piled on the earth, in the sky or in the heavens" (5.2.7.1.). Piling of fire in the sky is an impossible performance. Then why the prohibition? Again there are passages which in addition contain an address to some inanimate object. Thus in the same *Saṁhitā*, at one place (*TS* 2-1-1) the branch being cut with a sickle is involved to protect the tree, and then the sickle-blade which is cutting the branch is addressed and invoked to protect the branch. Finally, Kautsa draws attention to the difficulty of reconciling contradictory statements. Several examples are cited from the Saṁhitās — Thus, in the *Taittirīya Saṁhitā* (*TS*), at one place it

39. Nirukta, 1.15.

is asserted that "only one Rudra exists — no second" (*TS* 1-8-6) while at another place it is said that thousand, innumerable Rudras have being on this earth (*TS* 4-5-13). Śabara also on 1.2.1.2. of *Mīmāṁsā-Sūtra* cites examples from the *Taittirīya Saṁhitā* (7.2.2; 6.1.1): "who knows whether one lives in the other world or not."

Kautsa's reasoned scepticism stimulated a whole tradition of Vedic exegesis. As already noted, faced with the sensory rationality of the materialist thinkers, the Vedic philosophers and linguists responded by "interpreting" separately the portions of the Vedas that appeared irrational, implausible or contradictory, achieving in the process increasingly finer understanding of the nature of language, and of the relationship between language and reality. This, no doubt, in turn made possible the development of both linguistic and non-linguistic principles and devices of interpretation. For at the heart of these problems lay the three imperatives of logical, literal and plausible expectation. Once the learned *paṇḍits* had mastered the principles of judgement (*Nyāya*) and the essential symbolic mode of language, the foundation was laid for the organized, rejoinder of the Pūrva-Mīmāṁsā. Even in the much more ancient Yāska (eighth-ninth century BC), we have evidences of a thorough understanding of the issues involved (*Nirukta* 1.15, 16). His *Nirukta* is in fact, the first text devoted to the task of interpretation. The rejoinder formulates the concept of "suggested or indirect meaning," of what the words mean as against what they state, and this was a remarkable advance in the philosophy of meaning. This takes care of most of the objections. Commenting on *Mīmāṁsā* (1.2.1.1), Śabara mentions five "methods of indirect interpretation, — such as (a) supplying of ellipsis, (b) changing the form of words, (c) connecting what is disconnected, (d) disconnecting what is connected, and (e) in-putting a figurative meaning." (Ganganatha Jha 1933: 51). Examples of these methods are given by Kumārila Bhaṭṭa in *Śloka-Vārttika Sūtra* 1, verses 54-58 (Ganganatha Jha 1983 rpt.: pp. 9-10). This construct takes care directly of the objections based on unverifiability, implausibility and contradiction. "The four-horned bull" (unverifiability) stands for *yajña* (sacrifice) according to Śabara, and for language according to Patañjali (*MB* I.1.), and in each interpretation the *Ṛk* is given a consistent explanation that has the merit of illuminating the nature and structure of *yajña* in one case and of language in the other. The implausibility of addressing inanimate objects and of requiring or prohibiting impossible performances is similarly handled. Thus when the knife-blade, a seemingly violent agent cuts the branch, it is beseeched to protect the branch and the act is explained as protective and of a protector, very much after the surgeon who amputates a gangrenous limb. The contradiction between one Rudra and a million Rudras disappears when we are told that we are talking of quality and not of a being, very much as we say — "you are my father, you are my mother." The interpretation of opaque words is taken care of by the rules of *nirvacana*, "etymology," and complex and multivalent linguistic expression by *vyākaraṇa*, the science of linguistic analysis. The question of the status of sequence in *mantra*s which is used by Kautsa to set-up a rupture between the literary language of the Saṁhitās and the ordinary language is settled by Śabara by explicating Jaimini's theory of language which subsumes both and whose principle claim is that words in the Saṁhitās have the same meaning as in ordinary language and usage. The rest of the objections are taken care of by the rules of interpretation (*Nyāya*). The science of etymology, grammar, rules of interpretation (*Nyāya*), the principles of judgement prevalent in common life (*loka-nyāya*), and the philosophy of word-meaning relationship — each of these except the last, became a specialized branch of knowledge and was developed and refined as such to a degree where each of them became an independent "science" in its own right, complete with its theoretical framework and tools of analysis.

However, it is the Mīmāṁsā thinkers who explicitly formulated the theory and practice of interpretation. They made three great contributions :

1. They systematically analysed word-meaning relationship and set-up typologies of lexical, propositional and discoursal meaning.
2. They discussed the pros and cons of the role of grammar and metre and sharply defined and delimited their role in interpretation.
3. They formalised the concept of meta-rules, i.e., rules of interpretation which operate over the whole text and are the overriding conditions of, or constraints on, meaning.

These intellectual attainments were the product of a uniquely continuous and dedicated scholarship. Beginning before Yāska (eighth century BC) by the time of Kumārila Bhaṭṭa (sixth century AD), it had made available finished theories and methods of interpretation. Besides, in the prolonged contention between the Vedic and the materialist thinkers, the rules of dialectics had been laid down and an essentially acknowledged system of disputation had also been developed.

Vedic exegesis proved seminal; it generated methods that were possible of application and were extended to other fields of inquiry as — Smṛti and Kāvya — and, in turn motivated new constructs, besides generally refining the tools and techniques of interpretation. Smṛti exegesis may be sub-divided into the exegesis of (i) philosophic (*darśana*) texts, such as the *Bhagavad-Gītā*, and (ii) of grammatical (*vyākarṇika*) texts, such as the *Aṣṭādhyāyī*. The two differ a little. The Darśana-Smṛti texts are built on theories that may be characterized as metaphysical, in that they assume the existence of extra-sensuous entities — of course, the grounds of assumption of an entity such as atman, "self," for example, its rationality is logically demonstrated, and this demonstration is the primary task of exegesis. The grammatical texts emanate from theories that are grounded in the material facts of language, use, and its assumptions such as the grammatical categories of *kāraka, sup, ting,* etc., though abstract, are empirically inferred constructs. Therefore, the grammatical exegesis seeks to establish the validity of the theoretical constructs by testing and demonstrating their sufficiency describing the linguistic phenomena, their explanatory adequacy. For the rest, contradiction, tautology, discontinuity and implausibility may be identified as the major specific textual problems of Darśana-Smṛti. In Vyākaraṇa-Smṛti — contradiction, implausibility discontinuity, ambiguity and specially in the case of Pāṇini, incomprehensibility, are the major islands of reflection.

Kāvya-exegesis, literary criticism in our parlance, is different. *Kāvya* resembles grammatical exegesis in the nature of its theoretical constructs — *rūpaka, upamā, prabandha* are realities inferred from empirical phenomena though the "reality" of this phenomena, the literary artefact, is a second-order reality the *kāvya* constructs such as "metaphor" often differ from a construct such as "noun" (grammar) in not sharing the latter's capacity to enter into a duality of patterning to yield next higher order constructs. The task of *kāvya*-exegesis is not to show the integration and interaction of different constructs in the explanatory process but to identify the constitutive devices of expression, to measure and explicate their effect by determining their meaning. Since suggestion is the essence of poetry according to Ānandavardhana (ninth century AD), the *kāvya*-interpreters wrestle with the problems of symbolic language and try to give to the poetic statements "a local habitation and name." This is their chief task. In the Indian tradition, this generally boils down to analysing how the suggested meaning is constituted and successfully conveyed. Of course, the exercise begins with such textual "impertinents" as ambiguity, transparency, repetition, redundancy and proposition-internal-asymmetry.

The Smṛti exegesis banked heavily on Mīmāṁsā principles and methods. They accepted the epistemological role of language as detailed and exemplified by Jaimini and Śabara and Kumārila-Bhaṭṭa.[40] Secondly they borrowed and extended the concept of *Nyāya*, meta-rules, both logical and of common life (*loka-nyāya*).[41] Thirdly, they adopted and refined the mode of disputation — the *tarka-vidhi*. Ādi Śaṅkara's various commentaries on diverse Smṛti-texts, are supreme examples of Darśana-Smṛti exegesis.

The *kāvya* exegesis employs the analytical models of a long line of poeticians[42] from Bhāmaha (first century AD) to Jagannātha (seventeenth century AD), models that are built on the two sources of grammar and the Mīmāṁsā theory of word-meaning relationship. Grammar figures in a major way in Kuntaka's *vakrokti* (deviation) theory, while Mīmāṁsā theory of symbolic use — owing a debt to both Yāska and Pāṇini — led in successive stages to Ānandavardhana's final and authoritative *dhvani*-theory of literary meaning, besides influencing and making possible the Rīti and the Alaṁkāra

---

40. In his two major works *Tantra-Vārttika* and *Śloka-Vārttika*, Kumārila Bhaṭṭa exhausively examines language as epistemology in terms of the relationship that its different constitutive elements and levels-words, sentence, negation, etc. — bear to meaning.

41. In grammatical exegesis particularly, in the work of scholars temporally as distant as Patañjali (second century BC) and Nāgeśa Bhaṭṭa (eighteenth century AD), the concept of meta-rules was extended and refined, with Nāgeśa Bhaṭṭa discussing the structure and domain of as many as 133 *Paribhāṣās*.

42. For a brief survey see Gaurinath Sastri 1978: 293-302.

Schools. Theory of symbolic meaning inspired by Mīmāṁsā but fully formulated by the poeticians, must be recognized as the characteristic method of interpretation in *kāvya* exegesis.

In this manner, the principles and methods of interpretation conceived and sharpened by the Vedic exegetes became the foundation of all kinds of exegesis so that there is a common core of methodology to interpret texts of different disciplines. The term for this common core is *śāstra-paddhati,* and our next section is devoted to its brief exposition.

3

The Shared Mode of Interpretation

Śāstra-Paddhati

SCATTERED in literature here and there are references to the *Śāstra-Paddhati* — a universally accepted method of reading texts. This *paddhati*, customary practice, can be seen to have four parts: (1) the formal organization of the discourse in terms of *prakaraṇa, adhikaraṇa,* etc. (which we have already described in chapter 2); (2) the logical mode of discussion and argument; (3) *pramāṇas*, or epistemology (nature of evidence or proofs); and (4) strategies or instruments of interpretation.

The presence of shared *paddhati,* or mode of interpretation, employed by the competing *sampradāya,* schools, such as the Brāhmaṇa, the Buddhist and the Jaina, define India as an interpretative community.

There are two parallel interactive traditions in India — the learned tradition and the popular tradition of text-interpretation. The popular tradition exists in the form of collective, institutionalized reading — the *kathā* and the *pravacana* form. All over rural India, there is a cyclic occasion known in the north as *saptāh,* literally a "week," which is a meeting point for inhabitants of about twenty to fifty contiguous villages, and in which all kinds of socio-economic transactions take place, it is also an occasion for religious and cultural events. In all such *saptāhs*, the epics and the Pūraṇas are narrated and discussed and discourses are also given on important Smṛti-texts. Sometimes the same text is being expounded by more than one *paṇḍit* so that audience often move from one *kathā* or *parvacana* to the other. The expositions are no doubt based on the learned commentaries but are in the local dialect and are full of illustrative anecdotes and stories from mythology, epics, Pūraṇas, other texts not under exposition, and, of course the local events and folk wisdom. It is though these public readings that concepts of philosophies, such as the inseparability of form and substance, *ātman* and *Brahman*, first explained by some thinker such as great Ādi Śaṅkara through the analogy of wave and water, would become a part of the ordinary stock of wisdom held by the common people of India.

The learned tradition which forms the core of this popular tradition, seeks to determine the meaning of the text by analysing the text according to the accepted *paddhati* and in the shared metalanguage. This imposes certain conditions on the interpreter. There is in the tradition the concept of *adhikāra*, the concept of competence to interpret. "A process of saturation, resulting in a participation mystique, must set in before the eyes are ready to see and the mind to grasp" (Anirvan 1973: 326). This "process of saturation" involves mastering all the pertinent knowledge. The boundaries of this universe of knowledge have been described by Rājaśekhara — the four Vedas; the five sub-Vedas, *Itihāsa* (history), *Dhanurveda* (military science), *Gandharvaveda* (dancing), *Āyurveda* (medicine and surgery), *Gānaveda* (music); the seven ancillary sciences — *Śikṣā* (phonetics and phonology), *Kalpa* (ritual or conduct, individual and social), *Vyākaraṇa* (grammar), *Nirukta* (etymology), *Chanda* (metrics and prosody), *Jyotiṣa* (astronomy), *Kāvya* (literary compositions); and the six *vidyās* (disciplines) — *Vārttā* (commerce, agriculture, animal husbandary), *Kāma-Sūtra* (sex and sexual life), *Śilpa Śāstra* (sculpture, painting and architecture), *Arthaśāstra* (polity),

Sāhitya-vidyā (poetic) and *Āṇvīkṣkī* (philosophical disputation). Besides, says Rājaśekhara, each Śāstra, seminal scholastic work of a discipline, is like a river; small (*alpa*) in the beginning and grows vast (*vipula*) and more vast with the passage of time. It is the exegetical scholarship and the exegetical literature (*bhāṣya, vr̥tti, ṭīkā, samīkṣā, pañjikā, kārikā* and *vārttika*) which is responsible for the refinement, extension and increasing precision and profundity of knowledge. A learned man who takes upon himself the task of interpreting a Śāstra, has to have mastered all this knowledge — twenty-two sciences and the commentary literature — if he is to make an enduring contribution to knowledge.[1] Great exegetes of the Indian tradition — Yāska, Patañjali, Śabara, Kumārila Bhaṭṭa, Ādi Śaṅkara, Rāmānuja and Mādhavācārya — were such men.

The interpreter conducts his inquiry following a given pattern, *vyākhyāna-prakriyā*, that is a part of the *Śāstra-Paddhati*. A self-contained total act of interpretation includes (i) what the earlier thinkers of the same school (*sampradāya*) have said, (ii) the differing opinion (*matantara*), and (iii) the context (*prasaṅga*). Its method is of paraphrase, explanation, example, counter-example since an interpretation can be arrived at only through controversy. As Prof. Matilal points out —

> During the *śramaṇa* (post-Upaniṣadic) period of Indian philosophy, the intellectual climate was brisk, critical and controversial . . . in such an environment, debate . . . was the

---

1. One may be tempted to say that such a condition is futile because the requirement is impossible to meet. Not really so — education in the oral tradition has a different character and different possibilities. For one thing, the texts are really, very, brief, their length being determined in syllables (where as now we do it in pages). Secondly, the *guru* had a very important role — his learning was an alternative to years of self-study. Thirdly, learning was whole-time activity for the first quarter of one's life, and undertaken with great discipline and renunciation.

> order of the day. . . . No subject was considered too sacred for criticism and refutation. . . . These debates sometimes degenerated . . . it (was) necessary to enter into a debate if one has to . . . maintain, defend and propagate one's own religious and philosophic convictions . . . ordinary people may be misled by a crafty debater. . . . Therefore, some professional training in the art of debate is essential for a philosopher.
>
> —B.K. Matilal, 1985: 9

The *Śāstra-Paddhati* permits only one kind of *kathā* (controversy) — the *vāda*. This *vāda-kathā*, which is the best of *kathā*s will continue until truth is arrived at. Almost all the philosophical treatises we know of have adopted *vāda-kathā*. *Vijigīṣukathā* (discussion for scoring a victory) which includes *jalpa* and *vitaṇḍa*, is different. It is not resorted to for ascertainment of truth. . . . *Vijigīṣukathā* is employed to expose the ignorance or to demolish the contrary conviction of the disputant, and it ceases with his discomfiture. *Vāda-kathā*, on the other hand, does not come to an end till the definite ascertainment of truth is reached. Śrī Kṛṣṇa has also said in the *Gītā*, "I am *vāda*: *pravadatam aham*" (1.2.1-3) — suggests the superiority of *vāda* characterised by right type of reasoning. *Vāda* is explained as the correct and fruitful mode of disputation —

> The collection of sentences (i.e. a discourse) that mentions the protagonist's point of view and of the opponent as well, is in accordance with the protagonists' overriding principle (meta-assumption), follows the five-steps of syllogistic reasoning, establishes the protagonists point of view and refutes that of the opponent with the help of logic and different kinds of evidence, is *vāda*.
>
> — *Nyāya-Sūtra* (1.2.1)

Vāda is thus reasoned controversy — it involves postulating a thesis in relation to the object of inquiry. Since contradictory qualities cannot exist in the same object, an argument follows and continues till the contradiction is overcome or resolved. It is noted that when Indian philosophers write treatises or expound certain truths in the seclusion of their seminaries, even then they present the *prima facie* objections of their opponent (*pūrva-pakṣa*) and meet them. While doing so, they assume the presence of these opponents and invest them with the freedom of advancing contrary arguments. They also assume the presence of neutral persons, give expression to the latter's doubts, and suggest solutions. When an author writes a "treatise, he thus imagines himself to be present in an assembly of the enlightened." (Bagchi 1937: 564) It may be noted here that Patañjali's *Mahābhāṣya* is the supreme example of this mode. This *vāda*, according to Vācaspati Miśra (*Nyāya-Vārttika-Tātparyaṭīkā* 1, 2.1) yields three results — knowledge of unknown truths, removal of doubts, and confirmation of previous knowledge. Acts of interpretation, therefore, have a dialectical structure — Patañjali's *Mahābhāṣya* is entirely structured in this mode.

The structure of argument also follows a given logical process — one based in the system of Nyāya and given a formal shape by the Nyāya School[2] — *saṁśayā, prayojana, dṛṣṭānta, siddhānta,* and the five parts of a "syllogism" — *pratijñā, hetu, udāharaṇa, upanaya, nigamana* and the concept of *sādhya,* what is sought to be established, and *sthāpanā,* successful proof or establishment (*Nyāya-Sūtra* 1.1.23-36). This process has been thus explained by Prof. Bagchi:

---

2. We are presenting here one position — the Nyāya position. There are differences such as in the Mīmāṁsā and the Buddhist positions. But the Nyāya position is the most widely agreed one on the nature and structure of logical argument, e.g., Vācaspati Miśra, *Nyāya-Vārttika-Tātparyaṭīkā*.

> . . . after the presentation of the point at issue, the disputant[3] will take up one of the *pakṣa*s and his opponent will take up the other. That is to say, the two contradictory positions appearing in the *vipratipattivākya*[4] will be taken up by them. The disputants, after having taken up his position, should state the *hetu* (reason or middle termed that is capable of establishing his own position). This is called *sthāpanā*. To do this, the disputant will have to adduce a fact which is to be 'a cause of, and which has to be in the "locus" of, what is sought to be proved. As for instance, if doubt is generated by the *vipratipattivakya* — "Is sound non-eternal or not?" the disputant seeking to prove "non-externality" will employ the hetu "having an origin." That which has an origin is called *kṛtaka*. This *hetu* (having an origin) is "a case of" "non-externality." These two facts represent what is called *vyāpti* (invariable concomitance) and *pakṣadharmatā* (condition of being an attribute of the subject), which constitute the strength of a *hetu*. With the help of these two, the hetu establishes what is sought to be proved (the *sādhya*). That the *hetu* is "a case of" the *sādhya* has also to be demonstrated and this to be done by citing instances from experience, as for example, "whatever has an origin is non-eternal, e.g. a pot." This example shows that there is an invariable relation of the *sādhya* to the *hetu*. Now, a *sādhya* comes to be established in a *pakṣa* (subject of a syllogism), if a *hetu* with the *vyāpti* of that *sādhya* is found in that *pakṣa*. The disputant will therefore have to employ the *upanaya* (application). This will be done by saying that the *hetu* (here, having an origin) with the *vyāpti* of the *sādhya* (here, "non-

---

3. We have noted above that the "disputants" — *pūrva-pakṣa* and *uttara-pakṣa* — along with the natural observer are posited by the interpreters.
4. A disjunctive proposition generally in the form of a question which encodes the two contradictory position, viz., "Does *X* mean *A* or *B*?"

> externality") is actually found in the *pakṣa* (here, "sound"). The disputant will next end, with the *nigamana* (conclusion). "Therefore sound is non-eternal." The original thesis regarding the non-eternal character of sound is thus established on the ground of *Kṛtakatva*, i.e. "having an origin," for the mark *kṛtakatva* establishes *anityatva* i.e. non-externality. These statements constitute the five parts (*avayava*) of the comprehensive statement called Nyāya.
>
> — Bagchi 1937: 567-68

This structure of logical disputation is invariably followed in determining controversial propositional meanings. As is evident, the syllogistic reasoning in India is different from that in the west: the syllogism itself has five parts, as against the three of Aristotelian logic, and, more importantly

> The Indian syllogism . . . is not, as with us (the Western logician) an affair of pure deduction, but a sequence of inductions and it is characteristic of India's practical outlook and its practical conception of proof that not only some positive example, but generally one or more negative examples also, are inserted to demonstrate that *hetu* 'is a case of *sādhya*.' — Betty Heimann 1937: 87

Thus, syllogistic reasoning and different modes of discussion mentioned above are not mere eristic and futile logical games — their extensive employment in the *Śāstra-Paddhati* of commentary literature establishes the fact that

> their importance arises . . . from their applicability and use . . . from the earliest period of Indian thought discussion has been considered the most effective of all means of scientific research. — Heimann 1937: 89

The *Śāstra-Paddhati*, therefore, restricts itself to the given mode of discussion and adopts the logical structure of argument. This is evident in the formal textual divisions such as *adhikaraṇa* (which means "discussion," "consideration," "inquiry," "investigation"). With its five parts — (1) *viṣaya*, subject-matter, (2) *samśayā*, doubt arising in connection with that matter, (3) *pūrva-pakṣa*, the standpoint of the opponent, (4) *uttara* or demonstration of the validity of that standpoint, and (5) *siddhānta* (and *nirṇaya*), demonstration of the validity of the standpoint being upheld and the conclusion. "This system of discussion is adopted, more or less, in all the Sanskrit philosophical system"[5] (Ganganatha Jha, 1900, 1981 rpt, ii). This is how through a three-dimensional analysis — *pakṣāntropanyāsa* (examination, explication, of the other opinion), *khaṇḍana* (demonstration of its unacceptability) and, *svamatasthāpanā* (establishment of the *siddhānta*, the accepted position) — the exegetical goal of *yathārtha-nirdhāraṇa* (determination of meaning as truth)[6] is attained.

With the structure of argument, with syllogistic reasoning, we are already in the realm of *pramāṇa*, evidence. It is well known that Indian philosophical systems lend themselves to epistemological categorization and sub-categorization — thus systems fall into classes according to whether or not they accept Śruti as *pramāṇa*. They further get sub-categorized on the basis of both the strength hierarchy and the number of *pramāṇa* allowed — the broad divisions here are based on the relative strength of *pratyakṣa* (perception) and *anumāna* (inference) and on accepting *abhyāsa* (experience) and intuitive flashes as reliable evidence. There is statement of the means

---

5. Grammar and logic are included among "Sanskrit philosophical systems."

6. The phrase "meaning as truth" is Todorov's and occurs in stating the distinction he makes between "meaning as truth" and "true meaning." See Tzvetan Todorov, *Symbolism and Interpretation*, Catherine Porter (tr.), London: R.K.C. Paul 1973 (Original) 1982 (Cornell) 1983 (rpt.) pp. 136-42.

of knowledge accepted by different Indian schools of thought on p. 107.

Serious investigations in all fields, however, accept four *pramāṇas* in this strength *hierarchy* — *pratyakṣa* (perception), *anumāna* (inference), *upamāna* (analogy) and *āptavacana* or *śabda* (testimony of the texts). Direct perception of objects through sense-organs is the supreme means of knowledge . . . "there is no scepticism with regard to the knowledge, acquired through the senses. . . . Actual objects for the Indian mind . . . possess reality . . . whence it follows that the act of perceiving these realities is itself real . . ."[7]

Next is *anumāna* (inference) which may be regarded as "secondary measure," because all inferences are Smr̥tis — memories of the knowledge acquired through perception. The third *pramāṇa* is *upamāna*, "sub-measure," which is the criterion of truth by analogy. For Western logicians, analogy is one form of inference; but, for Indian thinkers analogy is an empirical association of two or more similar data. Analogical proof is central and plays a very important part both in Indian philosophy and in common belief and life — the Indian tends to regard everything "on a common belief and essentially alike, the tendency to identify apparently different objects being therefore always operative." (Heimann, 1937: 83) It is to be noted that in Indian poetics, simile, is the dominant figure of speech, not the metaphor, which is regarded by the Nyāya thinkers as a means of illusory knowledge (see Junarkar). The

7. This needs to be stressed, for the popular misconception, bred through two centuries of the British domination, is that the Indians deny objective reality. Nothing could be farther from the truth. The word *māyā* has been mistranslated as "illusion." *Māyā* is the individual eye's perception (image, if you please) of the objectively real object. *Pratyakṣa*, what the eye sees, is true, is knowledge, provided — the conditions of valid perception are met.

fourth logical canon, *śabda* is unique to Indian disputation and is accepted more or less by all the major schools of thought, barring the Buddhists, the Jainas and the Cārvākas. *Śabda* or verbal testimony, is treated as a form of direct perception — the perception of a man who has tried to control and focus all his faculties and achieve heightened consciousness. Either the Śruti-texts, or the founder-thinker's teachings, a part of the Smr̥tis, are accepted as authoritative axioms that need no further argument.

Śabda, in fact, is a very important and a widely employed instrument of exegesis in the commentary literature. A study of the *Śāstra-Paddhati* shows the employment of ten strategies or instruments of exegesis in the practice of the major exegetes:

A. 1. Śruti (The Vedas)

2. Darśana-Śāstras (primary texts of schools of philosophy)

3. Illustrations from *Itihāsa-Pūrāṇa*

B. 4. *Sārvabhauma Siddhānta* (assumption) or the principle upheld

C. 5. *Saṅgati* (Coherence)

6. *Paribhāṣā -Nyāya* (Rules of interpretation)

7. *Laukika -Nyāya* (judgement employed in common life)

8. *Vyākaraṇa* (grammar)

D. 9. *Nirvacana* ("etymology" for meaning)

10. *Śabdaśakti*: *Lakṣaṇāvr̥tti* (symbolic meaning), etc.

We treat these in the following section.

Instruments of Exegesis

Instruments of exegesis may be classed under four headings: those pertaining to —

School of Thought	*pratyakṣa*	*anumāna*	*śabda*	*upamāna*	*arthāpatti*	*anupalabdhi*	*sambhava*	*aitihya*
Cārvāka	√	—	—	—	—	—	—	—
Vaiśeṣika and Buddhist	√	√	—	—	—	—	—	—
Sāṁkhya and Yoga	√	√	√	—	—	—	—	—
Nyāya	√	√	√	√	—	—	—	—
Prabhākara	√	√	√	√	√	—	—	—
Bhaṭṭa and Vedānta	√	√	√	√	√	√	—	—
Paurāṇika	√	√	√	√	√	√	√	—

A. verbal testimony (nos. 1-3 above)

B. the interpreter's belief-system (no. 4)

C. general rules of language and logic (nos. 5-7)

D. the theory of language (nos. 8-10).

It has been noted in the preceding section that *śabda* is one of the widely accepted *pramāṇas*. The interpreter may cite from the Vedas,[8] the Śāstras,[9] or quote incidents, examples or statement from the Itihāsas or Pūraṇas.[10] Verbal testimony is employed as an instrument of interpretation in all types of exegesis — philosophical, grammatical and literary. Its use in philosophical exegesis is generally ancillary — the interpreter argues out a particular position, employing different kinds of evidence, and then adds, "Moreover, the Śruti also says,"[11] to support the position. Quite often a position — generally the *pūrva-pakṣa* — is rejected on the ground that it contradicts Śruti.[12] Philosophical exegesis is in fact replete with verbal testimony but it is rare for an interpreter to argue a position purely on verbal testimony, although it is not excluded completely.[13] Its use in grammatical exegesis is infrequent, although sometimes serious concepts are introduced by quoting from the Śrutis and putting an interpretation on the *Ṛk* — to

8. See *Śrī Rāmānuja-Bhāṣya*, on *Śrī Bhagavad-Gītā*, 11.24 where *ṚV*, 2-6-25-5 and 8-9-17-1 are cited.

9. Numerous examples. For instance *Śrī Rāmānuja Bhāṣya*, on *BG*, 13.2 *Bṛhadāraṇyakopaniṣad* (3-7-3; 3-7-22), *Śvetāśvataropaniṣad* (4-9; 4-10; 1-10; 6-9; 6-16; 1-9; 6-13; 1-6; 4-5), *Muṇḍakopaniṣad* (3-1-1:, 1-1) are cited along with *Māṇḍūkyopaniṣad*, *Taittirīyopaniṣad*, *Chāndogyopaniṣad* and *Kenopaniṣad* on the dichotomy of *kṣetra-kṣetrajña*, the "object and the agent."

10. See *Śrī Rāmānuja Bhāṣya*, on *BG*, 261, *Viṣṇu Purāṇa* is cited.

11. See Ādi Śaṅkara *Brahma-Sūtra Bhāṣya* on 2.3.16.

12. *Śrī Rāmānuja Bhāṣya* on *Bhagavad-Gītā*, 2.12.

13. Ādi Śaṅkara *Brahma-Sūtra Bhāṣya* on 2.3.17.

accord with the discipline's thesis. This is done by Patañjali, for example, with reference to the famous *catvāri-śṛṅga* . . . Ṛk 4-58-3 (*MB* I.i). Again, the primary Śāstra, say the *Aṣṭādhyāyī*, when not itself the object of exegesis, is in innumerable instances cited as authority. In *kāvya* exegesis again, the situation is very like the grammatical exegesis, except that Śruti use is by and large analogical, that is examples of parallel use are drawn from the source. It is in philosophical exegesis that *śabda-pramāṇa* has an extremely important place. This, of course, betokens the strong intertextuality of the philosophical texts and the philosophical debate. In one recent commentary on the *Gītā*[14] the exegesis ranges over the Vedas, the Upaniṣads, Darśana-Śāstras, Dharma-Śāstras, Pūrāṇas, epics and works of the *bhakti*-poets.

Consider now the *Sārvabhauma Siddhānta*, the interpreter's belief system.[15] In philosophical exegesis, we may distinguish two overriding principles or positions — one serves as the primitive in interpretation, the belief with which the whole exegesis begins; and, second the principle or proposition that the interpretation seeks to uphold. The two are understandably inter-related, one being the constraint on, and the other the goal of interpretation. In the polyvalent philosophical texts, the interpreters search for the Mūla-Siddhānta, the core or the true meaning of the text in accordance with the *sampradāya*, school, to which they belong. A text like The *Bhagavad-Gītā* is a good example of competing interpretations. Ādi Śaṅkara's

14. Jayadayal Goendka, *Śrīmadbhagavad-Gītā Tattvavivecanī*, Gorakhpur: Gita Press, Saṁvat 2042, p. 26.

15. It is the overriding assumption of the school — it is called Tantra, rightly "ideology." The *Nyāya-Sūtra* then goes on to sub-classify *siddhānta* into four sub-types shared or common (*sarva-tantra*), implicative or overriding (*adhikaraṇa-tantra*), belonging to the school (*prati-tantra*), and accepted but un-examined so far (*adhyopgamya tantra*). See *Nyāya-Sūtra*, 1.1.26-31.

celebrated *Bhāṣya* illustrates the point we are making here. His *meta-assumption,* which he shares with almost all major exegetes, is that *dharma* is the only test of valid action. And both as an adherent and as an exponent of the *nivṛtti-mārga,* he seeks to establish in his *Bhāṣya,* the principle that liberation from sorrow is achieved only through knowledge *brahmātmaikatva bodhena mokṣa siddhayati nānyathā* (*VC* 58). This according to Ādi Śaṅkara is the "true meaning" of the text. In upholding this "meaning," he is obviously contending against the interpreters of the school known as Bhartṛprapañca, who believed that such liberation flows from both *karma* and *jñāna* — action and knowledge together. Ādi Śaṅkara has referred to them in the text of his *Bhāṣya* and also refuted them. He has argued, instead, that unless one stabilizes one's experience generates *vairāgya,* non-attachment to transient objects and pleasures, one can not attain liberation. This then through several steps becomes the reason for liberation — no philosophy, no education, no action will produce that liberation.[16]

> *na yogena na sāṁkhyena karmaṇā no na vidyeyā.*
> *brahmātmaikatva bodhena mokṣa siddhayati nā anyathā.*
>
> — *Vivekacūdāmaṇi,* 58

With *Saṅgati,* coherence, we are beginning to deal with 'within the text' strategies. In a way, when the interpreter quotes from other texts, or cites instances from other texts, he is seeking *Śāstra-saṅgati,* coherence, with other texts, an external coherence in a total intellectual system.

---

16. Lest this may misrepresent Ādi-Śaṅkara's position, it is important to point out that Śaṅkara does not advocate renunciation of action — he has a concept of *vidvatsaṁnyāsa.* Just as a ripe fruit falls off the tree on it own, a wise man develops non-attachment for the world and its transient pleasures.

What we are talking about is internal coherence. The interpreter strives (i) to eliminate any contradictions that may be there and, also (ii) reinforces a thesis in one part of the text with the help of other portions of the texts which may repeat or elucidate the thesis. *Saṅgati* as "reinforcement" is an act restricted to the text while *saṅgati* as "contradiction-resolution" requires the application of meta-rules of interpretation. All exegesis relies heavily on *saṅgati* as reinforcement and the argument often begins with "Elsewhere also it has been said. . . ." Harmony or homogeneity of thought is the organizing principle. But it is not merely reinforcement — every such interpretive act also extends the concept by enriching it with another dimension. Thus Śrī Ramānuja in fixing the meaning of the fully inflected word (*pada*), *nabha* (sky) in the expression *nabhasparśam* (reaching the sky) which is used in *BG* (11.42) as a descriptive epithet for Śrī Kṛṣṇa's *virāṭa-rūpa* (permeating form?), notes that it is an attributive expression and is a part of the attempt to define *Brahman* in terms of its cosmic properties. Śrī Rāmānuja employs verbal testimony, cites from *Śvetāśvataropaniṣad* (3.18). *Yajur-Saṁhitā* (31.18) and *Ṛk-Saṁhitā* (8-9-17-7) to fix the meaning of *nabha* as *paramavyoma*, "space beyond the changeable material sky or nature," that element of universe which is not subject to change or decay. Does that mean that the material sky (nature) as we know it is not permeated by *Brahman*? Śrī Rāmānuja says: no for permeation of material nature has already been laid down as an attribute in 11.20, where the nominal stem *vyoma* has been employed in that sense. The exercise is philological/linguistic while the governing principle is reconciliation of thought.

Again, a text may lack *saṅgati*, coherence, because it says contradictory things at different places. In such a case coherence is achieved through *Paribhāṣā* or overriding rules of interpretation, whose domain is the entire text. An instance of this is the contradictory nature of statements made in the *Manu-*

Saṁhitā about approved forms of marriage, or permitted foods. In the absence of a rule of interpretation, the text makes little sense and leaves the reader perplexed, particularly scholars who, coming from outside the tradition, are unaware of the processes of reading in a given scholastic tradition. Professor Rāghavan explains with reference to such contradictions in the *Manu-Saṁhitā*:

> In regard to the current text itself, orientalists like Bühler were of the opinion that it has several contradictory passages which could be explained only on the theory of several recasts and interpolations and accretions. But as Kane has observed, the facts of the case do not require the assumption of many recasts and additions of topics like cosmogony, philosophy, etc. A closer examination of the context and of understanding of the passage concerned on the basis of accepted rules of interpretation would remove the need to resort in all cases to the theory of interpolations. The apparently divergent statements (see Kane, *History of Dharma-Śāstras*, vol. 1, pp. 148-9) on taking a *śūdra* wife, resorting to niyoga (levirate), and eating flesh found in the work are not really contradictory; for they are based on the doctrine of *nivṛttistu mahāphala* (greater benefit from abstention which Manu himself enunciates, and which is basic to the approach and philosophy of Manu . . .).
>
> — V. Rāghavan 1937: 337-38

Paribhāṣās,[17] meta-rules of interpretation, of which analogical reasoning is a sub-division, must be acknowledged as an achievement of the Indian logic-grammatical-philosophic system. These meta-rules have an important place in the task

17. In this discussion of meta-rules, I am indebted to my student Sri Vinay Kumar who allowed *me* to use materials from his term paper on meta-rules, particularly in the discussion about the use of *Paribhāṣās* in poetics, literature and in Śaṅkara's exegesis.

of interpretation and the determination of meaning — whether the discipline is grammar or philosophy, or even poetic and literature. Pāṇini's *Aṣṭādhyāyī* (seventh century BC), expressly includes some *Paribhāṣā*s (meta-rules). In the Nyāya-system, the *Paribhāṣā*s are given a logical foundation and explanation. It is not possible to settle relative chronology; and setting aside the question of historical evolution of the concept, it may be reasonably claimed that while the concept of meta-rule is the major contribution of the Mīmāṁsā thinkers, they had their birth in the grammatical tradition with the *Aṣṭādhyāyī*, though there are references to them earlier also as common-sense principles of judgement. Later they were widely employed by the philosophers and formed an essential part of Śāstra-exegesis. Thus, in their quest for meaning of the Vedas, the Mīmāṁsakas formulated rules of interpretation for all the five parts of the Vedas — *vidhi* (injections in the optative mood), *mantra* (a text that lays down the procedure of a *yajñya*, sacrifice), *nāmadheya* (proper nouns and their reading), *niṣedha* (negative precepts), and *arthavāda* (existential statements or declarative sentences). In all these, common problems of meaning arise — ambiguity, contradiction, implausibility. To handle these, the Mīmāṁsā system developed an elaborate apparatus of analysis and interpretation. The apparatus was no doubt specific to the object; but its generality, its rationality, and its procedural efficacy rendered it universal and ensured its application to all acts of interpretation in diverse disciplines.

But the discipline which really developed these meta-rules into a full-fledged system is Mīmāṁsā. These were employed to resolve contradictions and to arrive at the right meaning of the Vedic *mantra*s, answering the objections of such anti-Vedic sceptics as Kautsa in the process.

Consider for example the attempt to resolve contradictions. The Smṛtis are based on the Vedas, therefore the Mīmāṁsakas hold that every text of a Smṛti is supported by a Vedic text. If there is none available, the presumption is that Vedic text supporting it is lost. But if there be any contradiction between a Vedic text and a text of a Smṛti, the former prevails over the latter (*Mīmāṁsā-Sūtra*, 3.3).

Another kind of contradiction arises when a Vedic *mantra* is to be sung along with the *mantra*s of another Veda. The *mantra*s belonging to the *Ṛgveda* and the *Sāmaveda* are to be read aloud whereas those in the *Yajurveda* are to be read low. Therefore, if a *mantra* from *Ṛgveda* or *Sāmaveda* happens to be in *Yajurveda*, the question arises whether it has to be read aloud or low. The *Sūtrakāra* replies that it will be read low (*Mīmāṁsā-Sūtra*, 3.3). In other words, it is the nature of the Veda of which the *mantra* has to be read that determines the way of reading.

Another manner in which the *Paribhāṣā*s help the Mīmāṁsakas is in determining the fruit of the sacrifices and the punishment to be given to the offenders. When in a Vedic text an act is presented, but fruit is not mentioned, the presumption is that a fruit accrues from the performance of the act. For example, there is the utterance "let him perform the Viśvajita sacrifice." No fruit is here mentioned as accruing from the above sacrifice, but it is assumed that some fruit will accrue. The highest fruit that one can obtain is *svarga*, it therefore follows that one secures *svarga* by the performance of the Viśvajita. This manner of determining the fruit of a sacrifice is called Viśvajitayajña. Moreover, if the fruit of a sacrifice is not reaped in the present life, the presumption is that it will be obtained in the life hereafter. This *Paribhāṣā* is called *Yogasiddhi Nyāya*.

There are also *Paribhāṣā*s to determine the punishment to be meted out to the offenders, where the punishment inflicted is bodily restraint, it is always distributively awarded; but when the punishment is a fine consisting of gold, it is collectively awarded. This *Paribhāṣā* is referred to as *Gargaśatadaṇḍa Nyāya*.

How do we interpret the texts that lay down the procedure of sacrifice?[18] Six parts of the text (discourse) are identified for this purpose[19]: (1) Śruti, primary sense conveyed by a word without the help of any other is Śruti; (2) *liṅga*, the suggestive or the secondary sense of a word which can be inferred from another word or collection of words or from the same word itself; (3) *vākya*, when the meaning of a word or collection of words is gathered from the whole sentence, it is called the principle of *vākya*; (4) *prakaraṇa*, when a sentence or a clause or a sentence is not clear and its meaning cannot be gathered without the context in which it occurs, the construction is governed by the principle of *prakaraṇa*, viz., He eats no salt — we do not know why he eats no salt. To reduce his weight — the information would come from the context; (5) *krama* or *sthāna*, the location or order of words which help one in the interpretation. Thus — "pencil, pen, doll, let Ramesh, Rita and Saumya take." This would mean, "Ramesh" takes the pencil Rita 'pen' and Saumya, 'doll' and (6) *samākhyā*, the last mode of interpretation, the interpretation of compound denominations, which requires the compound to be broken up into its component parts to ascertain its meaning.

It is then laid down that in case of conflict among *śruti-liṅga-vākya-prakaraṇa-krama* (*sthāna*)-*samākhyā*, the one preceding prevails over the following. This is the rule of interpretation. There is a separate metarule which says that *prakaraṇa*,

18. *Vidhi*, procedure, the injunctive portion of the Vedas is of central interest to Mīmāṁsā. Hence all queries begin with reference to *vidhi*, the injunction.

19. We are of necessity giving a rather brief, almost simplistic but essentially accurate account of the concepts involved here. For detailed discussion see Mohan Lal Sandal (1980 rpt.): Vol. I, Introduction.

contextual meaning, cannot prevail over the propositional meaning and that in case of conflict, the contextual meaning has to be reinterpreted (see, *Mīmāṁsā-Sūtra* 1-11, 17-22).

The concept of *sthāna* or *krama* is very important from the point of view of meaning. *Krama* or order stands for succession or sequence. It is of six kinds:

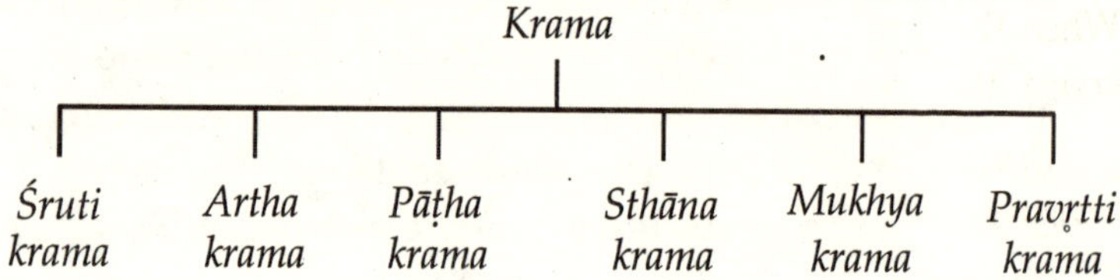

Śruti krama is the order determined by a direct text. It is of two kinds — (i) independent order as in "After meeting him, he came," and (ii) dependent order as in "He who reaches here first, gets the flower." *Artha krama* is the order determined by the object. In "He performs agnihotra and cooks *yavagu*," by "cooking *yavagu*." *Pāṭha krama* is the order of mention — "The car starts when he turns the key." The *pāṭha krama* is different from *artha krama*. *Sthāna krama* is reordered presentation due to requirements of variation in specific instances. *Mukhya krama* is the order of subordinate actions according to the principal action. "Offer whatever is left to your father and mother." In the indian context it will be offered first to the mother, for mother takes precedence over father according to the Dharma-Śāstras. *Pravṛtti krama* is the order which once adopted for one set of objects will apply to others as well. This is how the order of performances would be interpreted in the various injunctive sentences. And when there is conflict amongst them the left to right order of strength will prevail. The concept of *krama* or *sthāna* is very important for the determination of meaning, and conflicts are likely to arise between different kinds of *krama*s from the point of view of meaning — *śruti krama, artha krama, pāṭha krama, sthāna krama,*

mukhya krama and *pravṛtti krama*. According to the *sūtras*, if there is a conflict between *pāṭha krama* and *mukhya krama*, the former prevails (*MS* 5.1).

When there is a conflict between *śruti krama* and *artha krama* the *śruti krama* will have a preference. When there is a conflict between *pāṭha krama* and *artha krama*, the *artha krama* will prevail. When there is a conflict between the *śruti krama* and the *pravṛtti krama*, the *pravṛtti krama* will prevail.

Śruti krama-artha krama-pāṭha krama-sthāna krama-mukhya krama-pravṛtti krama : this is the *Paribhāṣā*, the rule of interpretation. The *Paribhāṣās* are also called *Nyāya* or principles of judgement. *Paribhāṣās* are of two kinds — *śāstra-nirdiṣṭa*, i.e., demanded by the inner logic of a discipline, and *loka-nyāya siddha*, based upon popular maxims. These *Paribhāṣās* may be expressly stated and incorporated in a text, or they may be implicit, in which case, commentators often take it upon themselves to explicate them.

In *Mīmāṁsā-Sūtras*, we can identify three kinds of *śāstra-nirdiṣṭa* meta-rules: (1) general meta-rules having to do with discussed values of order, transference and mutual relationship of parts of meaning; (2) lexical meta-rules, that help determine the reference of lexical units, and (3) sentential meta-rules, that have to do with the interpretation of sentential meaning. *Vaiśvānara Nyāya* which says that "a context cannot override a statement" is an example of the first kind of meta-rule.[20]

Gṛhaikatva Nyāya which says that "when an object in the singular number belongs to a class, what is predicated of one applies to the class," is an example of the second kind of meta-rule — one that limits or defines the referential domain of the lexical item. Thus, "Man is mortal" applies to all human beings.

---

20. *Āruṇi Nyāya, Mithosambandha Nyāya, Tadadi Nyāya*, etc., belong here.

The Mīmāṁsā school also focused its attention on Kautsa's charge regarding the meaninglessness of the Vedas and therefore a number of the Nyāyas used by the Mīmāṁsakas deal directly with the determination of meaning. These Nyāyas are an indispensable part of any treatise on meaning. For an example of how meaning is established by a Nyāya, consider: when an object in the singular number belongs to a class, what is predicated of one applies to the class; this principle is called *Gṛhaikatva Nyāya.* In a Soma sacrifice, what is said about one cup applies to other cups also.

Here we may also refer to the theory of negation, which was later developed more systematically by the Buddhists. Jaimini points out that the predicate will not apply to an object of a different class; when you predicate of a "cup," it can not apply to "pans" which are entirely different. Thus he seems to suggest that meaning is arrived at by the exclusion of all other meanings. The theory of meaning is further developed in other Nyāyas. Jaimini notes that the number in a noun is very important and conveys the oneness, duality or plurality of the materials. When a singular number is used, it means one only and does not include many. This principle is called *Paravaikatva Nyāya* and is applicable to other two numbers also. Similarly, a gender in a noun is also very important. Masculine gender, according to the same principle, does not include feminine or neuter, or vice versa.

Rathakāra Nyāya also belongs here — "where a word is used in a conventional sense by reason of the convention being stronger than the derivation," it is called *Rathakāra Nyāya.* The term *rathakāra,* thus, means "of mixed caste" — it does not necessarily follow that he follows the profession of chariot-making. The Mīmāṁsakas were also the first to note that the conventional sense of a word (*rūḍhārtha*) is stronger that the derivative sense (*yaugikārtha*) and prevails over the latter. The *sūtrakāra* cites the principle to determine the meaning of *rathakāra*. A *rathakāra* is of mixed caste; it does not necessarily follow (as the derivative sense of the word would suggest) that a *rathakāra* carries on the business of chariot-making it is an accident if he does so. Similarly, a *dvija* or a twice-born (i.e., a person who is not of mixed caste) even if he carries on the business of chariot-making does not become a *rathakāra*. This is termed *Rathakāra Nyāya*.

The principle is also referred to as *rudhiryogamapharati*, and is also employed by writers on poetics to sanction such usages as may otherwise be considered indecorous. These usages contain words or parts of words whose derivative significations are indecent. But if these words have acquired a very strong conventional sense and their sense is not generally known, they are sanctioned for use in *kāvya* (cf. Vāmana, *Kāvyālaṁkāra* 2.1.15-18). The *paribhāṣā, vākyaśeṣa* exemplifies the third kind of metarule, the one pertinent for sentential meaning. It says — when the meaning of a sentence or a clause can be understood by reading it with another, or without, it is called the *vākyaśeṣa* or ellipsis. Thus at a tea shop, to the tea-maker: "Give *me* one" means "You give *me* one cup of tea." "He hit a six" means, in the context of the game of cricket, "He hit the ball out of the ground for six runs."

The Mīmāṁsakas also employed the inductive method of arriving at a universal proposition from the observation of two or more particular individuals of the same class. They gave the following example to illustrate this : When rice or pulse is cooked, it is put with certain quantity of water into a cauldron that is placed on an oven and heated. The materials heated are not stirred by a spoon but after a certain time the cook wants to ascertain whether the material put on the fire is boiled or not. She takes it out of the cauldron by means of the spoon to ascertain the fact. From two or three grains of the material that are taken out and felt by the fingers, inference is made about the whole class. This Nyāya is called *Sthalipulak Nyāya*

It is, however, the grammarians who have employed, argued, explained and postulated a large number of meta rules. Nāgojī Bhaṭṭa's *Paribhāṣenduśekhara*,[21] in the Pāṇinian school, analyses 133 meta-rules and Hemahansagṇi's *saṁgraha*, enumerates 140 *Nyāya*s in Hemachandra's grammar. Besides securing right interpretation by resolving contradictions, these commentators of Pāṇini used these rules to refute objections raised against the *Aṣṭādhyāyī* rules, to extend the sphere of Pāṇini's rules so as to make them apply where apparently they would appear to be inapplicable and to render additional rules (such as some of those pointed out by Kātyāyana) unnecessary and sometimes to shorten and simplify these rules.

There are other *Nyāya*s also (which) come to the aid of the poetician. Such a Nyāya is *Ghaṭapradīpa Nyāya* or the illustration of a lighted lamp inside a vessel. Viśvanātha makes use of it in his treatise and according to him it teaches that as the lamp continues to burn even after it has lighted up the interior of the vessel and is indeed essential for the continuance of that illumination, so the *vācyārtha* (the expressed sense) of a sentence is absolutely essential as a basis for the *vyāngyārtha* (the figurative meaning) which it also conveys (cf. Viśvanātha, 4.2.ff).

A little later in the same chapter, he illustrates *Asaṁlakṣya-krama-Nyāya* with the analogy of the simultaneous blossoming

---

21. Prof. F. Kielhorn's translation of this into English completed in 1874 was published again in 1960 by Bhandarkar Oriental Research Institute, Poona. Our exposition is based on Prof. Kielhorn's preface.

forth of the hundred leaves of a lotus *Śatapatrapatraśata-Bheda-Nyāya*. To quote:

> Now, the perception of the suggested, caused as it is by, and hence succeeding, the perception of the accessories, etc., has necessarily a process, but from its quickness it is not perceived, like the process of the simultaneously blooming forth of a hundred lotus-leaves. — Viśvanātha, 4.4.ff

The *Nyāyas* also help the poeticians in defining certain figures of speech. The *Pradīpa-Nyāya* (i.e., the simile of a lamp) is used to define the figure *dīpaka* (illuminator). Just as one lamp, put at the doorstep, illumines both the inside and the outside of the house, similarly one and the same attribute may be associated with two or more objects. This is known as illuminator, e.g.:

> The wealth of misers, the head-jewel of serpents, the mane of lions and breasts of girls belonging to noble families — how can these be touched until they are dead?
>
> — Mammaṭa, *Kāvyaprakāśa*, 10.457ff.

Saṁsṛṣṭi (collocation) and *saṅkara* (commixture) are mixed figures, resulting from the union of two or more simple figures. The nature of the union is, however, different in each figure, and the poeticians apply the *Nyāyas* to bring out the difference in them. *Nyāyas* used are the *Kṣīranīra Nyāya* (the simile of milk and water) and *Tilataṇḍula Nyāya* (the simile of rice and sesame seeds). Milk and water represent the most intimate union of two things, so that no difference is perceptible between the two; the union of rice and sesame seeds is, on the other hand, less intimate, and illustrates a union where the parts are easily distinguishable.

Here we have the commixture of metaphor and alliteration in single words (in the shape of the two long compounds).

But the use of the *Nyāya*s is not limited to the discussions of poetics only; they have also found a place in literature. They are especially employed by the writers of didactic poetry to bring their advice home to the reader. The above illustration of water and milk, for example, is employed by Bhartṛhari in his *Nītiśataka* as an example of good friendship:

> In mixture with water, the substance of milk is diluted. Water, feeling milk's burning pain, yields itself to the fire's attack. Then, to relieve the plight of its friend, milk is willing even to burn; but mixed again with water, it is calmed.
>
> — Bhartṛhari, *Nītiśataka*, 28

Moving from didactic poetry to epic poetry, we come across the *Ardhavaiśasa Nyāya*, employed by Kālidāsa in his *Kumārasambhava*, in the lamentation of Rati, after the death of her husband Kāma. The *nyāya* means the slaying of one half of a body, whilst the other half is kept alive. It is based on the story of an Ionian who wanted both, to eat the flesh of the hen and also to get its eggs. He, therefore, cut-off the neck, etc., and ate it, and saved the remainder for procreation. in other words, the *Nyāya* is expressive of absurd contradiction, or incongruity. By using it Rati implies her own destruction, pointing out that by killing her husband fate has killed one half of her, and the other half will naturally perish (*Kumārasambhava*, 4.31-36 see also *Raghuvaṁśa*, 8.38-56).

In the second act of *Abhijñānaśākuntalam*, the Vidūṣaka or the king's jester tries to dissuade Duṣyanta from hunting, but when he fears that his attempts are in vain, he observes: "it seems I had only done *araṇyarodana* (wept in the forest)." (*Abhijñānaśākuntalam* 2.3 ff)

This *nyāya* in Śāstras is used to mean 'unregarded complaint.' Bhartṛhari uses *Nyāya*s of similar purport to drive home the truth that one should never argue with an obstinate fool:

> A man may tear a jewel from a sea-monster's jaws, cross a tumultuous sea of raging tides, twine garland wise a wrathful serpent on his head, might get oil from sand, drink water in the mirage, or somehow find the horns of a hare — but no man can alter the thoughts of obstinate fool.
>
> — *Nītiśataka* 9-10

In another context he provides more analogies of similar nature:

> He ventures to tether a vicious elephant with filaments of tender lotus, to cut an adamantine gem with petals of silk-tree blossoms, to render sweet the saline sea with a single drop of honey who tries to lead wicked men to the path of good with mellifluous words of wisdom.
>
> — *Nītiśataka*, 6

It is not only in Sanskrit literature, but literature written in other languages as well, that the writers take recourse to these *Nyāyas*. For instance Tulsīdās has his own string of analogies to illustrate the idea of wasted effort. Rāma is expressing his anger at the ocean, which had not responded to his prayers to give him a way. He tells Lakṣmaṇa:

> To plead with the wicked, to befriend those of crooked disposition, to talk of charity to a person who is by nature a miser, to impart *jñāna* to someone who is engulfed by worldly attachments, to discuss *vairāgya* with a person plagued with avarice, to talk of temperance with an angry person, all these are as futile as the attempt to sow seeds in a saline, barren soil, and then to expect fruit from it.
>
> — *Rāmacaritmānasa* 5.57

Tulsīdās and other *bhakti* poets also apply their own versions of the analogy *cintāmaṇi parityajya kacamaṇigrahaṇanyāya*. The expression, which means giving up the fabulous gem *cintāmaṇi* and taking instead a mere piece of quartz, had been earlier applied by the Vedāntins for a man who abandons the search for knowledge of the *Brahman* in order to enjoy the pleasures of the world. The *bhakti* poets employ it to highlight the folly of one who, instead of dedicating his life to Rāma or Kṛṣṇa hankers after wordily attainments.

Sometimes the *Nyāyas* are not directly quoted, but are indirectly suggested. An example is furnished by the well-known verse from the *Bhagavad-Gītā*:

> That which is the night of all beings, for the disciplined man is the time of waking; when other beings are waking, then is it night for the sage who seath. —2.59

This apparently has its source in the *kakotukanisavatanyāya* (the analogy of the crows and the owl's night-time). What is day to the former is night to the latter, and vice versa.

So also, the maxim "A brāhmaṇa does not become a *kirāta* (hunter) by living on a *śāligrāma* mountain filled with hundreds of *kirāta*s" is perhaps implicity suggested by Rahīm in the line:

> Sandalwood never absorbs poison, though snakes may be coiled around it.

Rahīm also echoes Bhartṛhari in the illustration of a raindrop falling at the time of the Swāti *nakṣatra* being transformed into different things, depending upon the object it happens to fall upon. If it falls in the mouth of a snake, it only adds to the poison, but if per chance it reaches into a sea-shell, it is transformed into a pearl (*Nītiśataka*, 68).

Also, cf. Rahīm:

कदली सीप भुजंग मुख, स्वाति एक गुण तीन ।
जैसी संगति बैठिये तैसी ही गुण दीन ॥

kadalī sīpa bhujaṅga mukha, swāti eka guṇa tīna ।
jaisī saṅgati baiṭhiye, taisī hi guṇa dīna ॥

This, no doubt, points to the handing down of folk-wisdom from generation to generation.

But by far the most interesting instance of the use of the *Nyāyas* is provided by the *Pañcatantra* (5.3). It is interesting, not only because it illustrates a *Nyāya*, but also because in the process of illustration, reference is made to several other *Nyāyas*. Here a story is given to illustrate the follies of some *paṇḍits* who, though well-versed in the Śāstras, are ignorant of the ways of the world. Their knowledge, says the learned author of the *Pañcatantra*, is as useless as a mirror for a blind man. Here is the gist of the story:

The four *paṇḍits*, when they were satisfied that they have mastered all the Śāstras, ask permission from their teacher to go home.

As they were going home, they reached a fork in the road. They did not know which way to go, therefore one of them read from a book? "That is the proper way (course of action) which is followed by the *mahājanas* (great men)." But they interpret *mahājana* as "money-lender," and follow a funeral procession of a money leader's son. As they reach the cremation ground, they see a donkey coming to their side, and one of them again read from a book:

> He is a true relative or friend who stands by (assists) one when there is a festival, in difficulty, when there is a famine, when there is a calamity arising from an enemy, at the royal court, or in the cremation ground.

The *paṇḍits* took the verse literally and decided the donkey was their relative, so that they touched his feet and embraced him like a dear one.

Just then a camel passes by. The *paṇḍits*, seeing its quick motion, conclude that it must be *dharma*, as the motion of *dharma* is quick. One of them cites a verse and points out that one should unite a desired thing with *dharma*. Therefore they tie the camel to the donkey.

As they are driven out by the washer man (who was the owner of the donkey) they proceed on their way home. At some distance they reach a river, and one of them quotes from a book, "Whichever *patra* (boat) will come, that will take us across the river." The *paṇḍit* takes *patra* to mean leaf, and seeing a leaf, jumps on it. As he is about to be swept away by the current, another grabs hold of his hair, and quotes another verse:

> when the destruction of the whole impends, a wise man foregoes half (if by doing so he can salvage the other half), and manages his business with the remainder.

Saying so, he cut the head of his drowning friend.

There are more instances of their folly but this will suffice to illustrate that the knowledge of the *loka* (world) is a prerequisite for the study of Śāstras. (This, incidentally, also explains the wide use of the maxims from folk-life in interpretation.)

The philosophers also employ *Nyāya*s in their arguments and propositions. We can illustrate this from Śaṅkara's *Vivekacūḍāmaṇi*. But, before we undertake to examine the use of analogical reasoning by Śaṅkara in his *Vivekacūḍāmaṇī*, let us first briefly consider a few *Nyāya*s especially favoured by the Vedāntins.

One of the postulates of the Vedānta system is that we are already *Brahman* and free but we are not aware of the fact until instructed by a competent *guru*. This is illustrated by the *Kaṇṭhacāmīkara Nyāya*, or the analogy of the golden ornament round the neck. A person is supposed to have a golden ornament round his neck and yet to be unaware of it until someone points it out to him. Another illustration for the same is furnished by the *Rājaputravyādha Nyāya* or the simile of the king's son brought up as a hunter. The story is that a young price abandoned at birth by his parents at this birth was adopted by a hunter and brought up as his own son. The boy remained in ignorance of his real origin until he was discovered by a kindly person and restored to his rightful position.

A problem the Vedāntins try to solve with the help of the *Nyāyas* is the problem of *nitya* and *anitya* and the nature of existence. To emphasize the *nityatva* of *Brahman*, they posit the *Nyāya*, *yatakṛtkam tadanityam*, i.e., anything that has been made is *anitya*, or, to put it another way, whatever has a beginning has also an end. Therefore this world that has a beginning has an end also but *Brahman*, which has no beginning, has no end.

This can also be established by another *nyāya* — *Ādivanta yannāsti vartamānepi tata tathā* (that which at the beginning and at the end has no real existence, has none either during the intervening period).

The Vedāntins hold that existence is of three kinds: *pāramārthika* (true), of which all *Brahman* is the sole representative; *vyāvahārika* (practical), to which all phenomena belong; and *prātibhāsika* (apparent), which includes such things as a snake surmised in a rope. But since the second and the third have a beginning and an end, they are *anitya*, and as such are only *Brahmavivarta*. Therefore they have no real existence from the beginning to the end of their supposed existence.

There is a very interesting Nyāya to teach the identity of the individual, the one's self, which is the primary proposition of the Vedānta system. The Nyāya is called *Ahibhukkaivarta Nyāya* (the analogy of the opium-eater and the fisherman). The story behind the Nyāya is as follows:

> A certain opium-eater got aboard a boat, and saw a lot of people there. Wishing that he may not be mixed up with

> somebody else, he tied a rope round his leg and fell asleep. To have some fun, a sailor untied the rope from his leg and tied it round his own leg. When the boat reached the other side, and everybody was getting down, the opium-eater, missing the rope and finding it round the fisherman's leg, decided that "This is I," and called out to him, "O fisherman, thou me."

The purport is that common man also behaves like the opium-eater not realizing his true identity with *Brahman* but deciding that he is just the body.

Let us now illustrate, Śaṅkara's use of the *Nyāyas* or analogical reasoning in his *Vivekacūḍāmaṇi*.

Vivekacūḍāmaṇi discusses the essential tenets of Vedānta, and there is a liberal use of analogies here. As the Vedāntins assert at the very outset that the only reality is *Brahman* and anything that seems to exist apart from it is an illusion, let us start by taking into consideration some analogies which express the illusory nature of things.

The analogy of the serpent and the rope is one such analogy, and is employed by Śaṅkara to bring out the illusory existence of this world (verse, 235). With the help of the same analogy, Śaṅkara argues that the connection between *ātman* and *jīva* is really non-existent;

> As long as there is this error, so long this connexion (of *ātman*) with *jīva*, created by false knowledge, exists; just as the illusion, produced by error, that the rope is the snake, lasts only during the period of error.
>
> — *Vivekacūḍāmaṇi*, 198

Another analogy drives the point home:

> Without error truly the *ātman*, the independent and non-acting, cannot be connected with objects, just as blue colour is attributed to the sky on account of our limited vision.

Since there is no other reality than the self the concepts of bondage and liberation, which are produced by *māyā* (one's perception), have no real existence. Śaṅkara compares their unreality to the ideas of a snake in a rope (verse, 570).

There are four more instances where this analogy has been used in the text for similar purposes (verses 7, 138, 388 and 405).

The simile of water in a mirage, used like the preceding one to express the idea of something that is a construct of one's mind, also figures here. In this manner thus, Śaṅkara employs several analogies: the analogy of water in a mirage (verse 27) of moon as seen by one's own eyes (verses 54, 523), of the tree's indifference to the failing leaf (verse 556), of indestructible space in the destructible jar (verse 134), of wave and water (verse 204), of gold and the ornament made of it (verse 262), of dream reality (verses 170-72). All seminal concepts are argued and established with the help of analogies, sometimes, in fact, a series of them. For example, to establish the need for self-knowledge or effort, three different analogies are used in verses 51, 52 and 53. Conversely the same analogy may be used to establish different concepts. For example, the dream-analogy is used in this way in verses 170-72, 252, 448 and 458.

> Thus, one observes that the *Paribhāṣās*, particularly the *Nyāyasiddha* ones are used extensively in the Indian intellectual tradition. It has been rightly said of them:
>
> *ekadeśasthita śāstra-bhavane yati dīpatāma* ।
> *parito vyāpr̥tam bhāṣam paribhāṣam prayakṣate* ॥
>
> Stationed at one place in the mansion of Śāstra, the light of *Paribhāṣā*, like a lamp, illumines all sides.
>
> — G.A. Jacob 1925: 49

The *Paribhāṣās* of grammar are maxims intended to guide and assist in the interpretation and application of the rules of Pāṇini's grammar. Nāgojī Bhaṭṭa suggests that there are three classes of *Paribhāṣās*: (1) Those which are needed and whose presence is indicated by some *jñāpaka*, "any term, any rule . . . any proceeding," in Pāṇini's grammar, which in the absence of the *Paribhāṣā* would not make sense. (2) Those universally accepted maxims whose validity is self-evident — the procedure stated in them is axiomatic and one would not proceed otherwise. They are called *Nyāya-* or *yukti-siddha*. Most of the latter are a part of folk-wisdom, and point at the close interaction between *loka* and Śāstra. *Loka* or *sarvaloka* is universally acknowledged as the ultimate authority in Śāstra-exegesis and we therefore have grammarians citing instances from *loka* in support of their arguments. These *nyāyasiddha Paribhāṣās* are based upon analogies from common life, and serve as final clinchers in a discussion.[22] *Vacanikia* — those maxims, the authority and validity of which can be ascertained only by an examination of the individual cause in which it may be applicable. The *jñāpakasiddha* include such rules as *tasminniti nirdiṣṭepūrvasya* (*Aṣṭādhyāyī* 1.1.66), which states the relation that is to be understood between the words in the genitive case are to be substituted by those in the nominative case, if they are preceded by words bearing the locative case — termination. Thus in *iko yaṇaci* (*Aṣṭādhyāyī* 6.1.76) *ik* (i.e., *i*, *u*, and *lr*) is to be substituted by *yaṇ* (i.e., *y*, *v*, *r*, and *l*) when the former is in proximity to *ac* (i.e., a vowel). Here the word to be substituted is in the genitive case, the substitution is in the nominative case, and *ac* which expresses the proximity of a vowel, is in the locative case.

Another meta-rule of this kind, *yathāsaṁkhasyāmanudeśaḥ-samānām* (*Aṣṭādhyāyī* 1.3.10) determines the order in which the

22. Three kinds of *nyāyas* are discussed pertaining to *loka* and *śāstra* (*mīmāṁsā* and *vyākaraṇa*).

substitution should take place. To take the above instance, "*i*" can be substituted by any one of the four sounds given as substitutes, but according to this rule the substitutes have the same order as the sounds to be substituted, and the substitution is to take place on that basis. So *i* is replaced only by *y*, not by *r* or *v*. Similarly, the meta-rule *paraśca* (*Aṣṭādhyāyī* 3.1.2.) provides for the suffixes to come after the base.

Besides this, the meta-rules also helped Pāṇini to avoid conflicts between his rules and to disallow *aniṣṭaprayoga* or the formation of undesired words. Such a meta-rule is *Aṣṭādhyāyī* 1.4.2. which paraphrases as *iṣṭavāci paraśabdaḥ* and states that of two conflicting rules, the subsequent rule in the order of the *Aṣṭādhyāyī* rules shall take effect in preference to the preceding rule.

Takrakauṇḍinya-Nyāya (i.e., whey for a Kauṇḍinya) is a meta-rule of the *nyāyasiddha* type, employed by the grammarians to account for exceptions. Though they are brāhmaṇas, the Kauṇḍinyas are given whey, while the other brāhmaṇas are provided with curd. Patañjali uses it to indicate a specific exception to a general rule. *Maṇḍūkaplutinyāya* (the analogy of a frog's jump) is another *Paribhāṣā* of this kind. Just as a frog leaps from one point to another, skirting some ground in between, so the grammarians read parts of some rules, together with succeeding rules, skipping the rules in between. *Ardhamatralāghavena putrotsavam manyante vaiyākaraṇaḥ* is another *Paribhāṣā* of this type, which states that grammarians rejoice as much at the saving of half short syllable as at the birth of a son (*Paribhāṣenduśekhara*, 133).

This has made it possible for later commentators of Pāṇini to read much more into the *Aṣṭādhyāyī* than might otherwise be apparent. Kātyāyana points out that the word *ca* is superfluous in a number of Pāṇini's rules, but the writers of the *Kaśikāvṛtti* refute the charge making use of this *Paribhāṣā* implicity asserting that every word set down by Pāṇini must have actually enumerated in some rule others that have not been mentioned; or, in other words, Pāṇini indicates by the particle *ca* that his rule applies to other words besides those actually mentioned by him. For instance, on 5.1.7. Kātyāyana has the note that *ratha* also takes the same suffix as the words enumerated in this rule. According to the *Kaśikāvṛtti*, by the particle *ca* at the end of the rule Pāṇini shows that the suffix taught by the rule is added to other words besides those actually enumerated (Kielhorn, 1887).

From the sphere of grammar the meta-rules moved to the domain of philosophy. Most of these meta-rules used in philosophy have a basis in *loka* and are therefore *nyāyasiddha*. In the Indian tradition, the simile is regarded as an instrument of right knowledge, and this explains why *Nyāya*s have so much authority. The Naiyāyikas talk about four instruments of right knowledge, which are termed "proofs." The Naiyāyikas recognize four kinds of proof: perception, inference, analogy and testimony. Analogy is recognized as an instrument of right knowledge by other systems also.

More than sixty *jñāpaka-siddha* meta-rules are applied in the interpretation of *Aṣṭādhyāyī*. For example, there is a maxim (*Paribhāṣā* 50 in *Paribhāṣenduśekhara*) that when an *antaraṅga* (inner) rule is to take effect, a *bahiraṅga* (outer) rule is regarded as not having taken effect (or as not existing). That is, if two rules apply simultaneously, one to an internal combination and the other to the external combination, the rule that operates on the internal combination takes effect. Thus in the formation of *syona* from (*siv-*)+ (*na*), *ū* is substituted for the *v* of *siv-* (by *P*. 6.4.19), we obtain thus (*si+ū+na*). Here two rules apply simultaneously, viz., *P* 6.1.77 which teaches the substitution of *ya* for i before *u*, and *P* 7.3.86 by which *guṇa* should be substituted for the penultimate i before the affix *na*, and the question arises which of these two rules should take effect?

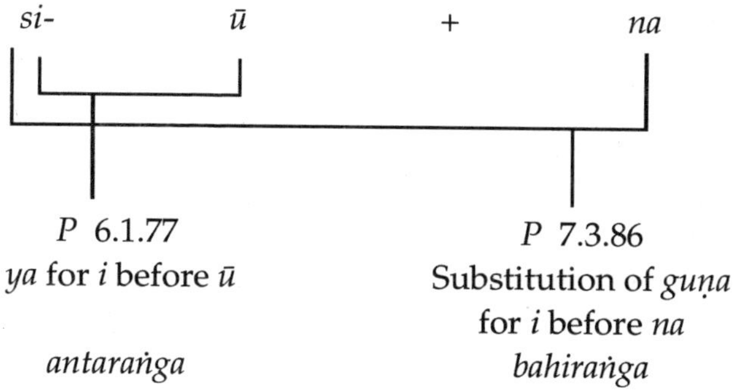

> The substitution of *ya* for i . . . is *antaraṅga* as the cause *u* lies before *na* . . . and the substitution of *guṇa* for i . . . is *bahiraṅga.* Accordingly, 6.1.77 must take effect because 7.3.86, so far as taking effect of 6.1.77 is concerned, does not exist.
>
> — Kielhorn 1960: 222-23

Paribhāṣā 42, *parannityam balavata,* is an example of *nyāya-siddha,* logical or self-evident meta-rule. It says:

> When two rules of which one would take effect under any circumstance while the other under certain circumstances would not take effect are both applicable simultaneously, it is natural to assume that the former (the *nityā*-rule) possesses greater force than the latter rule.

Kielhorn cites this example of its application

> . . . in the Present Indicative of *tud* etc. the affixes *S,* etc. (which are taught in 3.1.77, etc.) have, because they are *nityā,* superseded (the substitution) *guṇa* (for the penultimate *u,* etc.) notwithstanding that the latter is (taught in the) subsequent — rule 7.3.86.
>
> — Kielhorn 1960: 210-11

P 1.4.2, *vipratiṣedhe param kāryam,* is an example of the third kind of meta-rule, the *vacanika,* the rule whose validity is ascertained by its application in individual cases. It says — "When the rules of equal force prohibit each other; then the last in the order herein given, is to take effect." As an example, S.C. Vasu refers to 7.3.102 and 7.3.103: the first rule declares, "When a case-affix beginning with a letter of *yañ pratyāhāra*[23] follows, the long vowel is substituted for the final of an inflective base ending in short *a*. As *vṛkṣa* + *bhyam* = *vṛkṣābhyām*. The next rule 7.3.103 declares: "When a plural case-affix beginning with a letter of *jhal-pratyāhāra* follows, a *guṇa* vowel is substituted for the final short *a* of inflective base." As *vṛkṣa+su-vikṣesu*. But when the plural case-affix *bhyaḥ* follows, what rule are we to apply. For the sound *bh* belongs to both the *pratyāhāras-yañ* and *jhal*. Are we to lengthen the short a (by 7.3.102) or substitute (by 7.3.103)? The present meta-rule (1.4.2.) gives the reply — "the last rule applies." So we substitute. Thus *vṛkṣa+bhyaḥ-vṛkṣebhyaḥ* (S.C. Vasu 1891:168).

There is in grammar a sub-class of *nyāya-siddha Paribhāṣās*, which take us to our next instrument of exegesis — the *laukika-nyāya*. In grammatical exegesis, certain rules of interpretation, called *loka-nyāya siddha* are employed, "whose truth is established by the general practice of mankind" (Kielhorn 1960:x). Thus as in ordinary life a dog does not cease to be called a dog even if its tail is cut-off, so in grammar, a word which may have been partly changed by the grammatical process must still be considered to be the same word that it was before the change had taken place (*Paribhāṣā*, 37). With reference to *P* (4.1.92), *Patañjali* in the *Bhāṣya* states that the particular gender and a particular number that are given to the words that occur in the rules of grammar are not intended

---

23. *Pratyāhāra* is a class of sound generated from the *Pratyāhāra-Sūtras* (1-14) placed in the beginning of the *Aṣṭādhyāyī* and is an abbreviatory name for the class made up of the first sound of the class (*y* in *yañ* for example) and the closing indicatory and that immediately follows the last member of the sound (*n* in *yañ*). *Yañ-pratyāhāra* stands for the class of sounds that includes eleven sounds of Sanskrit — *y, v, r, l, ñ, m, ṅ, n, jh, bh*.

to teach anything — they are there because words cannot be without some gender and number, as little as it would be possible in ordinary life to get corn without straw. The last portion is a reference to the *laukika-nyāya-dhānyaphalanyāya*, the simile of grain and its husk. According to Col. Jacob:

> The earliest example of this figure is in the *Brahmabindu Upaniṣad*, verse 18 . . . (which) with others of similar import, is quoted in *Pañcadaśī*, IV . . . (Quoted) from *Bhāmati*, page 54, (it) appears also, without any acknowledgement, in the first chapter of *Śarvadarśanasaṁgraha*. . . . Vācaspati Misra, however, was not the originator of the illustration. It occurs four times in the *Mahābhāṣya* namely 1.2.39: 3.3.18: 3.4.21 (*vārttika* 2); and 4.1.92 . . . The *Nyāya* seems to have a different application in Marathi literature. Molesworth's definition is as follows: "The law of the corn and its straw. Conquer the King and you conquer his subjects; accomplish or a acquire a matter and you attain all it sustains or involves."
>
> — G.A. Jacob 1925: pp. 39-40

The above lengthy quote, illustrative of the loving and profound scholarship of Western civil servant scholars like Col. Jacob, shows how the logic of common life was employed as an instrument of exegesis in the learned discourse — this same *Nyāya* has been employed both in *Darśana* and *Vyākaraṇa*. *Laukika-nyāya* is extensively used in the Alaṁkāra-Śāstra (poetics) also. The employment of judgements from common life further reinforces the claim that there is no hiatus between life and learning in the Indian tradition, and " . . . (it is characteristic of India's practical outlook) . . . the assertion of practical examples . . . shows which facts are really important to the Indian mind even in "abstract" logic, the abstract idea being always elucidated by concrete illustration and comparison." The writer of these words, Prof. Betty Heimann (1937: 87) then draws attention to the entire literature of *laukika-nyāyas* in support of her contention.

The "instruments" of interpretation described so far are devices of judgement, decision-procedures to decide between competing meanings to resolve clashes of meaning and to establish the validity of a meaning posited for an apparently "implausible" or "meaningless" expression — they are not the process of interpretation, but auxiliaries in a process which is wholly linguistic as "meaning" is a matter of establishing a correlation between the word form, *śabda,* and its referent.[24] Successful establishment of this correlation constitutes *understanding* and language is the universal medium in which understanding itself is realized. The mode of realization of understanding is interpretation. All understanding is interpretation and all interpretation takes place in the medium of language. Interpretation is realized not just for whom it is being done but also for the interpreter himself. In the explicitness of linguistic interpretation . . . this process is simply the concretion of the meaning itself.[25] Therefore all interpretation, is a "philological" exercise — it begins and ends with *śabda*. *Śabda* therefore has been the object of much close investigation and study. In this context competing theories have been put forward about the relationship of language and thought on the one hand, and between language and reality on the other.[26]

In order to reconstruct the coherent universe signified by the signs, the words, the interpreter has to have a theory of the structure and system of words, the grammar of language, a theory of word-meaning relationship including a theory of the process of signification and methodologies for determining

24. The nature of referent "factual" or "imagistic," etc., is the consequent theoretical problem but not pertinent for us here.

25. H.G. Gadamer, Truth 350-60, quoted by Othmar Gachter *Hermeneutics and Language in Pūrva Mīmāṁsā. A study in Śābara Bhāṣya*, MLBD, 1983, pp. 3-4.

26. For a brief, incisive account see the first *kāṇḍa* of *Vākyapadīya*.

meaning. This is exactly what was done. Pāṇini laid down the structure of Sanskrit in a model that may well make claims about the structure of human language. Jaimini and Śabara related the categories of this grammar to categories of meaning and thus laid the foundation of objective linguistic exegesis. Bhartṛhari laid the foundations of a theory of word-meaning relationship and a long line of semanticists and philosophers of language from Jaimini to Kumārila Bhaṭṭa belonging to different schools built up the categorial structure of language as an epistemology. Poeticians beginning with Bharata, building on the foundation of grammarians and semanticists, examined the structure of meaning and their work culminated in the analysis of the symbolize of language by Ānandavardhana, "Who was perhaps the greatest of all theorists of textual symbolism" (Todorov 1973:12). It is these systems — the system of grammar, the system of meaning, and the system of symbolic meaning — which become exegetical apparatuses to handle textual problems.

Vyākaraṇa, grammar, sets up the elements, their arrangements and levels of language organization. Meaning is the function of arrangement of elements at several levels — *śabda* (word), *pada* (fully inflected word), *vākya* (sentence) and *prabandha* (discourse). In any text, one can envisage two kinds of situations — (i) some particular use itself requires a grammatical explanation; and (2) some particular meaning is to be explicated through the grammar of the expression. In both cases, knowledge of grammar is necessary in the ascertainment of both correct and incorrect words and hence it is that the *sūtra* speaks of the "learning" of grammar as the means of ascertaining the true expressiveness of words (Kumārila Bhaṭṭa, *Tantra-Vārttika*, on 1.III.9.27).[27] Jaimini in

27. Buddhists question the high status of Vyākaraṇa as an authority (*pramāṇa*), a position that Kumārila reports at great length in *Tantra-Vārttika* (I.III.9).

Mīmāṁsā-Sūtras makes the first organized attempt! to examine the categories of grammar for their significance and meaning in the interpretation of texts. He discusses, among other things, in particular:

I.1 the nature of words (*śabda*)

I.2 the meaning of words — nature of denotation, universal or particular and how words in the scriptures have the same meaning as in common usage

I.3 specific conditions — meta-rules — for the interpretation of proper nouns

II.1 the principles of syntactical unity *ekavākyatā*, syntactical split (*vākya bheda*) and syntactic ellipsis (*Anuṣaṅga*). A semantic typology of non-injunctive (declarative) sentences is also presented — reason, explanation, praise, doubt, command, description of an individual act, description of generic act, indirect statement, and comparison

II.2 the interpretation of different kinds of sentences, those with a series of verbs or nouns; co-ordinate sentences and complex sentences.

II.3 the interpretation of conditional sentences

III.1 the conditions on interpretation of complete sentences.

In fact, a number of meta-rules, *Paribhāṣās* having to do with interpretation of sentences have their basis either in grammatical categories or in the grammatical structure of sentences. Thus, *Āruni Nyāya* (*MS* 3.1) has its basis in the attributive constructions; *Gṛhaikatva Nyāya* (*MS* 3.1) is based on the category of number; *vākyaikatva* and *vākyabheda* (3.1) on the presence of more than one verb in the sentence; *pratyakamvākya-parisamāpti* (*MS* 4.3) on the coordination of objects in a sentence; *vākyaśeṣa* (*MS* 1.4.18) on syntactic ellipsis; *Prastaraparaharaṇa Nyāya* (3.2.14) is based in the category of case (*kāraka*).

Thus categories of grammar are available as exegetical devices in all kinds of textual situations: (1) to support an interpretation, viz., collective reference of a singular term, or singular reference of a plural form; (2) to disambiguate a construction; (3) to exclude a particular interpretation. Thus "He offers an oblation by going forward" means "After going forward, he offers an oblation" and not "in going forward, he offers an oblation," the latter being excluded by the principle of syntactic integrity (*vākyaikatva*). We may illustrate the use of grammar as a device by citing some examples from the interpretation of a philosophic text, the *Bhagavad-Gītā*. It is asserted in the tradition that in order to understand the *Gītā*, a knowledge of Sanskrit grammar is imperative (Swami Ramsukhadas, 1987: 201). There are *śloka*s and *pada*s in *Gītā* whose meaning and suggestion (*artha* and *bhāva*) are to be understood only with the help of grammar. Thus, for example, Arjuna, at places, refers to himself with singular pronoun (1.21: 1.22-23: 3.2: 11.4, etc.) and at other places he employs for himself the plural number (1.32-33; 1.36; 1.37; 1.39). The shift is important, as also the fact that Arjuna never employs the dual number although he is addressing and including Śrī Kṛṣṇa. This of course, defines the respective roles and the relationship of Arjuna and Kṛṣṇa. Śrī Kṛṣṇa is the arbiter and thus beyond the issues that are tormenting Arjuna and that are relevant for other participants in the battle as well. This explains the absence of the dual number — Śrī Kṛṣṇa is not included in the propositions. Again an analysis of the cases of the pronouns and the content of the propositions, in which the pronouns appear, shows that wherever the proposition is about an act actually performed, Arjuna employs the singular number thereby assuming full responsibility for the act. On the other hand, when he is talking about desirable actions he uses the plural, thereby suggesting that the propositions are valid for the other warriors as well and are therefore universal in their applicability. But what about the grammatical validity of using plural pronoun for reference to one individual, for the plural uses cited here have both collective and individual reference. And it is not the case of Caesar's imperial "we." Swami Ramukhadas says that the use of plural for singular reference is sanctioned by Pāṇini vide his rule 1-2-59, *asmado dvayośca*, which means "the plural of the first person pronoun is used optionally though the sense requires a singular or dual number the pronoun *asmad*, 'I' is used optionally though the sense requires a singular or dual number."

In the same way, interpreters have tackled problems of gender and agreement (*BG* 18.5, 2.38:, 5.11), person and agreement (*BG* 2.12: 3.11), significance of shift from *kartṛ-vācya* (agentive construction) to *karma-kartṛ* (impersonal construction) in the course of the same *śloka* (*BG* 2.68), significance of variation in the employment of demonstrative pronouns denoting greater or lesser proximity (*BG* 13.1; 11.51; 6.39; 11.19, 20; 11.33; 11.21, 26, 28; 11.45) and domain of the qualifiers (*BG* 17.9; 4.20; 12.17; 12.19), etc.

Consider now the use of a theory of meaning to interpret the texts. *Śabdārtha* in fact is the heart of this process — the relation between *śabda* and *artha*. The term widely employed for the power of words to evoke meaning is *śabda-śakti*.

Thus the study of word-meaning addresses itself to the question of (i) types of meaning, (ii) how they are generated, and (iii) how to fix or determine the meanings. In the Indian theories there is a consensus that words have four levels or kinds of meaning — *abhidhā, lakṣaṇā, vyañjanā* and *tātparya*. There is also good deal of agreement that *abhidhā* or primary meaning generates the other meanings through inferential processes (cf. Mahimabhaṭṭa: *Vyaktiviveka*). Before we proceed with typology of meaning, it is important to draw attention to the controversy about whether the meaning in language in directly referential or a mental object. Bhartṛhari's *sphoṭa* theory is the final product of this question.

The relationship between *śabda* and *artha*, between the linguistic elements we employ and what we talk about, is the central problem encountered by any philosophy of language. In our tradition, too, the discipline of grammar has had two clear divisions — one concerned with accepted usage (*sādhutva*) and the other with the linguistic form's potential to refer to objects (*pada-padārtha-sāmarthya*).

The second investigation has involved resolving a number of questions — the first one is the status of *śabda* and the status of *artha*, for neither the *śabda*, nor the *artha* can be understood as simple realities. The Indian grammarians have argued two levels of reality of both *śabda* and *artha*, a physical reality and an essential conceptual reality that lies beyond the physical reality. This makes the relationship between *śabda* and *artha*, a complex one:

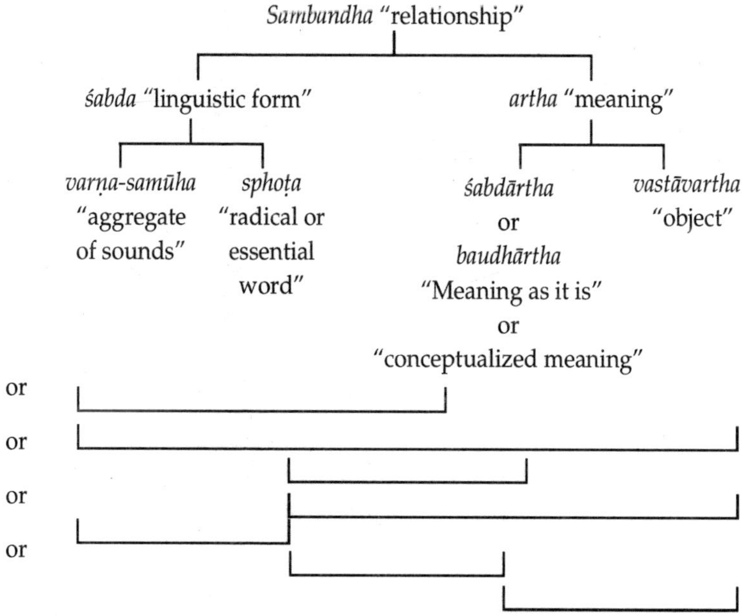

What is the nature and process of verbal cognition? Diverse and elaborate arguments have been put forward in this discussion. And on practically every issue in this problem, as is well-known, Nyāya, Mīmāṁsā and Vyākaraṇa generally take contending positions.

The first question is one of definition — what is *śabda*, and what is *artha*? Patañjali in *Mahābhāṣya* (*paśpaśā*) really laid down the basic duality of these in his famous definition —

"That which becoming manifest in articulated sounds brings/makes possible the cognition of cow-individuals, etc., with given attributes, horn, tail, etc., is the *śabda* (*Mahābhāṣya* I.1)."

The two levels of reality of both *śabda* and *artha* as shown in the above figure are posited in this definition besides other things such as sound-structure, the word in the mind (*sphoṭa*), cognitive meaning and the object referred to.

The second question or issue is — what are the different kinds of *artha*, meaning? Does the "word" have only one kind of meaning — a reference to some object? Or, is word essentially and potentially multivalent? For example, contemporary Western semantics distinguishes three kinds of potency — Sense, reference and meaning, (for example, in "Venus is the evening star," the two expressions, "Venus" and "the evening star" have the same reference but differ in both sense and meaning). Sometimes the distinction is also made between (i) conceptual meaning, (ii) connotative meaning, and (iii) thematic meaning. These categories criss-cross in the sense that the intrinsic structure of meaning is confused with factors that block or evoke meaning.

In the Indian theories, we said four kinds of *śabda-śakti* (potential of a word to evoke meaning) is posited — *abhidhā*, *lakṣaṇā, vyañjanā, tātparya.* Thus in the example, a settlement on the Gaṅgā, all the four meanings are read:

1. a settlement on the Gaṅgā (*abhidhā*, or primary meaning — blocked in this case)
2. a settlement on the bank of Gaṅgā (*lakṣaṇā* indicated meaning)
3. a settlement of good, pious people or a noble settlement (*vyañjanā* — suggested meaning)
4. A suitable place for settling down (*tātparyārtha* — the speaker's intended meaning, one of the several possible and one that is dependent on external factors).

Abhidhārtha is the "primary meaning" (texts often use the expression *mukhyārtha*), the "denotation" (texts use the term *padārtha*).

A fully worked out theory explains how the indicated, suggested and the intended meanings arise out of the primary meaning or when the primary meaning is blocked. The poeticians have made the study of meaning their major concern. Mammaṭa's *Kāvyaprakāśa* is the apt *saṁgraha*-text. Ānandavardhana's *Dhvanyāloka* is the final formulation of verbal symbolism.

The third question is the typology of the primary meaning itself. The *Mahābhāṣyakāra* is the formulator again —

The word has this four-fold external tendency or reference — Cow/Ox, White, Walking, *Ḍittha*.

In their primary meaning, the words refer to objects — but what all kinds of objects are in the outer world? The question is one of categories of meaning as they correspond to or are a statement of ontological categories. The linguistic meaning resolves really into four entities — *dravya, guṇa, karma, sāmānya* (substance, quality, activity and class or universal).

Though there are rival doctrines, the grammarians led by Patañjali maintain the existence of four different categories.

> And just as the cognizable universe is composed of these four different categories — viz., universal, quality, action and substance, — so too the words that are expressive of those things must of necessity differ in view of the difference in their import. . . . Thus . . . In the sentence — "The White cow *X* is running" . . . the four terms constituting the sentence — viz. *X*, white, cow and running are synonymous, though they refer to the self-same object which is *X* (*Ḍittha*).
>
> — Bishnupada Bhattacharya, 1962, p. 58

Questions that have been debated are — (i) Do the universals exist, i.e., is it necessary to posit them?; (ii) Is it valid to separate qualities from universals? (iii) How qualities differ from actions?; (iv) What is the significance of proper names?

An important question asked and answered in connection with *abhidhārtha*, is — Is the denotation of a particular term cumulative and composite (i.e., each term has all the four kinds of *abhidhārtha*) or isolationist and exclusive? The grammarians, along with the Naiyāyikas aver that the denotation of a particular term is a composite whole, a configuration.

The fourth question or issue is — for each of the four kinds of primary meaning, is the reference universal or individual or as the Buddhists assert, negation of the rest;

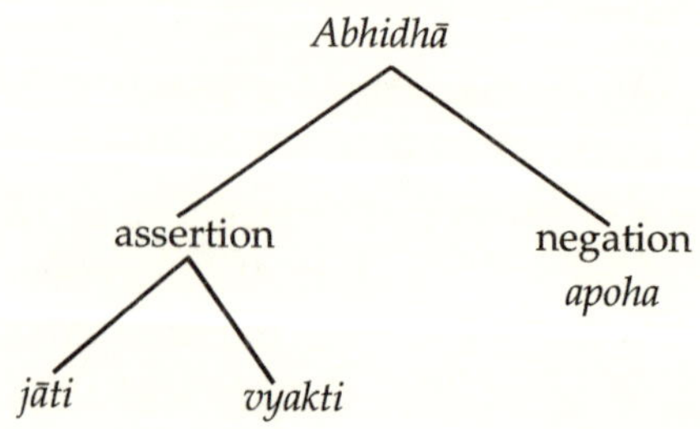

The significance of this is that both the *jāti* and the *apoha* theories make or render the process of verbal cognition an inferential process: abstraction of the individual from class, or identification of the individual by exclusion of the non-individuals. This problem has important implications for our understanding of the general cognitive processes.

The fifth question is equally important, and again concerns *abhidhārtha* basically (but provides the transition to all the secondary meanings)— is the linguistic meaning referential or conceptualized? Does the word refer directly to the object or to the concept of the object. Evidently the modern theories — viz., Ogden-Richard's theory of relationship between word and referent — are fundamentally not different from the Indian theories, particularly of the grammarians and the Mīmāṁsakas. Ogden-Richard in their basic triangle —

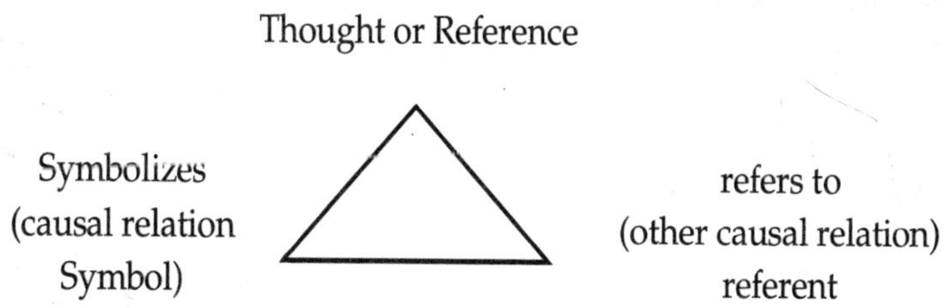

fig. 2

"point out that there is no direct relationship between a word and the referent and that the relationship is only imputed" (K. Kunjunni Raja, *Indian Theories of Meaning*, Madras, 1963, p. 12).

This is not different from one of the relationships suggested by Indian theorists (see *fig*. p. 141) If the meaning is essentially *baudhārtha/śabdārtha*, i.e., conceptualized, then the reality of what the word denotes is established only in terms of the word, and not by reference to some existing object in the outer world. This is categorically stated by Śabara. So "a barren woman's son" or "a horned tiger" may be asymmetrical with our knowledge of the outer world but is no less real for that. This leads directly to Bhartṛhari's constructivist view of language as against the representational. This has important consequence for the interpretation of texts as well — the texts mean exactly what they say.

This leads directly to the six issues involved — what if the linguistic meaning contradicts our knowledge of the reality? What is the status of expressions such as "Don't pile fire in the sky?" How are we to understand them? Questions such as these were faced very early in our tradition by the Vedic exegetes, viz., the famous critique of the Vedas by Kautsa, and Yāska's rejoinder to Kautsa, and Jaimini's whole science of interpretation (Mīmāṁsā) in response to Kautsa's assertion that Vedas are meaningless. Jaimini and Śabara closely investigate the structure of propositional meaning in relation to referential reality and develop a classification, a taxonomy of propositions — *anuvāda, bhūtārthavāda, guṇavāda* — and in doing so go intellectually far beyond the rather straight forward *yathārtha-ayathārtha* (real-unreal) dichotomy. They then handle the questions of (i) reality of linguistic meaning (*yathārtha*); and (ii) how to interpret the linguistic propositions. (In the process they are the first to formulate a theory of indicative and suggested meaning (*lakṣaṇā-vyañjanā vṛtti*) which finally led to the finished theory of verbal symbolism articulated by Ānandavardhana.) That reality is not necessarily *vāstvārtha* is one of the important claims — the *yathārtha* (the word we use even today in common parlance for "reality" or "real") could as well be *yathā-artha*. In any case, it is a highly complex network;

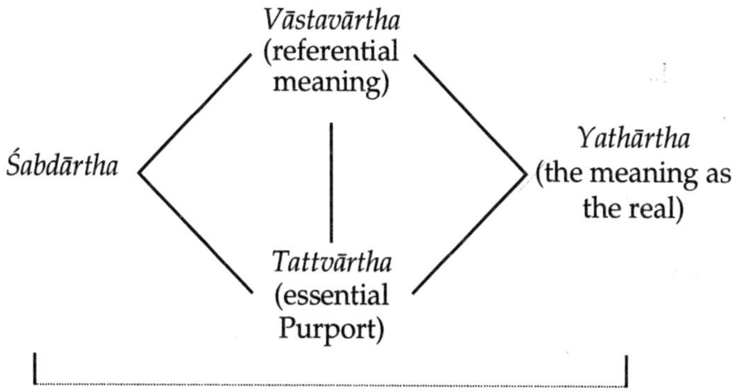

And to handle problems like contradiction, discontinuity, tautology, ambiguity, transparency and non-coherence that arise from the asymmetry between linguistic meaning and referential reality, they — the Mīmāṁsakas — formulated

(i) the concept of *śabda-śakti*, i.e., a general theory of meaning,

(ii) the concept of *lakṣaṇā-vṛtti*, i.e., figurative extension of meaning, and

(iii) the concept of Nyāya, i.e., meta-rules.

Finally, the seventh and the last issue involved is that of the process of communication of meaning. How does the word succeed in communicating or evoking the given meaning? As is well known, the grammarians propose two explanatory theories for the process — (i) *Śabdādvaita-vāda*, and (ii) *Śabda-adhyāsa-vāda*, the first assertion that all cognitions are determinate (*savikalpa*), i.e., with a word as the invariable concomitant, and the second assuming the mutual identity of *śabda* and *artha*, i.e., the theory of superimposition of *śabda* on the cognition and its object; both the theories have come in for elaborate criticism from the other schools —

> A diversity of opinions is to be found with regard to the specific character of the relation between words and objects.

> While in the one extreme we are confronted with the theory of *śabda-adhyāsa-vāda* of the Grammarians seeking to establish the identity of the two entities, in the other extreme we have to face the radical hypothesis of the Buddhists repudiating the reality of any sort of relation between *śabda* and *artha* and condemning all our conceptual cognitions as being illusory like the cognition of duality in the unitary lunar orb. — Bishnupada Bhattacharya, p. 53

There is also consensus that the association of word and meaning is conventional and given — *nitya sambandha* (*MB* I.1). In the work of semanticists and poeticians, in the rigorous typology of indirectly suggested meanings (cf. Mammaṭa, *Kāvyaprakāśa*) it has been shown that the global taxonomies are efficient devices to interpret symbolic meaning of transparent expressions and that the way to handle opacity on the other hand is to "etymologize" the word (in the Indian tradition of *nirvacana* which is not really "etymology" in the Western sense). These insights and frames of reference are available to the exegetes in their process of *śabdārtha* or *arthanirdhāraṇa*.

How important or widespread this is may again be illustrated from the philosophic exegesis. The recurrent question posed by the interpreters is — "What does the expression *X* mean here?" The question may be motivated by opacity (in the case of rare of "obsolete" words),[28] or by transparency (in the case of "symbolic" expression that has more than one meaning in a given use or in separate uses in the text). Swami Ramsukhdas, a recent interpreter of the *Bhagavad-Gītā*[29] has listed 69 polyvalent words which have been

---

28. There are no "obsolete" words, says Patañjali only words whose use is restricted in time, place or register (*MB* 1.1).

29. Swami Ramsukhdas, *op. cit.* What follows is a review of Swamiji's profound commentary.

employed in the text in more than one meaning: from two in the case of *svabhāva* (in *BG* 5.14 and 8.3) to fourteen different meanings in the case of *yoga* (in *BG* 4.2; 9.22; 2.48; 2.53; 7.1; 5.5; 18.75; 9.28; 12.1; 8.12; 6.16; 6.41; 8.10; 10.7). Each of the following seventeen words has six or more than six different meanings in the text, as identified below:

akṣara	-	6 (3.15; 8.3; 8.21; 10.25; 10.33; 15.18)
vyakta	-	8 (2.25; 2.28; 7.24; 8.18; 8.20; 9.4; 12.1; 8.21).
ātmā	-	11 (7.18; 6.26; 9.5; 4.42; 6.19; 3.13; 2.64; 6.15; 18.51; 12.14; 14.7).
eka	-	10 (6.12; 6.16; 7.17; 11.20; 18.3; 13.5; 13.30; 8.26; 11.7).
jñāna	-	9 (4.27; 3.39; 4.19; 13.17; 18.63; 12.12; 9.12; 7.2).
parā	-	10 (2.43; 5.16; 3.43; 6.45; 2.12; 4.4; 4.40; 3.35; 7.5; 14.19).
puruṣa	-	8 (9.3; 3.19; 2.21; 13.19; 15.16; 8.4; 8.22; 11.38).
priya	-	9 (5.20; 12.14; 9.29; 17.8; 17.15; 11.44; 11.44; 1.23; 18.69).
buddhi	-	6 (2.39; 2.65; 3.2; 7.10; 6.21; 13.5).
brahma	-	8 (4.25; 4.24; 5.10; 6.44; 8.13; 8.17; 14.4; 18.42).
bhāva	-	8 (8.3; 7.24; 8.4; 7.15; 8.6; 18.17; 10.6; 13.30).
bhūta	-	8 (7.11; 6.27; 9.4; 17.6; 13.34; 2.34; 13.27).
yajña	-	11 (3.10; 4.25; 4.25; 4.33; 4.28; 18.70; 4.28; 4.32; 9.16; 10.25; 16.17)/
yukta	-	10 (1.14; 6.29; 5.23; 6.17; 4.18; 5.8; 6.18; 12.2).
yogī	-	13 (5.11; 6.8; 15.11; 6.42; 8.14; 12.14; 6.15; 6.47; 6.45; 8.28; 8.25; 8.23; 10.17).

loka	-	10 (4.12; 5.14; 9.33; 11.30; 11.32; 10.16; 15.17; 18.7; 8.16; 15.18).
sukha	-	6 (1.33; 6.7; 2.66; 5.3; 5.13; 6.21)

The last word *sukha*, thus, for example has these meanings in its different uses: (1) ordinary worldly comfort (1.33); (2) conducive circumstances (6.7); (3) pure (*sāttvika*) happiness (2.66); (4) ease (5.3); (5) native or natural condition of being (5.13); and (6) spiritual pleasure (*ānanda*) (6.21).

All these words are thus loaded words, but all of them are part of the living, ordinary vocabulary of modern Indian languages. The attribution of a number of attested meanings to each of these words is founded either on (i) *abhidhā-vyāpāra*, primary meanings, or on (ii) *lakṣaṇā-vṛtti* (indirect or suggested meanings). Besides polyvalency, there is also the phenomena of using different words (*pada*) for the same object/meaning. Such use amounts to adding different shades or colours of meaning, i.e., defining an object exhaustively by explicating all its diverse properties. Thus, when twenty-one words are attested to have been used in the texts for *pṛthvī* "earth," the task is to show twenty-one different "sense" or attributes of "earth." Also, conversely, the word *pṛthvī* has twenty-one "meanings." With such meaning — potential, words in their particular uses have to be rooted to "a particular habitation and name," to the required meaning, in that use. This becomes the task of the exegetes and in order to be able to accomplish it, he has to be learned in the science of *Nirukta*, exposition of the meaning of words. When a word is invested with more than one meaning, the linguists try to account for them in terms of *nirvacana*, which may be rendered as "full exposition." Some of the meanings may result from the fact of the word having been derived from different verb-roots, and the respective forms collapsing phonologically into one word in the course of language. Or, the different meanings may result from the metonymic and the metaphoric extensions of the primary meaning. The exegetes therefore depend on both; the theory of *nirvacana* or exposition and the theory of *dhvani*, symbolic language.

Yāska's *Nirukta* lays down the principles of *nirvacana*. *Nirvacana* is not etymology in the Western sense; "etymology," as we now understand is concerned with tracing the history of a word of a modern language back to its source, the donor language: Eng. *conjoin* <(O)Fr. *conjoign* < L. *conjungere*. This is not motivated in Sanskrit — as the entire vocabulary is native (there are hardly any borrowed words). Yāska's concern is to interpret the Vedic text — he seeks to establish the meaning(s) of words as they are used in the texts by tracing them (both *nāma*, "all the words that undergo nominal declension" and *ākhyāta*, "all the words that undergo conjugation") back to *dhātus*, "verb roots."[30] He believes that without this exercise, "the exact meaning of *mantras* cannot be known" (1.15). Yāska was a semanticist, and unlike the better known ancient Sanskrit phoneticists, upheld the primacy of meaning over from — "The person who is only able to recite but does not understand the meaning is like a post, a mere load bearer" (*Nirukta* 1.18). He contended hard with his opponents who believed that the *mantras* merely chanted — the sounds alone — conferred merit. He says: "Whatever is learnt without its being understood is called mere cramming; like dry logs of wood on an extinguished fire, it can never illuminate" (1.18). "Meaning is the fruit and flower of speech" (1.20). In fact, Yāska speaks from a high pedestal — "Eternal is the scorn of the ignorant for knowledge;" he attaches great value to knowledge and

---

30. The details of the critical Gārgya-Śākaṭāyana controversy about whether in Sanskrit all nouns are derived from verb-roots or not cannot be presented here. For details, see Yāska, *Nirukta* 1.12, 1.13, 1.14.

shows deep contempt for ignorance (1.17). Just as he makes the first reasoned formulation of monotheism[31] Yāska is also to be credited with postulating knowledge as the great liberator (1.18), a concept that is given fuller exposition later in the *Gītā* (Chapter, V).

Yāska, in Chapter 2, first discusses the problem of why words become opaque and in the process presents an exhaustive critique of kinds of sound change: augment, loss, change and metathesis. The other explanation for opacity he finds in the history, how he cites the example of the verb-root $\sqrt{}$*dam*, "to burn": the derived noun *damunas*, "fire," was in use in the Vedic language but has gone out of use in *bhāṣā*, the language spoken in Yāska's time, although the verb, *dama* and the nominal *dama* continued to be used.[32] Conversely, the derived noun *uṣṇa* "hot" continues to be used in *bhāṣā*, but the verb *uṣ* "to heat" has gone out of use. As an example of geographic variation, he cites the example of *śava* which is still used in Afghanistan as a verb meaning "go," while in the Indo-Gangetic plains, it is used only as a noun meaning "dead body." Thus while articulating the meaning of a text, the historical and the geographical factors, and the possible sound changes that the word may have undergone, have to be kept in mind.

---

31. "It is because of his great diversity that they apply many names to him one after another — sub members of the one essence. . . . Their becoming is a birth from one another. . . . They are of one another's nature; they originate in function, in the variety of causal-factors (*karaṇa-tattva*) in any one object . . . just as material nature (*prakṛti*) though one, is manifest in a number of separately cognizable object . . ." (7.4). In the thirteenth and fourteenth chapters of *Nirukta* the concept of one *mahānātman* is explicitly discussed.

32. They still continue to be in use in current Hindī, viz., *damakala kendra*, "the fire brigade station."

Yāska lays down two principles of analysis: (1) the word must bear similarity of meaning to verb-root, to which it is traced; and, (2) there must also be phonetic similarity so that natural laws of sound change are able to account for the changes in form; (3) to establish similarity of meaning, we must have access to complete knowledge of the context — the syntactic context and the subject context; and, (4) we must also be aware of the possible polysemy of the basic word, in order to be able to determine which particular meaning is being articulated in the text and accordingly derive it from an appropriate verb-root.

With these assumptions, and with a grammatical structuration of the lexis,[33] he proceeds to establish the meaning of those *padas* — fully inflected words — in the texts which require *artha-nirdhāraṇa* or interpretation. He structures his entries around the classified word-list he had himself prepared, called *Nighaṇṭu*, a list of synonymous words, closed with the most unmarked word. In this the first entry lists 21 words for "earth," the last being *pṛthvī*. In *Nirukta*, 2.5, he starts by expounding the meaning of the first word in the list — *gauḥ*, "cow." He explains its use to denote "earth" to connote — (i) the "spread" of earth, and (ii) its "sanctity," and correspondingly then derives *gauh* from two verb-roots (i)$\sqrt{gam}$ (*Pāṇinīya Dhātupāṭha, juhotyādigaṇa*) which mean respectively "go" and "worship." Then Yāska gives the second meaning of *gauḥ*, "animal." He cites four *mantras* from the *Ṛgveda* (9.46.4; 10.94.6; 6.47.26; 6.75.11) illustrating the use of this word in its primary sense of "animal" and other figurative meanings. Thus

33. All vocabulary is divided into four classes — nominals (*nāma*), verbs (*ākhyāta*), pre-fixes (*upasarga*) and indeclinable or particles (*nipāta*) — and nominals are further classified into *yadṛcchā* (proper nouns), primary and secondary derived nominals (*taddhita* and *kṛdanta*) and *samasta* (compounds).

the word *gauḥ*, cow, is used to connote (i) milk, (ii) the leather-seat, (iii) skin, and (iv) the bow-string. Then, he proceeds to expound those words which appear in the citations, and which have the same meaning as one of the meanings of the word *gauḥ*. Thus, for example, the word *payas* appears as a signifier of "milk" in relation to the citation *Ṛ̥V* 9-46-4 and Yāska gives two sources of this word — (i) from the verb root $\sqrt{}$*pā*, to drink, and (ii) from the verb root $\sqrt{}$*pyay*, to nourish. Again he quotes illustrative passages from the Vedic texts, and so on.

Thus Yāska has expounded (i) words which appear in the *Nighaṇṭu*[34] list, (ii) synonyms which appear in the exposition of the *Nighaṇṭu*-words (viz., of *payas* in 2.5), (iii) words that appear in the quotation cited to illustrate the meaning of *Nighaṇṭu*-words (viz., of *mātṛ̥* in 2.8), (iv) words which appear in the exposition of these words from the quotations (viz., *parvat*, "mountain" which appears in the exposition of *giri*, "mountain" in *Ṛ̥V* 1-54-2, in 1.20), and sometimes, (v) other words which resemble in form or meaning (viz., *Bhīṣma* that resembles *Bhīma* in 1.20).

How does he order the meanings? He first gives the vedic meaning, the literary meaning and then he gives the *laukika* meaning, the meaning the word has in daily usage. Thus in 2.13, the word *vrata* is first expounded in its Vedic meaning (*karma* or action and then in its *laukika* meaning "abstinence from food, etc.").

Proceeding in this way, Yāska expounds the 21 synonyms for "earth." At the end of this all, he has built up (i) an exceeding rich universe of meaning — both direct and

34. This term is still used in some Indian languages, viz., Telugu, to designate a lexicon. Evidently, it was a common practice to prepare lists of those words from the Vedic texts which posed problems of lexical interpretation.

figurative — around "earth," (ii) correlated the words with different "verb-roots" to establish those meanings, (iii) cited textual support for these several meanings, and (iv) interpreted the cited texts in the given way.

His theory of meaning incorporates — (i) polysemy, (ii) synonymy, and (iii) metaphoric extensions and factors of meaning such as (i) usage, (ii) context, (iii) the speaker, his intention and the addressee (viz., 2.24). Besides, in the determination of meaning, Yāska takes into account the historical, geographic, social, cultural, psychological and philosophical dimensions of meaning. For example: in the exposition of *dama* and *śava* in 2.2, he has referred to historical and geographic variations; in the exposition of *gartaruk* in 3.5, he has made reference to a south Indian social custom; in the exposition of *puruṣaḥ* he has referred to the concepts of "self" and "inner consciousness," and in the explanation of suggested meanings in 3.18, he explains the psychological foundations of such figurative extensions.

No wonder that Yāska's methodology of interpretation, based on "total meaning," is at the head of the long tradition of exegesis, is the fountainhead of the subsequent theories of meaning. What is specific to Yāska is his effort to fix the meaning in terms of the root verb but the factors and the constructs that he demonstrates, as involved in this process, constitute a whole theory of meaning — *śabda-śakti*, the power of words to denote and connote a rich matrix of primary and associated meanings. And this *śabda-śakti* is our next, and last, instrument of exegesis.

The tradition offers competing theories of meaning — the Buddhists' *apoha-vāda* (meaning as the negation of objectively existing entities), the Mīmāṁsakas' and the Naiyāyikas' *vāstu vāda* (meaning as reference to objectively existing entities) and the grammarians' *sphoṭa-vāda* (meaning as that object which is brought to mind when the word is articulated)[35] and provides alternative modes of looking at the relationship between language and reality — both as it is (*vāstvārtha*) and as it is constructed (or, represented) by language (*śabdārtha*). These theories necessarily concern themselves with (i) classes of referential meaning (objects, actions, qualities and relations), (ii) nature of reference (universal or particular),[36] (iii) semantic conditions on the meaning of sentences, *ākāṅkṣā* "mutual expectancy," *yogyatā*, compatibility, and *sannidhi*, contiguity,[37] (iv) the process of comprehending the meaning of a sentence (*Anvitābhidhāna-vāda*, sentence meaning as aggregate of the meanings of constituting words),[38] (v) nature of word-meaning relation (*saṁketa*, conventional association, *anuvidhā*, merged in one another or *anumāna*, indication or inference),[39] (vi) multiple meaning in discourse (*samānārthaka vāc*, synonymy, *prakaraṇa* and *prasaṅga*, context and contextual factors, and *vācyārtha* versus *dhvanyārtha*, statement versus suggestion[40] and the role of etymology, convention and grammar.[41]

---

35. Reference may be made to (i) Bishnupada Bhattacharya, 1962, P.C. Chakravarti, 1930, and (ii) K. Kunjunni Raja, 1963. The exposition that follows is inspired by these discussions.

36. See K. Kujunni Raja, *op. cit.*, Ch. 2, and B. Bhattacharya, *op. cit.*, p.20.

37. Cf. B. Bhattacharya, *op. cit.*, pp. 128-58, and K. Kunjunni Raja, *op. cit.*, pp. 149-87.

38. Cf. K. Kunjunni Raja, *op. cit.*, pp. 191-213, and B. Bhattacharya, op. *cit.*, pp. 158-87.

39. Cf. B. Bhattacharya, *op. cit.*, pp. 19-54.

40. Cf. K. Kunjunni Raja, *op. cit.*, pp. 32-47.

41. Cf. K. Kunjunni Raja, *op. cit.*, pp. 48-58, for contextual factors, pp. 59-68 for role of etymology, etc., of Ānandavardhana's *Dhvanyaprakāśa* for *vācyārtha* versus *dhvanyārtha*; cf. Mammaṭa, *Kāvyaprakāśa*, 37-43 for the role of speech act factors in suggested meaning and Ch. IV, of the same book pp. 44-99 for an illustrated analysis of *dhvani* or suggested meaning.

The connotation of words in *mahāvākya* (discourse) is a very complex matter, depending on larger intuitive understanding as much as on systems such as etymology. Writing on the meaning of *Śrī Dakṣiṇāmūrti Stotram*, Sri D.S. Subbaramanya says —

> With the aid of Śāstras, taking into account the mental make up of the *adhikārī*, a suitable *prakriyā* (process) is designed by the Master, by accepting as it were, the situation to which the disciple is firmly attached to lead him on to understand the ultimate significance of the word 'that' and 'thou'. . . . The words by themselves have general connotations, but when brought together in meaningful sentences, they acquire determinate and unique significance. Says the *Naiṣkarmyasiddhi* (3-32) —
>
> *sāmānyam hi padam brute viśeṣo vākyakṛtṛka* ।
> *śrutyādipratibadhan sadā viśeṣārtham bhavetapadam* ॥

Of special significance here is the seventh element in the theories of meaning, the determination of meaning in discourse, and particularly the concept of multiplicity and variety of meanings — literal and suggested. We have in Yāska itself the first employment of a framework of *lakṣaṇā-vṛtti*, the figurative meanings (cf. *Nirukta*, 2.5, 3.13, 3.18, 4.1, 8.2, 8.22). Pāṇini's several *sūtra*s make reference to different figures of speech or are based on some figures of speech such as *upamā*, simile, faded metaphor, etc. (cf. *Aṣṭādhyāyī*, 5.2.72, 75, 76). However, it is Jaimini who in his *Mīmāṁsā-Sūtra* fully develops and employs as a hermeneutic device the concept of secondary, derived (figurative) meaning. Jaimini's principal concern, as we happen to have indicated earlier, is with sentence meaning. Many of the *Nyāyas*, meta-rules, he developed for the interpretation of sentence-meaning are in fact statements of how to generate figurative, secondary meaning from the literal or primary meaning. The following *Nyāya*s for example, are founded on various kinds of *lakṣaṇā*,

(i) *varhinyāya, MS* 3.2 (synecdoche)

(ii) *gārhapatya-nyāya* (*MS* 3.2) (metaphor)

(iii) *anarthakya-nyāya* (*MS* 3.1) (opposite of synecdoche — the whole stands for the part, viz., "the army enters" used to refer to the entry of a single solider).

However, it is the poeticians, who not only made exhaustive structural analyses of metaphorical meaning but also further extended the theory of literal and metaphorical meaning to include emotive and other associative meanings also under linguistic meaning (K. Kunjunni Raja 1963: 277). Thus, it is in the context of literary meaning that the Indian theories of meaning find full fruition. Tracing this evolution, Prof. K. Kunjunni Raja writes:

> Bhartṛhari had exposed[42] the unsatisfactory nature of a linguistic theory which depends entirely on individual words and their lexical meanings; the *Sphoṭa* doctrine which he brought forward emphasized the importance of taking the whole utterance as a significant unitary linguistic symbol. Bhartṛhari had also shown that the meaning of an utterance depends on contextual factors, and that the logical interpretation of the sentence meaning on the basis of the individual word-meaning is defective in many cases. At times, the meaning of the whole sentence is different from what the words indicate. Ānandavardhana took the cue from Bhartṛhari . . . since he was concerned with . . . literary appreciation . . . he confined his attention to . . . poetic meaning — Kunjunni Raja 1963: 277-78

Ānandavardhana accepted the distinction between the primary meaning (*abhidhā*) and the transferred meaning (*lakṣaṇā*) which he had inherited but went beyond and posited "a third

42. Reference is to Bhartṛhari's *Vākyapadīya* (sixth century AD).

potency" of language, the power of suggesting a meaning other than the literal, to which he gave the name *vyañjanā*. To this was added another power, or *vṛtti*, the *tātparyavṛtti*, the intended meaning. The four together represent what is called in the tradition, *śabda-śakti*: (1) *Abhidhā* — the power by which the signifier (*vācya*) directly manifests/communicates the signified (*vācaka*). For example, *BG* 13.1, Kṛṣṇa says, *idam śarīram kaunteya kṣetranityabhidhīyate* (This body, O Son of Kuntī, is designated by the word "field"). In this the word *kṣetra* has *abhidhā-śakti* — it denotes a field in which the seeds planted ("actions done") are bound to produce a crop (fruit or result). (2) *Lakṣaṇā* — the power which communicates the meaning that the speaker has as his object and which is different from the primary meaning. Thus in *BG* (1.33), *prāṇāṁstyaktvā dhanāni ca* (are standing after giving up life) cannot be understood in its primary sense for no one "Without life" can "stand up." So the transferred meaning "are standing giving up hope of remaining alive" is understood. Its substratum may be a word, words or a sentence. (3) *Vyañjanā* — the power that communicates a meaning that does not get communicated by *abhidhā* or *lakṣaṇā*, but rises as a resonance or suggestion. Thus in *BG* 3.16, ". . . *mogharṁ pārtha sa jīvati*," ". . . lives in vain" is understood as "should better die." Its substratum may be a word, phrase, sentence or a whole discourse. (4) *Tātparya* — the power that communicates in addition the desired or intended meaning of the speaker (through contextual factors). Thus in *BG* (2.11-30), the description of a bodied being as non-eternal (*anitya*) and of the self in the body as everlasting (*nitya*) has the purport, intention (*tātparya*) of removing or lessening Arjuna's sorrow — it is the meaning to secure which, the utterance meaning is constituted.

Ānandavardhana (ninth century AD) in his *Dhvanyāloka*, carried out a rigorous structural analysis of verbal symbolism with examples from literary texts (Prākṛta[43] poetry) and beginning with an archetypal division between statement (*vācyārtha*) and suggestion (*vyaṅgyārtha*) built up a systematic typology of suggestion (*dhvani*) in language. His work remains unique in the history of the study of literary language. To quote Todorov —

> To discover in the past a wide-ranging and incisive discussion of the problems of indirect language use, we have to step outside the Western frame of reference and turn to the Indian tradition. . . . At some point during the twelfth century, the Sanskrit poetician Mammaṭa (*Kāvyaprakāśa*) summarized . . . the prevailing idea of his day — ideas engendered by the fundamental work of Ānandavardhana, who was perhaps the greatest of all theorists of textual symbolism. — Todorov 1973, 1983 edn., p. 12

Ānandavardhana begins by claiming that *dhvani,* indirect meaning or suggestion is the essence of literary artefacts — *kāvyasyātmā dhvaniriti* (*D* 1.1.). The refined critics or readers (*sahṛdaya*) are agreed that poetry has two kinds of meaning — the explicit (*vācya*) and the symbolic (*pratīyamāna*), of which it is the symbolic or indirect meaning that is the determinant of literary language (*DL* 1.2-3). He asserts (*DL* commentary on III.33) that this meaning is compatible with the linguistic conceptions of the grammarians (vide their *sphoṭa*-doctrine) and of the logicians as well who may differ among themselves about the nature of denotation but not about suggestiveness, for suggestiveness as a fact of experience is amenable to perception and logicians never contradict perception. *Dhvani*

43. Prākṛta, the living speech of Ānandvardhan's times, the language of much of Jaina philosophy also. Thus Ānandavardhana was in fact applying Sanskrit poetics to a living literature, of the then "modern" language.

is a fact of experience as it is to be experienced even in sounds of music which are not even denotative, etc. — *gītadhvanināma śabdarūpanāma ca*. . . . The directly expressed sense is invariably an idea — but the suggested sense may be *vastumātramalaṁkāra rasūdaya* . . ., the idea, or figures of speech, or *rasa*, the evoked sentiment (*DL* 1.4). This suggested or symbolic meaning[44] is not grasped or understood as one understands or grasps the direct meaning; it is not understood by a mere learning in grammar and in dictionary. It is understood only by those who have the sensibility to penetrate into the significance of poetry — *Kāvyārthatattva* . . . (*DL* 1.7) — just as for a proper appreciation of *svaraśruti-ādi*, notes and tones of music, one has to be a good musician and it is not enough to have studied the science of music (*DL* commentary on 1.7). "Meanings evoked indirectly," says Todorov, "are meanings like any others; they differ only in their mode of evolution, which is precisely that of the association of something present with something absent" (Todorov 1973, 1983 edn. p. 15). And the poetic sensibility subsists precisely in an awareness of this association, in the ability to associate. So that, that meaning is immediately cognized and felt by those who have the ability to see this meaning the moment they turn away from the explicit meaning (*DL* 1.11). But the explicit meaning is definitely involved in the generation of this symbolic meaning (*DL* 1.10). This *dhvani*, the suggested meaning, is not to be confused with figures of speech (*DL* commentary on 1.13), nor is it to be confused with *lakṣaṇā-vṛtti*, the inferential extension of meaning or indication (*DL* 1.18), nor is it to be confused with the

---

44. It is in the twentieth century that this subject has come in for investigation in the work of Cassirer, Mukarovsky, Fry, etc., and lies at the heart of theories like Symbolism, Phenomenology, Reader-Response criticism and Structuralism. For a study of these affinities see Krishna Rayan, 1-15 (1987) : 230-33.

secondary meanings that the words have by convention (*DL* 1.16).[45]

Ānandavavardhana's contribution is his identification and definition of several varieties of *dhvani*. Several attempts have been made, both by the traditional commentators and modern scholars to understand the varieties of *dhvani*, the verbal symbolism. In spite of the lucidity of *Dhvanyāloka*, the understandings differ. One of the clearest statements is by professor (K. Kunjunni Raja, 1963: p. 306):

I. Literal sense not intended aside.

a. Literal sense completely set aside

b. Literal meaning shifted

II. Literal sense inten-ded but subserves the implied sense.

c. Stages of knowing the suggested sense imperceptible.

d. Stages of knowing the suggested sense perceptible.

It is a classification based on (i) the relationship between the literal and the suggested sense, and (ii) the process by which the suggested sense is generated. However, this is only a highly general taxonomy. We now present here a more comprehensive structural typology of symbolic meaning based on *Dhvanyāloka* (see the folded chart)

This theory of verbal symbolism superseded the extant literary theories — *rasa, alaṁkāra, rītī* — as a framework for the interpretation of literary texts. But more than that, its richness as a theory of meaning and its coherent and exhaustive

45. These aspects of the relationship of *dhvani* to direct meaning (*abhidhā*) and indication (*lakṣaṇā*) and intended meaning (*tātparya*) and defamiliarized language have been subjects of controversy in the tradition. For a review, see K. Kunjunni Raja 1963: 290-302.

categories ensured its application in all exegesis, even the Smṛti — exegesis. An equally integral part of this theory is the statement of text external factors that become conditions on textual symbolism in the sense that they control variation in the suggested meaning of a text. Mammaṭa, the eminent Kashmiri poetician of the twelfth/thirteenth century reported these contextual factors in the third chapter of his perennial work *Kāvyaprakāśa* which summarizes the major ideas of almost all the literary theories propounded till then, and which were evidently current in his times, He says:

> Suggestion is that function of the meaning which brings about the cognition of another meaning, by persons endowed with imaginative intuition, through peculiarities of (a) the speaker, (b) the person spoken to, (c) intonation, (d) the sentence, (e) the expressed meaning, (f) the presence of another, (g) context, (h) place, (i) time, and so forth.
>
> — *KP* (III.21-222.46)[46]

The meaning that thus arises is related to and different from the direct expression of meaning in the given ways that have also been examined. Mammaṭa reports in Chapter V these differences:

1. *In point of character*: (a) In the verse "The sandal paint is entirely rubbed out . . . though has not gone to the wretchedman," the expressed meaning is negative, while the suggested one is affirmative.
2. *In point of time*: The suggested meaning is comprehended after the expressed meaning.
3. *In point of the conveying medium*: The expressed meaning is conveyed by the word while the suggested meaning

---

46. We have taken this English rendering from Mahāmahopādhyaya Sir Ganganath Jha's authoritative translation of *Kāvyaprakāśa*, Allahabad, The Indian Press Ltd., 1925.

may be conveyed by the word, by a part of the word, by the expressed meaning of the word, by the sounds or by the style.

4. *In point of the means* (*of knowing*): The expressed meaning is understood with the help of grammatical rules, while the suggested meaning is understood with the help of those, as also with that of context and other conditions (mentioned above).
5. *In point of their effect*: The expressed meaning brings about a simple comprehension and that also in every one who hears the word, while the suggested meaning brings about a certain charm in the minds of only such persons as are endowed with linguistic and poetic sensibility.
6. *In point of number of meanings* As has been found in the case of expression "the sun has set" (where the expressed meaning is one only and the suggested meanings are ten or more).
7. *In point of the person addressed*: In the verse — who will not be annoyed at seeing the lips of his wife bitten? I warned you not to smell the lotus with the bee inside it: ". . . the expressed meaning is conveyed to the girl-friend, . . . while the suggested meaning . . . is conveyed to the husband." (*KP* 126-28)

The Indian poeticians went beyond the analysis of textual symbolism and described the relation between direct and indirect meanings both in terms of "global taxonomies" (Todorov's phrase, vide 1973 edn., p. 72), i.e., in terms of a universal theory of symbolic meaning and in terms of the rhetorical figures of speech. Mahimabhaṭṭa in his *Vyaktiviveka* worked out the "logic" of suggestion and sought to explain suggested meaning as a case of inference. Mammaṭa, on the other hand, clarified different varieties of suggestions in terms of categories arrived at by permutations and combi-nations. His (Mammaṭa's) model, naturally lends itself more readily for actual application of the theory of suggestion to the analysis of literary texts.

For a variety of reasons, in the middle ages, suddenly all scholarship receded into the background and the Indian society became engaged with quite different problems of survival and adaptation. But in modern times there has been a remarkable revival of interest and many Indian scholars are beginning to adapt and apply Indian models of literary analysis not only to texts of Indian literatures but also to Western literary texts. And ever since the Saussurean revolution, Western literary theorists have also started taking interest in Indian literary theory, which being essentially linguistic and rooted in the grammar of Pāṇini, can be seen to have close affinities with contemporary literary theories, particularly structuralism and formalism and those that have been generated or influenced by these movements.

In several ways, as Todorov has noted, the Indian analyses of textual symbolism got hold of insights which were missed elsewhere till very recently — among these unusual insights we may include the Sanskrit poeticians' early understanding that the human psyche is endowed with certain characteristic schemes that are always available and when it is confronted with unfamiliar actions and situations it reacts, on the one hand, by adapting old schemes to the new object (accommodation) and, on the other, by adapting the new phenomenon to old schemes (assimilation).

The interpretative process likewise includes two phases (which occur here in a fixed order). First, we have to distinguish the verbal sequence for which interpretation is required; this perception of difference is itself conditioned by the fact that the sequence cannot be absorbed by the available schemes. Thus, in an initial phase we recognize the new phenomenon while adapting to it (accommodation). Then we absorb this novelty and this non-integrability, until the verbal sequence comes into conformity with already constructed schemes (assimilation). This is something that the Sanskrit poeticians understand well. Mammaṭa summarizes their position[47] as follows:

> It is necessary, first, that an incompatibility between the primary meaning of the word and its context be manifest; second, that a relation of association exist, between the primary and secondary meanings.
>
> —Todorov 1973, 1983 edn., p. 27

Next, we must take note of the archetypal distinction made by the Sanskrit thinkers between lexical and propositional symbolism. To quote Todorov again —

> absent from Western works of rhetoric or hermeneutics in this specific form, the distinction between lexical and propositional symbolism seems to occur in the Sanskrit tradition. The phenomena . . . were first described separately, before anyone sought to characterize their articulation. The first to embrace the entire field seems to have been once again Ānandavardhana, author of the theory of *dhvani*; and his commentator Abhinavagupta is quite explicit on the point. . . . [48]
>
> — Todorov 1983 edn., p. 47

Ānandavandhana's theory of textual symbolism became, thus, a powerful instrument of interpretation in the Indian tradition and has retained its pre-eminent position in all the centuries that have elapsed since it was composed.

---

47. Cf. *KP*, Chapter V, commentary on Text 47.
48. See K. Kunjunni Raja 1963: 213-24 for a discussion of this distinction including a statement of the specific discussion by Abhinavagupta.

With this we have come to the end of our exposition of the different instruments of exegesis. It will be apt now to present, from the tradition, an example of exegesis, and, in the next section we illustrate the methodology through a presentation of Ādi Śaṅkara's interpretation of the second chapter of The *Bhagavad-Gītā*.

4

Ādi Śaṅkara on the Bhagavad-Gītā
An Example of Interpretation

BHAGAVAD-GĪTĀ (henceforward *BG*) is a timeless text dealing as it does with the global condition of man, the fact of his suffering. The fundamental question of Indian philosophy is the question of happiness — ever since Buddha, *sukha*, happiness is a contingent category, *duḥkha* being the primary reality. Quite contrary to the popular misconception, *mokṣa* (often wrongly translated as 'salvation') is not a metaphysical category at all — it is defined in Sāṁkhya as *dukh nivṛtti*, freedom from suffering. What is *duḥkha*, suffering? It is of three kinds, says Sāṁkhya — accidental, bodily and of the mind and spirit (*adhyātmika*). For the suffering of the body, Āyurveda provides a cure in the form of medicine. For the suffering of the spirit, we have *darśana*, philosophy, says Caraka of the Āyurveda. All systems agree that right knowledge is the answer to the fact of suffering but different definitions of 'right knowledge' are offered by the different systems — discriminating intellect (*nyāya*), proper knowledge of what is (*vaiśeṣika*), performance of ritual acts (*mīmāṁsā*), categorical knowledge (*jñāna*). *Bhagavad-Gītā* is unique because of all the texts, it is the only one that examines the nature and cause of human suffering — the other texts, particularly the six *āstika* systems, assume the existence of suffering and proceed with their analysis. The *BG* is important in the history of ideas because it investigates the cause of suffering in relation to a real life situation, a drastic situation involving killing and getting killed but one that epitomises all the dilemmas that one may encounter. The great sage Vyāsa examines this question and to give it authority makes Lord Kṛṣṇa the spokesman. Ādi Śaṅkara's seminal commentary establishes, articulates, the essence of Lord Krishna's *siddhānta* for attaining *mokṣa,* freedom from suffering — unattached action (*niṣkāma karma*) leads to purification of the self (*citta śudhi*) which leads to wise indifference (*vairāgya*) which leads to discriminating faculty (*viveka*) which leads to pure knowledge (*viśudha jñāna*) which then leads to freedom from suffering (*mokṣa*).

It is obviously a very important book as all the great Indian minds seem to conclude their life's work with a commentary on the *BG* — from Ādī Śaṅkara to Vinoba Bhave. The commentary tradition (*ṭīkā paramparā*) has kept this text alive. It is structured as a dialogue with Arjuna, who is both typical and common, asking 17 questions: his basic dilemma is — 'why to fight and kill 'our own people'? Dhṛtarāṣṭra in the very first *śloka* makes a distinction — that will not be made by any elder brother in India — between 'my sons' (self) and 'Paṇḍu's sons' (other) — and this is the cause of his misery. Arjuna on the other hand says 'they are *our* people'. Is he wiser than his elder uncle in considering his *opponents* also as his own people? No, obviously not, for as Kṛṣṇa tells him later, the problem lies in getting trapped in the dichotomies. Once you call somebody 'our,' there is room for 'not-our' and the misery begins. Even not wanting something is a desire and it binds (2.38). Arjuna is afflicted with grief, *śoka, moha* and he is paralysed, his will to act is paralysed, he becomes *'dharmasammūṛhaceta:'* (2.7), unable to decide in matters of *dharma,* matters involving questions of right and wrong. His is an ethical dilemma. Arjuna's inability to act, to decide between right and wrong stems from grief and distraction (*śoka-moha*) that stem from cognitions of 'me/mine' caused by oppositions affinity/otherness (*sneha-viccheda*). He wants no kingdom (1.32) *and* 'they, the Kauravas, are mine' (1.37). Why then fight and kill?

This is a blind alley, the kind all of us walk in some time or the other. Lord Kṛṣṇa says the concept of *dharma*, duty, is the way out. *Dharma* is the overriding category in Indian sociological thought as we have had occasion in this text to point out more than once. We have to perform the enjoined action, the enjoined duty (*niyata karma*) and it must be performed above and beyond our own needs, prejudices, predilections and desires. Now, we are told by the same text that action (*karma*) binds (*karma-bandhana*) and we have to look for freedom from bondage. But it is the action performed with some personal motive that binds and *Mīmāṁsāsūtra* says that men perform all actions in self-interest and for self-aggrandisement. That way all ritual, action of the *karma-kāṇḍa*, binds. But, and this is important, enjoined action (*niyata karma*) performed for *loka-saṁgraha*, welfare of all (3.25), liberates one from dichotomies, helps one to transcend the oppositions and become stabilized in the self (6.7), equable both in joy and sorrow.

In this sense, *BG* is the text of a civilization centered in *kartavya karma* (enjoined duty). Ours is a duty-centered civilization as against the rights oriented western society. 'Rights' are *self*-oriented while duties are *other*-oriented; *rights* promote discord and conflict as everyone is concerned with his self; *duty* promotes harmony as one seeks one's own good in the larger good of others. Ādi Śaṅkara says that liberation follows from realizing the identity of one's self and the larger self and that there is no other means of liberation.

This awareness is *jñāna*, knowledge, and 'nothing purifies like knowledge' (4.38). 'Then why do you push me into this dire action (*ghora karma*)?' asks Arjuna (3.1). Because, Śrī Kṛṣṇa tells him in chapter 3, one is in any case involved in action (*karma*) all the time. One has to act all the time — ". . . none can ever remain inactive even for a moment; for everyone is helplessly driven to action by nature-born qualities" (3.5). Inactivity (*akarma*) is also an action (*karma*). It is action that sustains life. Man obtains freedom from action only by performing action. And the paths of action (*karma*) and knowledge (*jñāna*) are not really different as 'all actions without exception culminate in knowledge' (4.33). Therefore of the three paths of devotion, action and knowledge, the path of *niṣkāma karma* (unattached action) is superior — performance of unattached action (*karma*) informed by knowledge (*jñāna*) is devotion (*bhakti*). This is therefore the key to freedom from suffering that everyone seeks.

The second chapter is the key chapter wherein the concept of non-transient *ātman* finds the first statement in the text. It is in his commentary on this second chapter in his celebrated Gītā *Bhāṣya* that Ādi Śaṅkara starts building the edifice of his liberating philosophy:

> Performance of unattached action for the welfare of others leads to purification of one's self that produces a discriminating intellect which establishes one in *vairagya*, dispassion in the objects of the world, which enables attainment of pure knowledge, which then leads to *mokṣa*, freedom from suffering, here and now.

Let us look at how Ādi Śaṅkara interprets *Bhagvad-Gītā* by reflecting on a small part of his commentary.

The second chapter of the *Bhagavad-Gītā* is described at the end of the chapter itself as the disquisition on Sāṁkhya Yoga, the Yoga of knowledge in which Śrī Kṛṣṇa calls upon Arjuna to give up his sense of attachment and consequent sorrow and perform his duty with the required dispassion. As all students of Indian philosophy know, this is an important chapter as it establishes some of the basic concepts central to the text and to Indian consciousness in general — the nature of being, the illusory sense of doership, the bounds of birth and death, and the conduct of a man of true wisdom. The chapter has 72 *ślokas* (couplets). Arjuna begins to mourn the fact that he will have to kill his kinsmen, his friends, his teachers and the elders of his race and is overwhelmed by deep sorrow at the moment when the battle is about to start. Śrī Kṛṣṇa tells him that his attachment (*moha*) and his sorrow (*duḥkha*) are not only inopportune but also rooted in ignorance, for as Śrī Kṛṣṇa says — "You are mourning for people and events that need not be mourned, for wisemen do not mourn either those who are dead or those who are yet to die" (2.11). This couplet is the cornerstone of the argument of the second chapter and the declarative sentence "you mourn those or that who do not need to be mourned . . ." (*aśocyānanvaśocastvaṁ* . . .) and contains the startling statement that the deaths of Bhīṣma and Droṇa, etc., need not be mourned — they are *aśocya* — "not to be mourned." Why not? Why is the death of grandfathers, brothers, "not worthy of mourning"?

In an exposition that displays a concentric enlargement of the idea, Ādi Śaṅkara bases his entire interpretation and thought on the key word — *aśocya* "unmournable." His purpose in the interpretation is to answer the question why the deaths of elders, kinsmen and friends are not to be mourned and in the process explicate the nature of *kartā* (agent), *kāraṇa* or *nimitta* (instrument), *moha-śoka* (attachment and sorrow), *sukha-duḥkha* (happiness and suffering), *ātmā* (self), *jñāna* (knowledge) and *sthita-prajña* (man whose minds rests in true wisdom), and the relationship between a *sthita-prajña* and *karma* (actions to be performed).

So, this is the first thing to notice. Ādi Śaṅkara's method is to isolate the key declarative sentence, that contains a proposition that is apparently unacceptable but which represents a conclusion arrived at the end of a long chain of reasoning. Śaṅkara rebuilds that chain of reasoning and explicates the grounds of the proposition.

First of all Ādi Śaṅkara identifies the overall argument by dividing the otherwise continuous chapter into sections — *prakaraṇa*. Each *prakaraṇa* is devoted to a major idea that forms a part of the over all argument. Movement from one *prakaraṇa* to the other is not marked in the text. So, Ādi Śaṅkara specifically indicates the argument with a structure like "so far this . . . now this." The 72 *śloka*s of this chapter fall into five sections :

Śloka 1-30 : *paramārtha-darśana* — *parama-artha* literally means, "the ultimate meaning." In this section, the nature of self (*ātmā*), sense of doership, and the process of birth-death rebirth are set forth.

31-38 : *laukika-nyāya*, "common real life wisdom." The argument of the first section is supported by citing matter-of-fact experience of common life.

39-53 : *viveka-buddhi*, "discriminating intellect." It explains how a man of discriminating intellect is able to separate real from unreal, grain from chaff.

54-67 : *sthita-prajña*, "man with mind stabilized in *viveka* (discrimination)." It describes the conduct of such men.

54-67 : *jñāna-niṣṭha*, the discipline of knowledge. The *uplabdhi*, gain in terms of true happiness, that accrues from knowledge.

Then the contents of the chapter are placed in the over-all purpose of the whole-text. It is well known that all Indian philosophy shows tension between *nivṛtti-mārga* (non-involvement, renunciation) and *pravṛtti-mārga* (involvement and participation). The *Gītā* lends itself to several interpretations and has been used as authority to support both the contradictory positions — *nivṛtti* and *pravṛtti*. Apparently this was so, both before and during the time of Ādi Śaṅkara. Even today, there is a widespread understanding among the common people that the *Gītā*'s central verb is "to do" — "doing" actions is its message. Ādi Śaṅkara, on the other hand considers the *Gītā* as a text of *nivṛtti-mārga*. Ādi Śaṅkara was, as is well known, a teacher of *nivṛtti-mārga*. This is Śaṅkara-Siddhānta, the meta-assumption within which the interpretation is carried out.

The argument is presented in the known structure of disputation — *pūrva-pakṣa* and *uttara-pakṣa*, the position taken by other learned interpreters is first stated (those interpreters are not named — the concern is with the logic of ideas only). Thus in the commentary on *śloka* 10, he states the position of *pravṛtti-mārga* interpreters who assert that man is liberated not through knowledge (of the self) alone but instead through *śrauta-smārtta-karma*, performance of actions laid down in the Vedas and the Dharma-Śāstras. The portions of the text which the *pūrva-pakṣa* cites in support of its position are also reported. The position then is controverted first broadly by pointing out the general flaw in reasoning and then in detail. Śaṅkara's contention is that they are not reading the text carefully — they overlook the fact that Lord Kṛṣṇa treats the two subjects — knowledge and action — separately. He identifies parts of the text where they are treated. They are thus guilty of collapsing a distinction that is explicitly made in the text. Śaṅkara then proceeds to expatiate on the distinction. In the process he carves out a close logical analysis of the text and demonstrates how the distinction coheres with the rest of the text and with the Śrutis. All doubts, *saṁśaya*, that arise, are resolved (*saṁśaya-nivāraṇa*). Then arguments for the *sva-siddhānta* are forwarded. This argument draws on a variety of sources and evidences. Thus, for example, the argument in the commentary after 2.10 depends on known philosophical frameworks (Sāṁkhya), on well known concepts attested in experience (*buddhi* "intellect", *niṣṭhā* "faith" or "discipline"), on known explanatory constructs and dichotomies common to different disciplines (*kartā*, "doer"; *akartā* "non-doer") and employed extensively in grammar, logic as well as philosophy, on verbal testimony (viz., *Śatapatha Brāhmaṇa* and *Bṛhadāraṇyak-opaniṣad* and on logical contradiction of invalid inference through "If-so-then-because-but-hence" structure.

We have noted (in Chapter IV) that verbal testimony, *śabda-pramāṇa*, is an important instrument of interpretation. Ādi Śaṅkara, too, employs verbal testimony to (i) support the principle he is setting up (cf. Goendka, 1932 : 39, 45), or (ii) attribute a particular meaning to a given expression (Goendka, 1932 : 32). It is important to note that in the first kind of use — to support the interpretation being given to a particular proposition — Ādi Śaṅkara, in conformity with accepted relative strength of epistemologies, employs verbal-testimony only as the final proof — *antima pramāṇa* — after perception (*pratyakṣa*) and logical inference (*anumāna*). Also, compared with some other interpreters, viz., Śrī Rāmānuja, Śaṅkara employs verbal testimony very sparsely. Thus in the extensive commentary on 72 *śloka*s of Chapter 2, verbal testimony is brought in as the supporting evidence only on thirteen occasions — two citations from the *Ṛgveda*, eight from *Bṛhadāraṇayaka Upaniṣad*, two from *Mahābhārata* and one from *Chāndogya Upaniṣad*. With Śaṅkara, the favourite sources are the *Bṛhadāraṇayaka Upaniṣad* and the *Mahābhārata*. And his citations are invariably prefixed by "And the *Śruti* also says . . ." Often appeal is made to felt experience to substantiate or establish a point, as for example when a qualitative distinction between pairs of opposites "Happiness-Sorrow" and "Heat-Cold" is being argued (Goendka 1932 : 34).

However his dominant epistemology is *anumāna*-logical inference, and again we find Śaṅkara delighting in the exercise of reason.

Among general rules of interpretation, all the three — *saṅgati, paribhāṣā* and *laukika-nyāya* — are employed. *Saṅgati* or coherence, is of two kinds. In the *Gītā* both *śloka-saṅgati*, coherence between couplets, and *prakaraṇa-saṅgati*, coherence between sections, are established, through "fillers" — explanations that provide continuity of argument between apparently discontinuous segments of the text. Thus, each commentary on a *śloka*, couplet, invariably ends in such statements as "Therefore it is said . . ., 'Why is this so?', 'Even with all this . . .', 'The example of this is . . .' etc. to link that couplet with the one that follows. There is of course the other kind of coherence — the mutual agreement of ideas — which is also reiterated to strengthen an argument by going back and forth over the whole text (cf. Goendka 1932 : 27). The *prakaraṇa-saṅgati*, coherence of sections of the text is a slightly different matter. Ādi Śaṅkara's *prakaraṇa*s thematically facilitate the understanding of the text. *Nyāya*s are also employed — but they come chiefly from Nyāya philosophy, the science of logic. For example, the use of principles of *samānādhikaraṇatā* and *ekādhikaraṇatā* in the comment on *śloka* 16. *Lokanyāya*, common day-to-day logic is rarely resorted to. But *dṛṣṭānta*, example or analogy is sometimes brought in to give further explanation of some idea. Thus *śloka* 13 is read as an example of what *śloka* 12 says. Such uses are restricted to those that appear in the text itself — portions are read as examples of ideas presented elsewhere.

Ādi Śaṅkara's explanations always or usually begin after he himself expresses a doubt, *saṁśaya*, and in the process of explanation he anticipates doubts and resolves them. The expression of doubts generally takes these forms : "How is *X*, *Y* ?" or, "Why are homonymous expressions used?," or "Why is the expression *X* repeated?," or, "What does *X* mean here?," "It is not right to understand it this way — because . . .," "Why two separate *śloka*s are there to say practically the same thing?," "Does *X* contradict *Y* ?," "Why does the *śloka*. *X* suddenly shift to another topic?," "What is the relationship among the members of a series?"[1] These are some of the recurrent questions and indicate the kinds of textual problems handled — seeming irrationality, repetition, contradiction, discontinuity or incoherence, the opacity or *parokṣa-vṛtti* of words or expressions.

Quite a few of these problems are resolved through linguistic exegesis — (i) *śabdārtha*, meaning of words and particular lexical choice, (ii) *vyākaraṇa*, grammar, and (iii) *dhvani*, suggestion or *lakṣaṇā-vṛtti*. Śaṅkara takes care to define the crucial terms — for example, the concept *mātra-sparśa* is explained in the comment on 2.14, and *tatva* in the comment 2.16. Definition of course, is only one of the several means of fixing the meaning of words. Sometimes Śruti is cited, i.e., established usage, to determine the meaning — for example the word *paṇḍit* is interpreted through a quotation from the *Bṛhadāraṇyaka Upaniṣad* in the comment on 2.11. Far more frequent is the derivational analysis of words to establish the meaning — this is particularly true of primary and secondary derived nominals. Thus, for example, the *tattvārdarśī* "one who perceives correctly," *tata* "essence" (comment on 2.16); *manasā* "of mind," *mana* "mind" (in the course of an extended comment on 2.21). There are innumerable instances of this. As an example of interpretation through lexical choice and meaning (*śabdārtha*) we may draw attention to the comment on 2.20 in which Ādi Śaṅkara dwells one after the other on the meanings of seven words — three indeclinables, three adjectives, and one verb : *vā* "not be," *kadācita* "any," *na* "not be," *ai* "that does not die,"

1. As in the case of a series of modifying adjectives for example.

śāśvata "not subject to decay," *purāṇā* "that does not grow," *hanti* "coming into being of a result" and shows how all the meanings through proscription or exclusion contribute to the general meaning of the self being not subject to the six processes of birth and decay.[2] To give just one example of this attribution of meaning to words, the indeclinable *vā*, which primarily means "or" is restricted to mean *ca*, "also," and it is then correlated with the negative particle *na* that occurs as the first word in the *śloka* (*na jāyate mṛyate vā kadācinnāyam* . . . 2.20), for in the sense of "also" it refers back to *na*, "not," and is thus finally given the meaning — "not."

By referring back to *na*, "not," the practicle *vā* "also" acquires the same grammatical function — negation, and with this, we are already talking of the use of grammar by Ādi Śaṅkara in his interpretation. Śaṅkarācārya we know, was also an original thinker in grammar — witness his denial of Bhartṛhari's concept of *sphoṭa*, his discussions of *mahāvākya*, the axiomatic sentences of philosophy, and his focus of analysis on the declarative sentences as against the indicative sentences on which the Mīmāṁsakas centered their analysis. Therefore, references to grammatical categories abound in his commentaries. Thus in the comment on 2.12, the plural form of the verb is highlighted and its use explained, to refer to so many separate bodies of so many individuals, and to the "self" which is an indivisible whole. Here was a case of seeming contradiction for while talking of indivisibility the verb referred to plurality of being. Again in the comment on 2.16, Ādi Śaṅkara proceeds from a grammatical category to a philosophic category : *tata* in the compound, *tattvadarśī*, says the Teacher, is a *sarvaṇāma*,

2. Ādi Śaṅkara's reference is to the six general meanings of the verb — *bhāva-vikāra* — which Yāska spells out in *Nirukta* (1.2) and which are archetypal activities and process of life: (1) birth, (2) existence, (3) change, (4) growth, (5) decay, and (6) death (*Nirukta*, 1.2).

a pronoun that includes in its domain of reference all objects, all existence, and *sarva* (all) continues the *ācārya*, is nothing but *Brahman* and *tattavadarśī* consequently is one who has known *Brahman*. Similarly the *ācārya* refers to the semantico-syntactic category of "agency," *kartṛtva*, and argues for its absence in all actions. At the level of syntax, we have instances of splitting up the sentences grammatically in order to build up the total meaning of the sentence — this is in line with the Mīmāṁsaka principle of *vākyabheda* as against *vākya-aikatva* (*MS* 3.1). An example of this occurs in the extended comment that follows *BG* (2.10).

We may add here a brief statement about the recurring linguistic forms in the *ācārya*'s sentences. They are : "If . . .;" "And . . .;" "So also . . ." "Because . . .;" "But . . .;" "Besides, . . .;" "Just as . . . so also;" "Therefore . . . ." It is the language of logic and argument. It follows perhaps from this that the *ācārya* only very rarely takes recourse to *lakṣaṇā-vṛtti*, figurative extension, to assign a meaning to a word or an expression. May be it holds true of all Śāstric (Smṛti) exegesis. The attempt to attribute symbolic meanings to items is practically absent. This radically separates Smṛti exegesis from the Śruti-exegesis in which, as we have noted (cf. chapter 2), explaining verbal symbolism is the overwhelming task as well as the explanatory mode of the interpreters. Even *kāvya*-exegesis, literary interpretation, makes this demand on the interpreters. But not the Śāstras which are more or less scientific treatises dealing with intellectual constructs and systems. Because of this, *Vyākaraṇa-ṭīkā*, the interpretation of grammar or rules of grammar, is closer to the interpretation of philosophy than to the interpretation of literature. But, evidently, on account of its subject-matter — the universe of language-use, rather than the universe of being — its categories and constructs are different and its statements, unlike statements in philosophy, have a different relationship to their objects, the correlation being verifiable in Vyākaraṇa. Hence, grammatical exegesis takes a different form and answers a different set of questions — questions of domain, application, conditions and result, questions such as :

> Does *X* include *Y* ?
> Does *X* apply to *Y* and/or *Z*?
> Under what conditions does *X* apply to *Y* ?
> When *X* applies to *Y*, what is the nature of the result *Z*?

But the instruments of exegesis remain the same although their relative strength becomes different. Thus in Vyākaraṇa interpretation even more than in philosophy, a much greater need is felt for *Paribhāṣās*, meta rules of logical interpretation and *laukika-nyāya*, judgements of common life. We have had the occasion to mention in chapter 2 that the history of grammar-commentaries shows a gradual refinement of, and an accretion in, the *Paribhāṣās*. The problematics also differ, for meaning in "a rule of grammar" subsists in its application and applicability, in its reference to a well-defined or definable class of linguistic objects. Much rigour and precision thus must mark the interpretation of a rule of grammar. Patañjali's monumental *Mahābhāṣya* is an acknowledged testimony of this.

Final Remarks

The Indian interpretive tradition is essentially linguistic and philological. From the very beginning and from the time of Yāska (ninth century BC) its foundations as a discipline are laid. Elements of India's cultural history and world-view no doubt contributed to this development. There wasn't any father-text — the concept is absent — no 'sacred' text to be worshipped and which had to be tied down to a meaning given in advance. So the Indian mind each time confronted the texts afresh on free and equal terms — in fact, again and again we see the mind triumphing over the text, playing with it, bending it, colouring it. Each text therefore has multiple interpretations. At the same time, the exigencies of the need to preserve oral texts intact generated the science of phonetics which has its origin in the unknown hoary past and which involved empiri-cal study and investigation — collection and processing of data, development of systems for classification and hierarchies, working out the networks of interelations between different elements of the sound system of Sanskrit, and evolution of predictive models for the generation of continuous speech.

This was structuralism or empiricism, call what you will, a habit of mind that was a product of rigorous enquiry and analysis, a precisely enunciated method in Indian scholarship. It led ultimately to Pāṇini's *Aṣṭādhyāyī* (seventh century BC) the only complete grammar extant in the world. From the categories of grammar to Jaimini's correlations between types of meaning and types of grammatical categories, we see a continuous development and from there to Śabara's credo that language is constructivist rather than representational and that once we have a word as a name, the object it names constitutes the real.[3] Add to this his other assertion that words in texts have the same meaning that they have in actual usage and we have a clear basis of linguistic interpretation in the Indian tradition which till today treats, *śabdārtha*, "word-meaning," *yathārtha* "meaning as it is" and *vāstavārtha* "objects as meaning" as *practically* synonymous. The interpreter begins with the materiality of language and looks for its meaning as it is — in this process he constrains his method through modes derived from different systems which had developed as independent disciplines — logic (including meta-rules and principle of coherence *saṅgati*), grammatical theories, theories of meaning

3. See *Śābara Bhāṣya* 1.5. Also see Othmar Gachter, 1983, *Hermeneutics and Language in Pūrva Mīmāṁsa*, MLBD, pp. 93-108.

and the *Pramāṇa-Śāstra* or the science of epistemology. The rigour and precision, as part of a scientific objectivity and habit of mind, are evident even in a text like *Dhvanyāloka* dealing with the symbolics of language — an area notorious for its amorphousness, flux and, quite often, subjectivity.

The questions being recurrently asked are directed at the linguistic constituents and are answerable and answered only in terms of the word-meaning relationship : "What does the expression *X* mean?;" "Does *X* contradict *Y* ?;" "Why is *X* used to repeat the content of *Y*?;" "Is the denotation of *X* plausible, or acceptable?;" "What is the link between *X* and *Y*?" "Does *X* include or exclude *Y*?;" "Why do the mutually contradictory *X* and *Y* appear?;" "Why is *X* repeated?" These questions are asked and answered at all the levels of language-structure-*pada* (fully inflected word), *vākya* (sentence) and *caraṇa* (a unit of meaning that may or may not transcend the *vākya* which is a syntactic unit). All the instruments of exegesis function both sometimes as means of, and sometimes as conditions on, the determination of meanings of the elements and of the relationships that hold among or between them. The categories employed for interpretation, the filters through which meaning is seen to emerge, come from diverse disciplines but they are chiefly categories of grammar and of poetics. Many of these categories of grammar are shared as we noted with logic and philosophy as well.

The method slowly evolved into a convention common to texts of all discipline — the *Śāstra-Paddhati* — a method of interpretation well-defined in terms of (i) the structure of argument, (ii) the nature of evidence, and (iii) the instruments of exegesis. It began with the application of the techniques to the earliest symbolic poetry of India and attained maximum rigour and richness in the Smṛti exegesis, particularly the interpretation of the Upaniṣads and underwent final categorial extension, once again, in a work addressed to the problem of verbal symbolism in poetry, the *Dhvanyāloka*.

The origin, evolution and existence of *Śāstra-Paddhati* is a marvellous fact of India's intellectual history and is a testimony of our early recognition that "truth" is a matter of correlation between language, thought and reality and knowledge is the process of establishing and recognizing this correlation. As we said in the beginning, the freedom to interpret betokens a freedoms to think, a not so common attribute of cultures. The Indian tradition has not only allowed contending views and diversity of beliefs, but has actually considered this freedom of thought as an essential civilizational value. Bhartṛhari (fifth century AD) in the first Kāṇḍa of his *Vākyapadīya* says that by differently interpreting the same Śruti sentence '*ātmaiva dehamayaḥ*,' thinkers argue contending positions such as dualism, non-dualism and numerous other systems (*pravādā bahudhāmatāḥ*).[4] This eclecticism has kept the Indian thought systems alive and relevant and the Hindu mind open.

---

4. *Vākyapadīya, Kārika* 8.

Annotation of Major Terms

abheda	:	non-difference
abhidhā	:	primary/denotative meaning
abhyāsa	:	experience
ācāra	:	conduct
ādeśa	:	instruction in a rule of grammar
adhikāra	:	entitlement; eligibility; having sufficient learning to read and interpret a text
adhikaraṇa	:	section in a book
Advaita philosophy	:	non-dualist philosophy
āgama	:	appearance (of an element in language operations); knowledge; the Vedas and Tantra literature
alaṁkāra	:	figure of speech; theory of literary language as essentially figurative
ākṛti	:	form
anarthaka	:	unprofitable; without sense or meaning
anityatva	:	transience
aniṣṭaprayoga	:	linguistic forms that are not "desirable"
antaraṅga	:	internal, inclusive
anumāna	:	inference

anuṣaṅga	:	connection of word with word (in grammar)
anuvṛtti	:	application or bearing of a preceding rule or a part of it to or in the following rule
apoha	:	difference or contextual exclusion (*atadvyāvṛtti*); negation or absence as the essential meaning
āpta vacana	:	verbal testimony, the opinion of or wisdom received by word of mouth
arthavāda	:	meaningful statements
artha krama	:	meaning contingent on sequence
artha-nirdhāraṇa	:	determination of meaning
apaśabda	:	unacceptable usage; dialectal variant
*āśrama*s	:	secluded places for recluses; stages of life
atī-parokṣa-vṛtti	:	tendency in words for their meanings to become totally opaque
ātmā	:	self (of beings)
avayava	:	a part, a portion; a limb
bahiraṅga	:	external; less close
bhāṣya	:	explanatory commentary
bheda	:	difference separateness
dharma	:	customary observance; morality; right; duty; piety; disposition; an essential quality; a sacrifice
dharma niyama	:	a prescription to promotes *dharma*
dharma sādhāraṇa	:	common duty or morality
dharama viśeṣa	:	duty or conduct specific to a group or an individual

dhvani	: suggestion; suggested meaning; sound
dravya	: substance
dṛṣṭa	: perceptible
dṛṣṭānta	: example; analogy
ekādhikaraṇatā	: fact of being treated in or analysed in one place
ekavākyata	: principle of belonging to one sentence
gaṇapāṭha	: classified arrangement of nominal stems in ordered sets (in grammar)
guṇa	: attribute; quality
hetu	: cause, reason, object, motive; the middle term in a syllogism
jñāna-dharma	: pursuit of knowledge as duty
jñāpaka-siddha	: meta-rules inferrable from suggestive statements
kalpavṛkṣa	: a tree supposed to grant all desires
kāmadhenu	: the divine cow that fulfils all desires; anything that has the power to grant a boon.
karma	: act or action
karaṇa	: instrument
kārikā	: a verse-form
Kāraka-theory	: theory of "case" in grammar; of objects that interact to produce another object in metaphysics
kartā	: creator, agent
karma-kartṛ	: a "voice" in Sanskrit grammar in which the true object functions as the agent

kathā	:	disputation (in philosophy); narrative (in literature)
kāvya	:	verbal composition
khaṇḍana	:	refutation
krama	:	sequence
kṛti	:	a work; a creation; a composition
kṛta	:	created; accomplished
lakāra	:	a tense form, any one of the ten in Pāṇini's grammar
lakṣaṇa	:	a sign; rule of grammar; definition
lakṣya	:	the thing defined or referred to
liṅga	:	a sign; gender
liṅgānuśāsana	:	ordered assignation of gender to words of language
loka	:	world, life; usage
loka-nyāya siddha	:	proved to bc so and so by the wisdom of common life.
lokā-vyavhāra	:	worldly practice
mahāvākya	:	'grand' sentence; a literary work, specifically an epic; a great proposition or principal sentence in philosophy
maṇḍalas	:	a sub-section in the *Ṛgveda*
mantra	:	a Vedic verse form
mohā-śoka	:	delusion of mind which prevents discernment of truth and causes the resulting sorrow
mukhya krama	:	dominant or primary sequence
mūla siddhāanta	:	the core overriding principle

nāda	:	resonant nasal sound represented by a semi-circle in Yoga-philosophy
nigama-vāda	:	Vedic literature
nigamana	:	the conclusion in a syllogism
nirṇaya	:	decision (in logic)
nirvacana	:	exposition; semantic explanation of a word
nitya	:	given; existing
nivṛttistu mahāphala	:	"greatest merit is in abstinence," a *subhāśitā*
nivṛtti-mārga	:	the way of life that seeks fulfilment through non-involvement, withdrawal
nyāya	:	judgement; principle of judgement
pada	:	fully inflected linguistic form
paribhāṣā	:	meta-rule
pāṭha krama	:	the order of mention in a text
paddhati	:	mode, method
parokṣa-vṛtti	:	opacity
pramāṇa	:	proof, evidence, process of acquiring valid knowledge
pramāṇa śāstra	:	epistemology
pravṛtti mārga	:	the way of life that seeks fulfilment through active pursuit of wordly goals and participation
pratyakṣa	:	perceptible to the eye or senses
prakaraṇasaṅgati	:	coherence of treatment in a section/ between sections
prakaraṇa	:	section, chapter
prasaṅga	:	context

prakṛti	:	nature
prātibhāsika	:	apparent
pratyaya	:	affix; knowledge
prokta	:	a type of composition; knowledge already available but re-stated by someone
pūrva-pakṣa	:	the opponent's point of view
Rītī	:	a school of Indian poetics based on lexis
rūḍhārtha	:	conventional meaning
śabda	:	sound; note; a significant word; a declinable word; verbal authority; grammar; language
śabda pramāṇa	:	verbal testimony
śabda śakti	:	potential power of words to evoke meaning(s)
sādhya	:	to be accomplished
samīkṣā	:	investigation; close analysis
sammudeśa	:	section devoted to a particular topic;
sampradāya	:	a school
saṁskāra	:	imprint in the self; sixteen enjoined Hindu rituals
saṁśaya	:	doubt
sambandha	:	relationship
samānādhikaraṇatā	:	similarly governed; identity of treatment
śānta-ātman	:	the peaceful miner self
saṅgati	:	coherence
sārvabhauma	:	the overriding principle; meta-assumption
siddhānta		

śāstra : technical/philosophical texts; system of thought

saptāh : week; festival lasting a week; traditional trade fair lasting a week; narration of *Śrī Bhāgavata Purāṇa* over a week

śāstra-nirdiṣṭa : as laid down in the Śāstras

śāstra-paddhati : method of interpretation

siddhānta : principle

Śiva-Sūtra : fourteen rules in the beginning of *Aṣṭādhyāyī*, setting down the syllables of Sanskrit in given morphophonemic sets

Smṛti : the body of technical literature that includes grammar, philosophy, etc.

sphoṭavāda : a theory of Indian grammanians that considers a word (language) as that entity in the mind which manifests in speech or in working and evokes the cognition of an object.

Śruti : Vedic literature

śruti-krama : order of elements in a text

sthāna : location; place in a sequence

sūktas : Vedic hymns

sup : case affixes

sūtra pāṭha : Pāṇini's *Aṣṭādhyāyī*

Sūtrāmaka : expresely stated

sūtrakāra : writer of a treatise; also a term reserved for Pāṇini

sūtras : primary texts of philosophy and other technical subjects

svabhāva	:	inherent nature of an individual; natural constitution
Svamatasthāpana	:	establishment of one's thesis
Tarkavidhi	:	mode of disputation
tātparya	:	intention
tattvārtha	:	essential meaning
tiṅ	:	verb-affixes
ṭīkā	:	a type of explanatory commentary
upajñāta	:	a category of verbal compositions (created by an individual)
upamāna	:	simile, analogy (a mean of knowledge)
uttara pakṣa	:	exponents' point of view; a rejoinder
Va	:	other; or
vācyārtha	:	the expressed meaning
Vacanikī	:	expression
vāda kathā	:	argument to reach commonly agreed truth (a construct of Nyāya)
Vaikharī	:	manifest speech
vāk	:	language
vakrokti	:	non-normal (deviant) expression; a figure of speech using evasive speech
vākya-bheda	:	splitting a sentence for interpretation
vākya-śeṣa	:	ellipsis; resedual element
vāṅmaya	:	verbal composition
varga	:	set
vārttika	:	a form of critical commentary; Kātyayans's critical commentary on some Pāṇini rules
Vārttikakāra	:	Kātyāyana

vāstavārtha	:	referential meaning
vedanā	:	experience or feeling; suffering born of knowledge/experience
vibhakti	:	inflectional affix; case-marker
vibhāṣā	:	an option; optionality of a rule
vidhi	:	method
vidyā	:	a doemain of knowledge
vivarta	:	a changed form of something
vivarta-vādī	:	a thinker who believes the visible world is a transformed manifestation of a non-manifest principle
viveka	:	discrimination
viṣaya	:	subject
vṛtti	:	brief commentary
vyākaraṇa	:	grammar
vyākhyān	:	explanation
vyañjanā	:	indirect suggested meaning
vyāpti	:	invariable concomitance in logic
vyavahārika	:	common sense; of practical life
yajña	:	sacrifice; sacrificial act
yathārtha	:	meaning as it is; the meaning
yathā-darśanam	:	as perceived or conceptualized
yaugikārtha	:	compounded meaning

Bibliography*

Abhinavagupta (tenth-eleventh century AD) 1891, *Locana*, Bombay: Kāvyamālā Series (KMS), (Sanskrit).

Abhyankar, K., 1928, *Nyāyakośa of Jhalakikar* (Dictionary of Technical Terms of Indian Philosophy), Poona: Bombay Sanskrit and Prakrit Series, 49.

———, 1955, "A Short Note on the Paribhaṣa works in Sanskrit Grammar," *Annals of Baroda Oriental Research Institute* (ABORI), 36: 157-62.

———, 1969, "Dramatic, Pictorial and Verbal Representation of Past Events at the time of Patañjali," *Festschrift Gopinath Kaviraja*, Lucknow: Akhil Bharatiya Parishad.

———, 1977, *A Dictionary of Sanskrit Grammar*, Baroda: Oriental Institute.

Ādi Śaṅkara (eighth century AD), *Vivekacūḍāmaṇī*, Gorakhpur: Gita Press (Sanskrit Text with Hindi paraphrase), 1932.

———, *Bhāṣya on Gītā* (*Śāṅkara-Bhāṣya*) see under Sir Ganganath Jha (Sanskrit Text with Hindu Paraphrase).

———, *Brahma* (*Vedānta*) *Sūtra Bhāṣya* (*Śāṅkara-Bhāṣya*), see under Thibaut.

---

* This is a listing of, mostly, modern writings.

From among the classical Sanskrit works, only the major ones used in the book are included here. Other Sanskrit works and writers including those referred to in the text of this study have been published off and on by the following oriental publishers, and are generally available with them:

1. Chaukhamba Sanskrit Sansthan, Varanasi, India.
2. Chaukhamba Orientalia, Varanasi, India.
3. Chaukhamba Sanskrit Pratishthan, Delhi, India.
4. Gita Press, Gorakhpur, India (for Ādi Śaṅkara's exegetical works).

Agarwala, V.S., 1953, *India as Known to Pāṇini*, Lucknow: University of Lucknow.

———, 1963, "The Thousand-Syllabled Speech" (Being a study in Cosmic Symbolism in its Vedic Version), Delhi: Motilal Banarasidass..

Aitareyopaniṣad (with Śāṅkara-Bhāṣya), 1936, Gorakhpur: Gita Press (Reprint 1968), Text with Hindi translation.

Aiyar, C.P. Ramaswamy, 1937, "Introduction," to *Cultural Heritage of India*, vol. II, 2nd rev. edn., 1962 (rpt. 1969), pp. xxi-xxviii.

Aklujkar, Ashok N., 1970, "Ancient Indian Semantics," *Annals of Bhandarker Oriental Research Institute*, 51: 11-29.

Amarjit Kaur, 1979, *Influence of Indian Philosophy on Sanskrit Poetics*, Delhi: Bharatiya Vidya Bhawan.

Ānandavardhana (ninth-century AD), *Dhvanyāloka*, see under K. Krishnamoorthy.

Anirvan, Shrimat, 1937, "Vedic Exegesis," in *Cultural Heritage of India*, vol. I, Calcutta, 2nd rev. edn., 1958.

Apte, V.M., 1937, *The Vedāṅgas*, in *Cultural Heritage of India*, vol. I., Calcutta: Ramakrishna Mission Institute of Culture, 2nd rev. edn., 1958, pp. 264-92.

Atharvaveda Saṁhitā (*Sanātan Hindi Bhāṣya Sahit*), Varanasi: Chaukhamba Orientalia (Text with Hindi commentary).

Bādarāyana, *Brahma/Vedānta-Sūtra* see, under G. Thibaut.

Bagchi, Yogendranath, 1937, "The Art of Philosophical Disputation," in *Cultural Heritage of India*, vol. III, Calcutta, 2nd rev. edn., 1953 (rpt. 1969), pp. 562-80.

Banerjee, Anukul Chandra, 1978, "Buddhist Literature," in *Cultural Heritage of India*, vol. V, pp. 184-210.

Barlingay, S.S., 1964, "Theories of Language in Indian Logic," New York: *International Philosophical Quarterly*, 4: 94-109.

Bedekar, V.M. and G.B. Palsule (trs.), *Sixty Upanishads by Paul Deussen*, vols. I and II.

Bhagavad-Gītā, 1997 (with Hindi commentary and Analysis of the Text into Padas-inflected Word Forms and Indeclinable), 1929, Gorakhpur: Gita Press.

Bhāmaha (sixth-seventh century AD), 1927. *Kāvyālaṁkāra*, with English Translation and Notes, P.U. Naganatha Sastry (ed., tr.), Tanjore: Wallace Printing House.

Bhandarkar, R.G., 1873, "On the Interpretation of Patañjali," *Indian Antiquary*, 2.94-96.

———, 1877, "Dr. Goldstücker's Theory about Pāṇini's Technical; Terms," *Indian Antiquary*, 6.107-13.

———, 1879, "Ācarya, the Friend of the Student, and the Relation between the Three Ācaryas," *Indian Antiquary*, 5. 345-50.

———, 1883, "Development of Language and of Sanskrit," First Wilson Lecture, *Journal of the Bombay Branch of the Royal Asiatic Society*, 16, 1883-1885, 245-74.

Bharata (second century BC to second century AD), *Nāṭyaśāstra*, See under Ravishankar Nagar.

Bharata, 1926-54, *Nāṭyaśāstra*, with the commentary *Abhinavabhāratī* by Abhinavagupta, *Gaekwad Oriental Series*, 36, 68, 124, vol. I, 1926, vol. II, 1934; vol. III, 1954, Baroda.

Bhartṛhari, *Vākyapadīya*, see under Subramania Iyer, K.A.

Bhaṭṭa, Annam, *Tarka-Saṁgraha*, see under Ramacandra Bhara Shukla.

Bhaṭṭa, Jayanta, 1936, *Nyāya Mañjarī*, Kashi Sanskrit Series.

Bhaṭṭa, Kumārila, *Śloka-Vārttika*, see under Sir Ganganath Jha (tr.).

———, *Tantra-Vārttika*, see under Sir Ganganath Jha.

Bhaṭṭa, Nāgeśa, 1901-21, *Mahābhāṣya Pradipodyota*, Bibliotheca Indica, 142.4 vols.

———, *Vyākaraṇa-Siddhānta Mañjūṣā*, Varanasi: Chaukhamba Orientalia

———, (18th century) *Paribhaṣendusekhara*, see under Kiehorn and Vishvanatha Mishra.

Bhaṭṭa, Nārāyana (seventeenth century), *Mānameyodaya*, see under C.K. Raja and S.S. Suryanarayana.

Bhattacarya, Bishnupada, 1956, "Constitution of Words: Sphoṭa Theory and its Opponents," *Our Heritage: Bulletin of the Sanskrit College*, Calcutta.

———, 1957, "Connotation of words" (A Comparative Study of the Viewpoints of Grammarians, Mīmāṁsakas, and Naiyāyikas), *Our Heritage: Bulletin of the Sanskrit College*, 5: 147-67.

———, 1958, *Yāska's Nirukta and the Science of Etymology: An Historical and Critical Survey*, Calcutta: Mukhopadhyaya.

———, 1962, *A Study in Language and Meaning: A Critical Examination of some Aspects of Indian Semantics*, Calcutta: Progressive Publishers.

Bhattacharya, G.N., 1937, "A Study in the Dialectics of Sphoṭa," *Journal of the Dept. of Letters*, University of Calcutta.

Bhattacharya, Kalidas and Amiya Kumar Majumdar, 1978, "Philosophical Literature," in *CHI*, vol. V., Calcutta, pp. 371-89.

Bhattacharya, Ram Shankar, 1950-52, "Pāṇinian Principles of Determining the Desired Import of Words," *Journal of Andhra Historical Research Society*, 21: 133-141.

———, 1952-53, "Significance of the Examples in the Mahābhāṣya," *Journal of Ganganatha Jha Research Institute*, 10: 39-48.

———, 1953, "Kinds of Agents (Kartā) as Depicted by Pāṇini," *Vāk*, 3: 129-33.

———, 1954-55, "On the Original Reading of a Pāṇinian Sūtra," Baroda: *Journal of Oriental Institute*, 4: 268-29-69 (on the rule 6.1.115).

———, 1955, "Kinds of Exposition in Sanskrit Literature," *Annals of the Bhandarkar Oriental Research Institute*, 36 : 123-32.

Bhattacharya, Surendranath, 1937, "Buddhism in Relation to Vedānta," in *CHI*, vol. I., Calcutta, 2nd rev. edn., 1958, pp. 547-58.

———, 1937, "The Philosophy of Śankara," in *CHI*, vol. III, Calcutta, 2nd rev. edn, 1953, rpt. 1969, pp. 237-44.

Bhawe, Shrikrishna Sakharam, 1953, "Pāṇini's Rules and Vedic Interpretation," Ahmedabad, *Proceedings of the All India Oriental Conference*, 17: 231-40.

———, 1954, "Interpretation of Some Ṛgvedic Compounds," Baroda: *Journal of Oriental Institute*, 4: 315-29.

———, 1957-62, *The Soma Hymns of the Ṛgveda: A Fresh Interpretation*, 3 vols. (MSURS 3, 5, 6), Baroda: Oriental Institute.

Bhojarāja (eleventh century AD), *Śṛṅgāraprakāśa*, see under V. Raghavan.

Bṛhadāraṇyakopaniṣad with Śāṅkara's-Bhāṣya, 1891, Ānandāśrama, Sanskrit Series, Poona.

Bloomfield, L., 1933, *Language*, New York, Holt, Rinehard Winston, 1965.

Brough, J., 1952, "Audumbarāyaṇa's Theory of Language," *TPS*: 73-77.

———, 1953, "Some Indian Theories of Meaning," *TPS*: 161-76.

Burrow, T., 1936, "Indian Theories on the Nature of Meaning," *TPS*: 93-93 (summary of paper).

Cāndravyākaraṇa, See under Kshitish Chandra Chatterji.

Cardona, George, 1967, "Pāṇini's Syntactic Categoriesm," Baroda: *Journal of the Oriental Institute*, 16: 201-15.

———, 1970, "Some Principles of Pāṇini's Grammar," Dordrecht: *Journal of Indian Philosophy*, 1: 40-74.

———, 1971, "Cause and Causal Agent: the Paninian View, Baroda: *Journal of the Oriental Institute*, 21: 22-40.

———, 1974, "On Pāṇini's Metalinguistic use of Cases," *Festschrift Charudeva Shastri*, Delhi : The Charudeva Shastri Felicitation Volume Committee, pp. 305-26.

———, 1974, "Pāṇini's Kārakas: Agency, Animation and Identity," Dordrecht: *Journal of Indian Philosophy*, 2. 231-306.

———, 1973, "On the Interpretation of Pāṇini," 1.4.105-8. *Adyar Library Bulletin*, 37: 1-47.

Chaitanya, Krishna, 1965, *Sanskrit Poetics: A Critical and Comparative Study*, Delhi: Asia Publishing House.

Chakravarti, P.C., 1930, *The Philosophy of Sanskrit Grammar*, Calcutta: University of Calcutta.

———, 1933, *The Linguistic Speculations of the Hindus*, Calcutta: University of Calcutta.

Chakrabarti, Tarapada, 1971, *Indian Aesthetics and the Science of Language*, Calcutta: Sanskrit Pustak House.

Chatterji, Kshitish Chandra (ed.), 1933, "Pāṇini as a Poet," *Calcutta Oriental Journal*, 1 : 47-56.

———, 1953-61, *Cāndra Vyākaraṇa* of *Candragomin* 2 vols., Poona: Deccan College.

———, 1955, "On the Interpretation of a Rule of Pāṇini," *Festschrift S.K. Chatterji*, (Indian Linguistics. 16), pp. 194-95 (Rule 1.1.36).

———, 1964, Technical Terms and Technique of Sanskrit Grammar, Kolkata : University of Calcutta.

Chatterjee, Heramba Nath, 1960, *Comparative Studies in Pali and Sanskrit Alaṁkāras*, Calcutta: Sanskrit Pustak Bhandar.

Chatterji, Suniti Kumar, 1937, Editor's Preface, *The Culture Heritage of India*, vol. I, 1958, 1958, rpt., iii-iiii.

Chaudhary, Satyadev (tr.) 1965, "Kāvyālaṁkāra (of Rudrata)," Delhi: Vasudev Prakashan (Text with Hindi commentary).

Dandekar, R.N., 1937, "Literature of Brahmanism in Sanskrit," in *The Culture Heritage of India*, vol. V, Calcutta, 2nd rev. edn., 1978, pp. 13-48.

Daṇḍin (seventh century AD) 1924, *Kavyadarṣa*, Sanskrit Text and English Translation, S.K. Belvalkar (tr.), Poona: The Oriental Book Supplying Agency.

Dasgupta, S.N. and S.K. De, 1947, *History of Sanskrit Literature*, Calcutta: University of Calcutta.

Dasgupta, S.N., 1932-1449, *A History of Indian Philosophy*, vols. I and II, 1932; vol. III, 1940; vol. IV, 1949, and Vol. V, Cambridge: Cambridge University Press.

Datta, Dhirendra Mohan, 1932, *The Six Ways of Knowing*, London: George Allen and Unwin.

Datta, Dhirendra Mohan, 1937, "Indian Epistemology," in *The Culture Heritage of India*, vol. III, Calcutta, 2nd rev. edn, 1953 (rpt. 1969), pp. 548-61.

De, S.K., 1925, "The Theory of Rasa in Sanskrit Poetics," *Sir Asutosh Mookerji Silver Jubilee Volumes*, vol. III, pt. 2, pp, 207-53, Calcutta.

———, 1925, *Studies in the History of Sanskrit Poetics*, London: Luzac Co.

Devasthali, Govind Vanayak, 1965, "Pāṇini as an Aid to Ṛgvedic Interpretation," *Festschrift H.D. Velankar*, Bombay : Prof. H.D. Velankar Commemoration Committee, pp. 20-26.

———, 1967, "Pāṇini and Ṛgvedic Exegesis," in *Indian Antiquary*, 2.3 : 1-8.

———, 1981, *Apropos of Vibhāṣa*, in International Seminar on Pāṇini — Summaries of Papers (*ISP-SP*), University of Poona. 1981.

Dharma Kirti, *Pramanavartika*, see under Swami Dwarikadas Sastri.

Dīkṣita, Bhaṭṭojī, *Siddhānta Kaumudī*, see under S.C. Vasu.

Divanji, P.C., 1949, "Bhagavad-Gītā and Aṣṭādhyāyī," *Annals of Bhandarkar Oriental Research Institute*, 30; 263-76.

Dwivedi, R.C., 1969 (ed.), *Principles of Literary Criticism in Sanskrit*, Delhi: Motilal Banarsidass.

———, (tr.), 1970, "The Poetic Light," *Kāvya Prakāśa of Mammaṭa*, Delhi: Motilal Banarsidass (Sanskrit text and with English translation).

Dwivedi, Rewaprasad, 1979, *Alaṅkāra Sarvasva of Śrī Rājānaka Ruyyaka and Maṅkha*, Varanasi: Chaukhamba Sanskrit Sansthan.

———, (ed.), 1982, *Vyaktiviveka of Rājānaka Śrī Mahimabhaṭṭa*, (3rd edn.), ed. with a Sanskrit commentary of Rājānaka Ruyyaka and Hindi commentary and Notes (Hindi), Varanasi: Chaukhamba Sanskrit Sansthan.

Edgerton, F., 1936, "Indirect Suggestion in Poetry : A Hindu Theory of Literary Aesthetics," *Proceedings of the American Philosophical Society*, vol. 76.

Edgerton, F., 1938, "Etymology and Interpretation," *Proceedings of the American Philosophical Society*, vol. 79., pt. 4, pp. 705-14.

Gachter, Othmar, 1983, *Hermeneutics and Language in Pūrva Mīmāṁsā: A Study in Śābara-Bhāṣya*, Delhi: Motilal Banarsidass.

Garge, Damodar Vishnu, 1949, "Jaimini-Śabara and the Science of Grammar," *ABORI*, 30: 254-62.

Ghatge, Amrit Madhav, 1968, Pāṇini 1.4.32., *Festschrift S.M. Katre, S.M. Katre Felicitation*, Vol. 2, pp. 150-54.

Gode, Parashuram Krishna, 1953-56, *Studies in Indian Literary History*, Bombay: Bharatiya Vidya Bhawan.

Goendka, Sri Hari Krishandas (ed., tr.), 1932, *Śāṅkarabhāṣya on Śrīmadbhagvad-Gītā*, Gorakhpur: Gita Press, rpt. 1968.

———, 1948, *Śrīmadbhagvad-Gītā*, Śrī Ramānuja Bhāṣya with Hindi translation, Gorakhpur: Gita Press, rpt. 1952.

———, 1948, *Śrīmadbhagavad-Gītā Tatva-vivecanī* with Hindi Ṭīkā, Gorakhpur: Gita press, rpt. 1986.

Gonda, Jan, 1974, "Nimitta," *Festschrift Charudeva Shastri*, pp. 233-40.

Granoff, P., 1978, *Philosophy and Argument in Late Vedānta*, Dordrecht.

Griffith, R.T.H., tr., 1889-92, *Ṛgveda*, 2 vols., Banaras.

Haradatta, 1892-9, *Padamañjarī*, Banaras: Pandit Series.

Hattori, M., 1968, *Dignāga on Perception*, Cambridge, Mass.

Heimann, Betty, 1937, *Indian and Western Philosophy, A Study in Contrasts*, London: George Allen and Unwin Ltd.

———, 1941, "Sphoṭa and Artha," A Volume of Studies in Indology, presented to Prof. P.V. Kane, pp. 221-27, Poona: Oriental Book Agency.

Induraja (commentator), 1925, *Kāvyālaṅkārasāra Saṁgraha of Udbhaṭa*, Poona: Bhandarkar Oriental Research Institute.

Īṣāvāsyopaniṣad (with *Śāṅkara-Bhāṣya*) 1935, Gorakhpur: Gita Press, Reprint 1969 (Text with Hindu translation).

Jacob, G.A., 1925, *Laukikānyayañjali*, 2nd part, A second Handful of Popular Maxims, Bombay: Nirnaya Sagar Press.

Pt. Jagannātha (seventeenth century AD), *Rasagaṅgādhara*, Pt. Madan Mohan Jha (ed.), 1969, Varanasi: The Chaukhamba Vidya Bhawan.

Jaimini, *Mīmāṁsā-Sūtra*, see under Sandal M.L.

Jain, Hiralal, 1978, "Literature of Jainism," in *CHI*, vol. V, Calcutta, pp. 152-63.

Jaini, Padmanabh S., 1959, "The Vaibhāṣika Theory of Words and Meanings," *BSOAS*, 22 : 95-107.

Jawalaprasad, 1939, *Indian Epistemology*, Lahore: Motilal Banarsidass.

Jha, Madanmohan (ed.), 1969, *Rasagaṅgādhara* (of Pt. Jagannatha), Varanasi: The Chaukhamba Vidya Bhawan.

Jha, Sir Ganganatha, (tr.) 1900, 1908, *Śloka-Vārttika*, 2nd edn., 1983 rpt., Delhi: Sri Satguru in *R̥V*, 4.48.1: 6.44.6 and 8.19.33, Poona: University of Poona.

———, (tr.) 1903-24, *Kumārila Bhaṭṭa's Tantra-Vārttika*, 2 vols., 2nd edn., 1983, Delhi: Sri Satguru Publications.

———, (tr.), 1925, *Mammaṭa's Kāvyaprakāśa*, Allahabad.

———, (tr.), 1933, *Śābara-Bhāṣya*, in 3 vols., Baroda: Oriental Institute, 1973 (edn.).

———, 1942, *Pūrva-Mīmāṁsā in its Sources*, Varanasi: Banaras Hindu University.

Jolly, Julius, 1885, *Outlines of a History of Hindu Law*, Calcutta, Tagore Law Lectures.

Joshi, S.D., 1966, "Patañjali's Definition of a Word — An Interpretation," *Bulletin of the Deccan College Research Institute*, 25: 65-70.

———, 1966, "Two Methods of Interpreting Pāṇini," Poona, *Journal of the University of Poona*, 23-53-61.

——— and Roodbergen, 1971-73, J.A.F., *Patañjali Vyākaraṇa-Mahābhāṣya*, Poona: University of Poona.

Junarkar, N.S., 1978, *Gautama: The Nyaya Philosophy*, Delhi: Motilal Banarsidass.

Kane, P.V., 1951, *Sāhityadarpaṇa*, (ed. and tr.), Bombay: Nirnaya Sagar Press.

———, *History of Dharma-Śāstra*, vol. IV, Poona.

———, 1961 (2nd edn.), *History of Sanskrit Poetics*, Delhi: Motilal Banarsidass.

———, 1962, *History of Dharma-Śāstra*, vol. V, Poona.

Kapoor, K., 1985, "Metaphor in Sanskrit and English Criticism," *Journal of Literary Criticism* 2 (no. 2), Delhi, 29-44.

———, and R.N. Srivastava, 1988, "Semiotics in India," in *The Semiotic Web*, Sebeok and Sebeok (eds.), Berlin: Mouton de Gruyter.

———, 1989, "Alaṁkāra and the Theory of Metaphor" in *Sanskrit Poetics and Western Thought*, ed. M.S. Kushwaha, Lucknow: Agro.

———, 1991, "Bhartṛhari on lexical meaning" in *Linguistics at Large: S.K. Verma Festschrift*, ed. V. Prakasam, Hyderabad: Bookslinks Corporation.

———, 1992, "Oral Narrative and Tense: A Description" in *Aspect, Tense and; Mood in Hindi*, ed. Chaturbhuja Sahay, Agra: Central Institute of Hindi.

———, 1992, "Norm and Variation: Pāṇini to Kumārila Bhaṭṭa — A Classical Indian Debate" in R.N. Srivastava, ed., *Text and Language, Papers in Honour of A. Kelkar*, Delhi: Kalinga Publishers.

———, 1993, "Pāṇini's Aṣṭādhyāyī: Questions of Theory and Order" in S.M. Katre Felicitation Volume, (1991-92, Vols. 51-52), Poona: Deccan College.

———, 1994, *Language, Linguistics and Literature — The Indian Perspective*, Delhi: Academic Foundation.

———, 1994, "Vivakṣā and Tātparya: Bhartṛhari on Speaker's Perception/ Intention" in *Linguistics and Linguistics*, ed. J. Srihari Rao, Vol. 2, Our: Indian Scholar Publications.

———, 1996, "Concept of *Padārtha* in Language and Philosophy" in Sir William Jones (1794-1994) Bi-centenary Volume, Pune: *Bulletin of the Deccan College Post-Graduate and Research Institute.*

K. and Ranga Kapoor, 1994, "Mahāvākya: The Indian Theory of Literary Couse" in *Confederate Gestures: Search for Method in Indian Literature Study*, ed. Charusheel Singh, New Delhi: Associated Publishing House.

Kaṭhopaniṣad, 1973, (11th edn.), Text with English Translation, Madras: Sri Rama Krishna Math.

Katre, S.M., *Dictionary of Pāṇini*, Parts I-III, Deccan College, Poona, 1968.

Keith, A.B., 1924, *The Sanskrit Drama*, Oxford: Clarendon Press.

Kenopaniṣad (with *Śāṅkara-Bhāṣya*) 1935, Gorakpur: Gita Press (Reprint 1969) (Text with Hindi translation).

Kielhorn, F. (ed.), 1960, "The Parihbāśenduśekhara of Nagoji Bhaṭṭa," Part II, 2nd edn., K.V. Abhyankar, Poona: Bhandarkar Oriental Research Institute.

———, 1962 (ed.), The Paribhāṣenduśekhara of Nāgojī Bhaṭṭa, Part I, New edition with an Introduction by K.V. Abhyankar, Poona: Bhandarkar Oriental Research Institute.

———, 1882, 1883, 1885, *Mahābhāṣya of Patañjali*, vols. I, II, III, Bombay Sanskrit and Prakrit Series.

———, 1887, "Some Devices of Indian Grammarians," *Indian Antiquary*, 16: 244-52 (Rpt. Stall, 1972: 123-34).

———, 1898, "The Jatakas and Sanskrit Grammarians," *JRAS*, 17-21.

Kishore, Sri Nanda, 1990, *Aṣṭādhyāyī Sūtra Pāṭha* (*Vārttika-Gaṇapāṭha-Sahita*), Panipat: Anita Arya Prakashan, Halwai Hatta.

Kiparsky, Paul and Stall, J.F., 1969, "Syntactic and Semantic Relations in Pāṇini," *Foundations of Language*, 5 : 83-117.

Kosambi, D.D., *The Culture and Civilisation of Ancient India*, Vikas, Delhi, 1970.

Krishnamoorthy, K., 1964, *Essays in Sanskrit Criticism*, Dharwar: Karnataka University Press.

———, (ed., tr.), 1974, *Dhvanyāloka* of *Ānandvardhana*, Delhi: Motilal Banarsidass, 1981 (2nd edn.).

———, 1977, *Varkrokti-Jivita of Kuntaka*, critically ed. with variants, introduction and English translation, Dharwad : Karnataka University.

Kulkarni, N. (ed.), 1953, Tarkabhaśa, Poona.

Kulkarni, V.M., 1988, *Some Aspects of the Rasa Theory*, Delhi: Bhogilal Khemchand Institute of Indology.

Kumārila Bhaṭṭa, *Tantra-Vārttika*, Ganganath Jha (tr.), Sri Satguru Publications, Delhi, 2nd edn., 1983 (rpt.).

Kunjunni Raja, K., 1954, "The Theory of Meaning According to the Buddhist Logicians," *Adyar Library Bulletin*, 18 : 178-95.

———, 1955, "Indian Theories on Homophones and Homonyms," *Adyar Library Bulletin*, 19: 193-222.

———, 1957, "Ākāṅkṣā: The Main Basis of Syntactic Unity," *Adyar Library Bulletin*, 20: 282-95.

———, 1957, "Yāska's Definition of the 'Verb' and the 'Noun' in the Light of Bhartṛhari's Explanation," *Annals of Oriental Research*, Madras.

———, 1958, "The Elliptic Sentence — Indian Theories," *Adyar Library Bulletin*, 22: 25-31.

———, 1958, "The Indian Influence on Linguistics," *Journal of the Madras University*, 30: 93-111.

———, 1963, "Indian Theories of Meaning," Madras: *The Adyar Library Bulletin*.

———, 1964, "Bhartṛhari's List of Sentence Definitions," *Adyar Library Bulletin*, 28: 206-10.

———, 1965, "Pāṇini's Attitude Towards Lakṣaṇā," *Adyar Library Bulletin*, 29 : 177-87.

———1956, "Transfer of Meaning — A Buddhist View," *Adyar Library Bulletin*, 20: 345-348.

———, K., 1961, "Tātparya as a Separate Vṛtti," *PAIOC* 20, Bhubaneshwar (1959), 319-32.

———, 1955, "The Theory of Suggestion in Indian Semantics," *ALB*, 19: 20-26.

Kuntaka (tenth and eleventh century AD), *Vakrokti-jivita*, see under K. Krishnamoorthy.

Laddu, Suresh Chandra Dhyaneshwar, 1971, "Ancient Sanskrit Grammarians and the Literary Records," *Hoshiarpur: Vishveshvarananda Institute Journal*, 9: 315-22.

———, 1972, *The Device of Contiguity as a Key to Interpreting Pāṇini's Rules*, Poona: Centre of Advanced Studies in Sanskrit Studies.

Lahiri, P.C., 1937, *Concept of Rīti and Guṇa in Sanskrit Poetics*, Dacca: The University of Dacca, Reprint: Oriental Books Reprint Corporation, Delhi, 1974.

Lele, Jayant, and Rajendra Singh, 1987, "Pāṇini, Language Theories and the Dialectics of Grammar" in *Papers in the History of Linguistics*, Hans Aarsleff, Louis G. Kelly and Hans Josef Niedereha, eds., Amsterdam/Philadelphia: John Benjamins Publishing Co.

Mādhavācārya, *Sarva-Darśana-Saṁgraha*, E.B. Cowell and A.E. Gough (tr.), 1878, K.L. Joshi (ed.), Ahmedabad: Parimal Publications, 1981 (new edn.).

Mahimabhaṭṭa (eleventh century AD), *Vyaktiviveka*, see under Rewa Prasad Dwivedi.

Mahulkar, D.D., 1981, The Prātiśākhyan Tradition and Modern Linguistics, Baroda: M.S. University.

Mammaṭa (twelfth century AD), *Kāvyaprakāśa*, Ganganatha Jha (tr.), 1925, Allahabad.

Mammaṭa's *Kāvyaprakāśa*, see under Ganganatha Jha.

Manusmṛti (with the *Mānavārtha-Muktāvalī* commentary of Kulluka Bhaṭṭa with the *Maṇiprabhā* Hindi commentary by Pt. Haragovind Sastri), 1970, Pt. Gopala Sastri Nene (ed.), Varanasi: The Chaukhamba Sanskrit Series Office (Sanskrit text with Hindi commentary).

Māṇḍūkyopaniṣad (with a summary of GauḍapādaÆs Kārikā), 1956, Text with English translation, Madras: Sri Ramakrishna Math.

Matilal, B.K., 1968, *The Navya-Nyāya Doctrine of Negation*, Cambridge: Mass.

———, 1971, *Epistemology, Logic and Grammar in Indian Philosophical Analysis*, The Hague, Paris.

———, 1977, *The Logical Illumination of Indian Mysticism*, Oxford.

———, 1982, *Logical Ethical Issues of Religious Belief*, Calcutta.

———, 1985, *Logic, Language and Reality*, Delhi: Motilal Banarsidass.

Mehendale, M.A., 1965, Nirukta Notes, Series I, Poona: Deccan College.

Mishra, Kesava, *Tarkabhāṣā*, see under N. Kulkarni.

Mishra, Narayan (ed., tr., exegete) 1972, *Kāśikā* (of Vāmana and Jayāditya), Varanasi: Chaukhamba Sanskrit Sansthan (Sanskrit text with Hindi explanation).

Mishra, Vidyaniwas, 1970, "Structural Meaning: An Indian Standpoint," *Actes du ... Congress International des Linguists*, 10.2: 555-59.

Mishra, Viśvanātha (tr. and commnt.), 1985, *Paribhāṣenduśekhara*, Varanasi: Chaukhamba Surabharati Prakashana.

Moghe, S.G., 1971, "Paribhāṣās of Vyākaraṇa and the Mīmāṁsā Rules of Interpretation," *Festschrift Rajeswar Shastri Dravid*, Allahabad: Bharati Parisad, English Section, pp. 90-100.

Mohanty, J.N., 1966, *Gangeśa's Theory of Truth*, Shantiniketan, 1966.

Mukerji, Radhakumud, 1923, "History of Sanskrit Literature from the Works of Pāṇini, Kātyāyana and Patañjali," *Indian Antiquary*, 52 : 21-24.

———, *Hindu Civilization*, Bharatiya Vidya Bhavan, Bombay, 1957, Rpt. 1977.

Muṇḍakopaniṣad with Śāṅkara-Bhāṣya, 1935, Gorakhpur: Gita Press (Reprint 1969) (Text with Hindi Translation).

Nagar, Ravishankar (Chief ed.), Joshi, K.L., (ed.), 1984, *Bharata's Nāṭyaśāstra*, Ahmedabad: Parimal Publications.

Narayana, Murti M.S., 1973, *Sanskrit Compounds, A Philosophical Study*, Varanasi: Chaukhamba.

Narayana Murti, M.S., 1973, "Philosophy of Grammar," *Proceedings of the Seminar on Andhra's Contribution to Indian Culture*, Tirupati, *Sri Venkateshwara University Oriental Journal* : 37-54.

Narendra, Chandra Nath, 1969, *Pāṇinian Interpretation of the Sanskrit Language*, Varanasi: Banaras Hindu University.

Oswald Ducrot and Tzvetan Todorov, 1981, *Encyclopaedic Dictionary of the Sciences of Language*, Catherine Porter (tr.), Oxford.

Palsule, Gajanan Balakrishnan, 1961, *The Sanskrit Dhatupāṭhas — A Critical Study*, Poona : University of Poona.

Palsule, Gajanan Balakrishnan, 1970, *Some Views of Pāṇini and his Followers on Object-language and Meta-language*, University of Poona: Publications of the Centre of Advanced Studies in Sanskrit, A36.

Pandey, Kanti Chandra, 1963, *Abhinavagupta, an Historical and Philosophical Study*, Varanasi: Chaukhamba.

Pandey, Pt. Ramanarayanadatta Sastri, 1955, *Mahābhārata*, 6 vols., Gorakpur: Gita Press (Sanskrit text with Hindi translation).

Pandey, Ram Chandra, 1963, *The Problem of Meaning in Indian Philosophy*, Delhi: Motilal Banarsidass.

———, 1962, "Zero in Pāṇini," *Journal of the Maharaja Sayaji Rao University*, Baroda, 11.1 : 53-66.

———, 1971, *Pāṇini and the Vedic Interpretation, Festschrift Rajeshwar Shastri Dravid*, Allahabad: Bharati Parishad, English section, pp. 49-53.

Pāṇini, *Dhātupāṭha*, sea under J.L. Shastri.

Pāṇini, *Aṣṭādhyāyī*, S.C. Vasu (ed. & tr.). MLBD, vol. I and II, 3rd Reprint, 1980.

Patañjali, *Māhabhāṣyam*, Part 1, Yudhiṣṭhira Mīmāṁsaka (tr. & explanator), Bahalgarh: Ram Lal Kapur Trust Press, 1979 (Sanskrit Text with Sanskrit/Hindi explanation).

Pathak, C., 1976, "Brahma-Jijñāsā as a Fundamental Hermeneutics," in *Bharata Manisha Quarterly*, I. No. 4, 13-27.

Pathak, Kashinath Bapuji, 1912, Daṇḍin, Nyāsakāra and Bhāmaha, *Indian Antiquary*, 41 : 232-36.

Pathak, Kashinath Bapuji, 1932, "On the Text and Interpretation of some Passages in the Mahābhāṣya of Patañjali," *Annals of Bhandarkar Oriental Research Institute*, 13: 17-24.

Paul, Kiparsky, 1980, *Pāṇini as a Variationist*, University of Poona, Poona.

Praśnopaniṣad (with *Śāṅkara-Bhāṣya*), 1935, Gorkhpur: Gita Press (Reprint 1969), Text with Hindi Translation.

Pramathanath, Tarkabhushan, 1937, Pūrva-Mīmāṁsā, in *The Cultural Heritage of India*, vol. III, Calcutta, 2nd rev. edn., 1953 (rpt. 1969), pp. 151-67.

Pusalkar, A.D., 1937, "The Ramāyaṇa : Its History and Character," in *The Cultural Heritage of India*, vol. II, Calcutta, 1962 edn. rpt., 1969, pp. 14-31.

Quine, W.V.O., 1964, *From a Logical Point of View: Logico Philosophical Essays*, Cambridge, Mass.: Harvard University Press.

Radhakrishnan, S., 1923, *Indian Philosophy*, vols. 1 and 2., London: The Macmillan.

Radhakrishnan, S., 1953, *The Principal Upaniṣads*, London: George Allen and Unwin.

Rāghavan, V., 1937, *The Manu Saṁhitā*, in *CHI*, vol. II, Calcutta, 2nd rev. edn., 1962, rpt. 1969, pp. 335-63.

———, 1940, "The Number of Rasas," Madras: Adyar Library Series, 23.

———, 1942, "Studies on Some Concepts of Alaṁkāraśāstra," Madras: The Adyar Library Series, 33.

———, 1963, *Bhoja's Śṛṅgāra Prakāśa*, Madras: Punarvasu.

———, 1978, "Sanskrit Kāvya Literature : A General Survey," in *The Cultural Heritage of India*, vol. V, Calcutta, pp. 211-33.

Raja, C. Kunhana and S.S. Suryanarayana, 1933, *Mānameyodaya*, Madras: Theosophical Publishing House.

Rajaśekhara (ninth century), *Kāvya-Mīmāṁsā*, see under Pt. Kedar Nath Sharma Sarasvat.

Rajvansha Sahay 'Hira,' 1973, *Dictionary of Indian Poetics*, Patna: Bihar Granth Academy (Hindi).

Rāmānuja, Śrī, *Bhāṣya on Śrīmadbhagvad-Gītā*, see under Sri, Harikrishandas Goenka.

Ramsukhdas, Swami, 1987, *Gītā Darpaṇa* (2nd edn.), Gorakhpur: Gita Press.

Randle, H.N., 1926, *Fragments from Dinnāga, London : The Royal Asiatic Society*, 1981, rpt., Delhi: Motilal Banarasidass.

Ranganath, S., 1985, *Arrangement of Ṛgveda in Tattvaloka*, Sri Abhinav Vidya Teertha Educational Trust, Madras, 49-52.

Rayan, Krishna, 1987, *Text and Sub-text — Suggestion in Literature*, Delhi: Arnold Heinemann.

Renou, Louis, 1954, "The Dhvani in Sanskrit Poetics," *ALB*, vol. 18, pp. 15ff.

Ṛgveda, The Hymns of *Ṛgveda*, T.H. Griffith, tr., Varanasi: Chaukhamba, 1963.

Rudraṭa, *Kāvyālaṁkāra*, see under Satyadeva Chaudhary.

Ruyyaka *Alaṁkārasarvasva*, see, under Rewa Prasada Dwivedi.

Śābara-Bhāṣya, see under Sir Ganganatha Jha.

Sandal, M.L. (tr.), 1923-25, 1980 (rpt.), *Mīmāṁsā Sūtras of Jaimini*, vols. I, II, Delhi: Motilal Banarsidass.

Sankaran, A., 1929, *The Theories of Rasa and Dhvuni*, Madras: University of Madras.

Sarkar, Mahendra Nath, 1937, "The Bhagvad-Gītā: Its Early Commentaries," in *CHI*, vol. II, Calcutta, 2nd edn. (rev.), 1962, rpt. 1969, pp. 195-203.

Sarma, K. Madhava Krishna, 1962, *Pāṇini, Kātyāyana and Patañjali*, Delhi: Shri Lal Bahadur Shastri Rashtriya Sanskrit Vidyapeeth.

Sarup, L. (tr. and introduction) 1967, *The Nighaṇṭu and the Nirukta*, Lahore: University of the Panjab (Second Rpt. Delhi: Motilal Banarsidass).

Saraswati, Sri Dayananda, *Aṣṭādhyāyibhāṣyama*, Ajmer, Vedic Pustakalaya, 1961.

Śatapatha Brāhmaṇa (with *Sāyaṇa-Bhāṣya*), Varanasi: Chaukhamba (Sanskrit).

Shastri, Gaurinath, 1959, *Philosophy of Word and Meaning*, Calcutta: Sanskrit College Research Series 5.

———, 1978, "Sanskrit Poetics," in *CHI*, vol. V, pp. 293-302.

———, 1987 (rpt.), *History of Classical Sanskrit Literature*, Delhi: Motilal Banarsidass.

Shastri, S. Suryanarayana, 1932, "Vācaspati's Criticism of the Sphoṭa Theory," *Journal of Oriental Research*, 6 : 311-321.

Shastri, Charudeva, 1957-58, "Paniniye Dhātupathertha-Nirdeśah (The Statement of Meanings in Pāṇini's Dhātu-Pātha)," Madras: *Journal of Oriental Research*, 27: 79-84 (in Sanskrit).

Shastri, Charudeva, 1962, *Vyākaraṇa-Mahābhāṣya*, Prathama Āhnika, Delhi: Motilal Banarsidass (text with Hindi commentary).

———, 1968 (tr.), *The Mahābhāṣya of Patañjali*, tr. into Hindi with comments: first nine *āhnikas*, Delhi: Motilal Banarsidass.

Shastri, Charudeva, 1988, *Pāṇini Reinterpreted*, Delhi: Motilal Banarsidass.

Shastri, Kapil Deva, 1964, "Bhartṛhari's Discussion on the Relation Between Upamāna and Upameya in his *Vākyapadīya*," *Festschrift Baburam Saksena*, pp. 229-33.

Shastri, Kapil Deva, 1965, "Upamāna, Upameya and Sāmānyavacana According to the *Vākyapadīya* of Bhartṛhari," *Vishveshvarananda Ontological Journal*, 3, Hoshiarpur, 19-28.

Shastri, Satyavrat, 1978, "Sanskrit Grammar," in *The Cultural Heritage of India*, vol. V., Calcutta: Sri Ramakrishna Mission Institute of Culture.

Shastri, Satyavrat, "Pāṇini's Regard for Usage" in International Seminar on Pāṇini — Summaries of Papers (*ISP-SP*), University of Poona, 1981.

Shastri, Satyavrat, 1964, *The Rāmāyaṇa — A Linguistic Study*, Delhi: Munshiram Manoharlal.

Shastri, Shivnarayaṇa, 1972, *Nirukta*, Delhi, Published by Shrimati Taradervi Kokila.

———, Shivnarayana, *Ṛgveda Saṁhitā me Vyutpatti Cintana*, in B.N. Tewary, see 1.45, 1971-72.

Sastri, Swami Dwarikadsa (ed.), 1984, *Śarvadarśana Sūtra Saṁgraha*, Varanasi: Sudhi Prakasan (Sanskrit Text with Hindi Introduction).

———, 1968, *Pramāṇavārttika*, Varanasi.

Shastri, V.A. Ramaswami, 1932-33, "The Doctrine of Sphoṭa," *Annamalai University Journal*, 1: 233-40, 2: 109-20.

———, 1952, "Mukhya and Gauṇa Words in Language," *Bulletin of the Deccan College Research Institute*, Poona 14 : 183-94.

———, 1942, *Jagannātha Paṇḍita: A Study*, Annamalai University.

———, 1955-56, "Bhartṛhari's Interpretation of *grahaṁ saṁmārṣṭi* and *paśunā yajeta*," Madras: *Journal of Oriental Research*, 25: 74-78.

Scharfe, Hartmut, 1971, *Pāṇini's Metalanguage*, Philadelphia: American Philosophical Society.

Schauer, Ellen and Ellen Spolsky, 1986, *The Bounds of Interpretation, Linguistic Theory and Literary Text*, California: Stanford University Press.

Seschachalasarma, Sri, 1985, "Dharma — Its Utmost Significance in Tattvāloka," Madras: Sri Abhinava Vidyateertha Educational Trust.

Shrimat Anirvan, 1937, 1962 rpt., "Vedic Exegesis," *The Cultural Heritage of India*, vol. I., Calcutta: Sir Ramakrishna Mission Institute of Culture.

Singh, Jagdev, 1972, "Pāṇini's Theory of Language," *International Journal of Dravidian Linguistics*, 1 : 80-96.

———, 1974, "Pāṇini's Theory of Kārakas," *International Journal of Dravidian Linguistics*, 3: 287-320.

Solomon, E., 1976, *Indian Dialectics*, Ahmedabad.

Spinoza, "The Interpretation of Scriptures" in *The Philosophy of Spinoza*, New York: Carlton House.

Sreekrishna, Sharma, 1959, "Syntactic Meaning — Two Theories," *ALB*, 23: 41-64.

Śrīmadbhāgvat Mahāpurāṇa, 1940, "Sanskrit Text with Hindi Paraphrase," Gorakhpur: Gita Press.

Srinivasachara, P.N., 1937, "The Viṣiṣṭādvaita of Rāmānuja," in *CHI*, vol. III, Calcutta, 2nd edn., 1953, (rpt. 1969), pp. 300-12.

The Śrī-Bhāṣya, 1899, M. Rangacharya and M.B.V. Aiyangar (trs.). Madras: The "Brahmvādin" Press, vol. I.

Stall, Johan Frederick, 1962, "Negation and the Law of Contradiction in Indian Thought : A Comparative Study," *Bulletin of the School of Oriental and African Studies*, 25 : 52-71.

———, 1966, "Indian Semantics," *International Journal of the American Oriental Society*, 86: 304-11.

———, 1966, "Analyticity," *Foundations of Language*, 2: 67-93

———, 1969, "Sanskrit Philosophy of Language," *Current Trends in Linguistics*, vol. 5 (ed. sebeok); pp. 449-531.

———, 1972 (ed.), *A Reader on the Sanskrit Grammarians*, Cambridge, Mass: The MIT Press.

———, 1973, "The Concept of Pakṣa in Indian Logic," *Journal of Indian Philosophy*, August.

Śvetāsvataropaniṣad, 1964, Swami Tyagisananda (ed., tr.), Madras: Sir Ramakrishna Math.

Subramania, Iyer, K.A., 1935, "Who are the Anitya Sphoṭavādinaḥ?" *Proceedings of the All India Oriental Conference*, no. 8, Mysore, 258-63.

———, 1941, "Pratibha as the Meaning of a Sentence," *Proceedings of the All India Oriental Conference*, no. 10, Tirupati : 326-32.

———, 1947, "The doctrine of Sphoṭa," *Journal of Ganganatha Jha Research Institute*, vol. 5, pt. 2, 121-47.

———, 1965, "Bhartṛhari on Dhvani," *Annals of Baroda Oriental Research Institute*, 46: 49-65.

———, 1965a, *Vākyapadīya of Bhartṛhari with the Vṛtti*, Chapter I, tr., Poona: Deccan College.

———, 1968, "Bhartṛhari on the Primary and Secondary Meaning of Words," *Festschrift S.M. Katre* I, pp. 97-112.

———, 1969, Bhartṛhari : A Study of the Vākyapadīya in the Light of Ancient Commentaries, Poona: Deccan College.

———, *Bhartṛhari*, 1969, Poona: University of Poona.

———, 1971, *The Vākyapadīya of Bhartṛhari*, Chapter III, Part I, English tr., Poona : Deccan College.

———, 1973, *Vākyapadīya of Bhartṛhari with the Prakīrna Prakāśa of Helarāja*; Kāṇḍa III, Part II, Poona: Deccan College.

———, 1977, *Vākyapadīyā of Bhartṛhari*, Kāṇḍa II, Delhi: Motilal Banarsidass.

Subbaramanya, D.S., 1985, *Śrī Dakṣiṇāmūrthi Stotram, Tattvāloka* VIII, 1 and 2, pp. 5-28.

Subramanian, A.V., 1988, *Aesthetics of Wonder*, Delhi: Motilal Banarsidass.

Sukla, Sri Ramacandra Dhir, 1976, *Annam Bhaṭṭa's Tarka-Saṁgraha*, Varanasi: Chowkhamba Orientalia.

Taittirīyopaniṣad, 1958, Text with English translation, Madras : Sir Ramakrishna Math.

Thibaut, G., 1890, 1896, *The Vedānta-Sūtras with Śaṅkara's Commentary*, The Sacred Books of the East, vol. xxxiv, F, Max Müller (ed.) Delhi: Motilal Banarsidass, 1962 (edn.).

Tiwari, Kapil Muni, 1971, "Asiddham Bahiraṅgam Antaraṅge: A Metarule of Rule-ordering in Pāṇini," IL, 32: 241-57.

Tiwary, R.S., 1984, *A Critical Approach to Classical Indian Poetics*, Delhi and Varanasi: Chowkhamba Orientalia.

Todorov, Tzvetan, 1973, 1982 (Eng. tr.) *Symbolism and Interpretation*, Catherine Porter (tr.), London: Routlege and Kegan Paul.

Udbhaṭṭa, *Kāvyālaṁkāra Saṁgraha*, see under Induraja.

Upadhyaya, Baldev, 1984, *Bhāratiya Darśana*, Varanasi: Chaukhamba Orientalia.

Upaniṣads, see under S. Radhakrishnan and under V.M. Bedekar.

Vaidya, P.L., and Pusalker, A.D., 1973, "The Mahābhārata: Its History and Character," in *CHI*, vol. II, 2nd rev. edn., 1962, rpt. 1969, pp. 51-70.

Vajpeyi, Sri Kishoridas, 1958, *Hindi Sabdanuśāsana*, Prayag: Nagari Pracarani Sabha.

Vāmana and Jayāditya, *Kāṣikā-vṛtti*, see under Narayana Mishra.

Vāmana (the ninth century AD) 1928, *Kāvyālaṁkāra*, tr. into English, Ganganath Jha (tr.), Poona: Oriental Book Agency, 2nd rev. edn.

Varma, Siddheshwara, 1925, "Analysis of Meaning in the Indian Philosophy of Language," *Journal of the Royal Asiatic Society*, London: 21-35.

———, 1929, *Critical Studies in the Phonetic Studies of Indian Grammarians*, London: Royal Asiatic Society.

———, 1950-51, "The Vedic Accent and the Interpreters of Pāṇini," *Journal of the Bombay Branch of Royal Asiatic Society*, New Series, 26 : 1-9.

———, 1953, *The Etymologies of Yāska*, Hoshiarpur: Vishveshvarananda Vedic Research Institute.

———, 1963, "Scientific and Technical Presentation of Patañjali as Reflected in the Mahābhāṣya," *Vishveshvarananda Ontological Journal*, Hoshiarpur, 1: 1-36.

———, 1968, "Plurality — philosophical and Grammatical — In Sanskrit Tradition," *Sri Venkateshwara University Oriental Journal*, 11: 1-4.

———, 1969, "Object — philosophical and Grammatical — In Sanskrit," *SVUOJ*, 12: 39-44.

———, 1972, "The Concept of 'Agent' — Philosophical and Grammatical in Sanskrit," *Festschrift K.C. Chattopadhyaya*, pp. 713-21.

Varnin, Vedavrata (ed.), 1962-63, *Mahābhāṣya*, 5 vols., Jhajjar, Gurukul.